fifth edition

SMOKING AND POLITICS: Policy Making and the Federal Bureaucracy

A. Lee Fritschler
James M. Hoefler

Dickinson College

Prentice Hall, Upper Saddle River, New Jersey 07458

Library of Congress Cataloging-in-Publication Data

FRITSCHLER, A. LEE
  Smoking and politics : policy making and the federal bureaucracy /
  A. Lee Fritschler, James M. Hoefler. — 5th ed.
    p. cm.
  Includes bibliographical references and index.
  ISBN 0-13-435801-5
  1. Cigarettes—Labeling—Government policy—United States.
2. Advertising—Cigarettes—United States. 3. Cigarettes—Labeling—
Law and legislation—United States. 4. United States. Federal
Trade Commission. I. Hoefler, James M. II. Title.
HF6161.T6F75 1996
659.1'967973'0973—dc20

95-5578
CIP

For our students at
Dickinson,
we salute their talents and
their willingness to learn

Editorial/production supervision
  and interior design: **Joan E. Foley**
Editor in chief: **Nancy Roberts**
Acquisitions editor: **Michael Bickerstaff**
Editorial Assistant: **Anita Castro**
Copy editor: **Nancy Savio-Marcello**
Buyer: **Bob Anderson**

Printed in the United States of America
10 9 8 7 6

ISBN 0-13-435801-5

PRENTICE-HALL INTERNATIONAL (UK) LIMITED, LONDON
PRENTICE-HALL OF AUSTRALIA PTY. LIMITED, SYDNEY
PRENTICE HALL CANADA INC., TORONTO
PRENTICE-HALL HISPANOAMERICANA, S.A., MEXICO
PRENTICE-HALL OF INDIA PRIVATE LIMITED, NEW DELHI
PRENTICE-HALL OF JAPAN, INC., TOKYO
PEARSON EDUCATION ASIA PTE. LTD., SINGAPORE
EDITORA PRENTICE-HALL DO BRASIL, LTDA., RIO DE JANEIRO

Contents

Preface *vii*

1

Cigarettes and the Policy Process *1*

      Tobacco Subsystem, 5
      Tobacco Power and Government Regulation, 7
      Nicotiana: The Beginnings of the Controversy, 9
      A Challenge to the Subsystem, 11
      Administrative Policy Making, 12
      Bureaucrats and Members of Congress, 14
      Notes, 17

2

Smoking and Administrative Politics *20*

      Research Uncovers a Health Hazard, 21
      Industry's Response, 22
      Birth of a Lobby, 23
      Congress Rebuffs Health Proponents, 27

Smokers Sue Manufacturers, 28
Bureaucratic Conflict, 30
Notes, 35

3

The Advisory Committee and New Policy Directions*   *37
Support for a Health Warning, 39
Advisory Committees in the Bureaucracy, 41
The Surgeon General's Committee at Work, 42
The Advisory Committee's Report, 43
Impacts of the Advisory Committee's Report, 44
Notes, 45

4

Development of Administrative Policy-Making Powers*   *47
Congressional Delegation of Authority, 48
Regulatory Authority Delegated to Federal Trade
    Commission, 52
The Supreme Court on Delegation, 55
Change in Emphasis at the Federal Trade
    Commission, 58
Notes, 60

5

Procedures Used in Administrative Policy Making*   *62
Adjudication and Rule Making at the Federal Trade
    Commission, 63
The Federal Trade Commission's Experience with
    Cigarette Regulation, 67
The Federal Trade Commission Adopts Rule-Making
    Procedures, 69
Notes, 70

6

The Rule-Making Hearings*   *72
Cigarette Hearings at the Federal Trade Commission, 73

Witnesses, 75
Position of the Industry, 76
The Commissioners Respond, 77
The Federal Trade Commission's Defense of Its Action, 79
Promulgation of Rules, 81
Tobacco Interests Object to the Rule, 82
Notes, 83

7

Congressional Power and Agency Policy Making 85

Congressional Oversight, 86
The Federal Trade Commission's Oversight Struggle, 87
No Victory for Health, 88
Strategy for Success, 92
The Health Lobby, 95
The Congressional Hearings, 97
The Cigarette Men Testify, 98
The Federal Trade Commission Rescinds Its Rule, 101
Notes

8

Congress and the Bureaucracy: A Balance of Power? 104

Bureaucracy Continues the Controversy, 105
Federal Communications Commission Intensifies
    the Controversy, 110
Regulatory Update, 114
Notes, 123

9

The Bureaucracy and Democratic Policy Making 126

Bureaucrats Have Too Much Power, 127
External Checks on Bureaucratic Autonomy, 130
Administrative Procedures Act, 134
Written Records, 136
Administrative Law Judges, 138
Advisory Committees, 140
Accessibility, 143
Media as Watchdogs, 145

Reflective Representation and Bureaucratic
    Pluralism, 145
The Policy-Making Role of Bureaucracies
    Reconsidered, 148
Notes, 150

Appendix I

**Chronology of Important Events
in the Cigarette Regulation Controversy   157**

Appendix II

**Federal Trade Commission's Trade Regulation Rule
on Cigarette Labeling and Advertising (29 FR 8325)
Subchapter D—Trade Regulation Rules   167**

Suggestions for Further Reading   171

Index   175

Preface

The bureaucracy is an important focal point of the policy-making process in modern governments. Society relies upon bureaucracies to make policy decisions that in less complicated times were made exclusively by elected executives, legislators, and judges. These elected officials presently find themselves responding more and more frequently to the initiatives of bureaucrats and to decisions made by administrative agencies.

Although bureaucratic activities are the heart of the policy-making processes of modern governments, they are far from being of central importance in most government courses and curricula. This book attempts to correct that deficiency by providing students of government with some understanding of why bureaucracies have become important and how they operate in the policy-making process.

Too often the policy-making activities of bureaucracies are overlooked because the procedures used by agencies are complex, complicated, usually quite dull, and conducted away from the glare of publicity. The primary reason for the ascendancy of agencies to power—that is, the technical complexity of modern society and the resulting intricacies of administrative procedures—is, ironically, the factor keeping students from devoting time and attention to these important governmental functions. The implications of accelerated-depreciation accounting techniques for the electric power industry, for example, are tremendously important to industry and the public, but both the public and students of government should be forgiven if they find it impossible to give this complicated issue much concentrated attention.

Centering upon the policy-making process, the present study explores a public controversy that affects millions of Americans but which few understand except for the personal dilemma it presents. While the use of cigarettes has often been damned by clerics and scorned by health experts, citizens suddenly found their government requiring that a health warning appear in advertisements for, and on packages of, cigarettes. The controversy generated over the requirement for a health warning label provides an exceptionally good opportunity to study the processes of agency policy making. The issue was uncomplicated. Simply stated, it was: Should the government require cigarette manufacturers to inform consumers of the results of studies by the medical-scientific community that indict cigarette smoking as a cause of lung cancer and other diseases?

The cigarette labeling issue broke forcefully into public view on January 11, 1964, when the Surgeon General released the report of the Advisory Committee on Smoking and Health. One week later the Federal Trade Commission (FTC) prepared a regulation requiring a health warning to appear in all cigarette advertising and on cigarette packages. The processes and procedures used to write this rule were not exactly the same as those used by all agencies in policy making because these procedures differ slightly from agency to agency. Furthermore, most bureaucratic policy making does not draw as much attention from the public, Congress, and interest groups as the labeling controversy did. The extra attention that this issue received serves a useful purpose for students, however, by providing the opportunity to examine more ramifications of the policy process than might otherwise be possible.

Utilizing a policy issue involving a maximum number of public officials and institutions, the study illustrates the "whirlpool" or subsystem effect in public policy formulation as interest groups, members of congressional committees, and bureaucrats conspire quietly but effectively to steer government activity in directions that are mutually agreeable to these interested parties; a phenomenon explored perhaps first by Ernest S. Griffith in his studies of Congress, beginning over a half century ago. This study also reveals how in recent years these cozy triangles of power have been challenged by "dissidents": public interest–minded bureaucrats, members of Congress, and interest groups looking to take back the tiller from those who have quietly done the steering for so long.

In this book, the focus is on the bureaucracy. The rule-making and adjudicatory procedures of the Federal Trade Commission have not changed dramatically over time and are generally the same as those of other independent regulatory commissions or the Cabinet-level executive departments. This substantial degree of similarity in procedures allows the student to gain insight into the process of bureaucratic policy making regardless of which bureaucratic institution one selects for study. Also, the significance of bureaucratic power vis-à-vis other political institutions, democratic theory, and the policy-making process does not change significantly as one moves from one administrative body to another. Although specifically concerned with one policy question and concentrating primarily on one regulatory commission, the study illustrates generally the procedures and politics of bureaucratic policy formulation in contemporary American government.

The extent to which the cigarette and health controversy was a harbinger of things to come is rather surprising. The controversy was one of the first major events in a consumer movement that made consumerism an important political force. The processes of agency policy making illustrated by the cigarette labeling controversy are being used today by well-organized, highly skilled groups representing consumer interests. Citizen advocates at all levels of government have discovered that change can be brought about by manipulation of the rules and regulations that govern agencies and by participating in the processes agencies follow to write rules. The use of agency powers is the cornerstone of the successes of the groups founded and inspired by consumer advocate Ralph Nader and his followers. They started a movement. The movement puts the study of administrative law and administrative politics high on the list of skills needed by students of government. Public participation in agency policy processes was minimal until recently. Now, bureaucracy-centered politics is more fruitful both as a field of study and as a means of influencing public policy than it was when the first edition of *Smoking and Politics* appeared in 1969.

Many millions of Americans have died from smoking-related diseases since reliable scientific evidence about the hazards of the habit began accumulating in the 1950s, and more than 1,000 smokers are added to the tally every day. For the first time in history, however, former smokers outnumber smokers in America, suggesting that education campaigns, warning labels, and advertising restrictions promulgated by government in recent decades may be having some salutary effect. Effective or not, the controversy over smoking regulations is alive and well, making this fifth edition of *Smoking and Politics* as timely as ever.

While being careful not to disturb the basic structure of the book, we have made several changes that we hope will make it more useful to students of government and policy. First, we have covered important developments on the regulatory scene and put those developments into historical context. In addition, we have updated and streamlined the chronology of important events so that it, too, may be more useful and accessible to readers. Also included in the fifth edition are visual aids that will help students bring the sometimes complex material covered here into sharper focus. Finally, we have added a ninth chapter to the book where we review the democratic checks on bureaucratic discretion that keep the policy process more responsive to a variety of interests—and, at the same time, less efficient in advancing the public interest—than it might be otherwise.

Over the years, *Smoking and Politics* has been used in a variety of academic settings, from introductory courses on American government to intermediate-level courses on public policy, public administration, and administrative law. Graduate-level seminars on policy making, public law, and government–business relations have also found the book useful. We hope the renovations we have made in the latest version of this timeless story will make it possible for yet another generation of students in courses such as these to learn about how their government works—and doesn't work—so that in the end, they will better understand the policy process, and, ultimately, so they will be better equipped as responsible citizens to shape their own destinies.

A. L. F.
J. M. H.
Dickinson College
Carlisle, Pennsylvania

Chapter

1

Cigarettes and the Policy Process

Tobacco is a dirty weed.
    I like it.
It satisfies no normal need
    I like it.
It makes you thin, it makes you lean,
It takes the hair right off your bean.
It's the worse darn stuff I've ever seen.
    I like it.

"Unrepentant" by G.L. Hemminger

As the evening variety show ends and the late news is about to begin, a panorama of traffic signals, danger signs, and cautionary flashing lights dance across the television screen. A chest X ray appears, a man coughs, and a voice announces, "We receive many warnings in our lives." The camera then closes in on a cigarette package so that the viewer can read, "Caution: Cigarette Smoking May Be Hazardous to Your Health."

Today there are no cigarette ads on television, although a few anti-smoking commercials continue to appear. Beginning in January 1966, a health warning has been printed on all cigarette packages sold in this country: "Caution: Cigarette Smoking May Be Hazardous to Your

Health." In 1970, legislation was passed to make the warning more emphatic.[1]

The warning no longer appears only in small print on the side panel of cigarette packages. In 1972, it also began appearing in all billboard, newspaper, and magazine advertising in the United States. In 1985, the Surgeon General's warning became a series of statements, rotating every three months: "Smoking Causes Lung Cancer, Heart Disease, Emphysema, and May Complicate Pregnancy"; "Smoking by Pregnant Women May Result in Fetal Injury, Premature Birth, and Low Birth Weight"; "Cigarette Smoke Contains Carbon Monoxide"; "Quitting Smoking Now Greatly Reduces Serious Risks to Your Health." In each case, government agencies played a key policy-making role in bringing these regulatory changes about.

Since these early years of the cigarette labeling controversy the public has been deluged with various kinds of publicity about the ill effects of cigarette smoking. Even so, the American smoker, to whom all these messages have been addressed, has reacted slowly and a bit grudgingly. One year after the warning appeared there was no evidence that cigarette sales had been adversely affected. In fact, U.S. consumption increased to 549 billion cigarettes during that year, an increase of 8 billion over 1966 consumption figures. Two years later cigarette sales dropped slightly, but by 1970 trends reversed themselves. Consumption had dropped to 595 billion in 1985, but the decrease may have resulted from higher cigarette excise taxes. There was some positive news for health advocates, however—per capita annual consumption for those over the age of 18 dropped from 4,345 cigarettes in 1963 to 3,384 in 1985. By 1993, consumption had reached a historical low of 2,539 cigarettes per capita, a figure 25 percent below the 1985 mark, and 42 percent below the level of consumption in 1963.

Whether or not there is any relationship between the decrease in smoking and the appearance of the health warnings is a matter for speculation. It is not known whether the government-required health warnings persuaded people to quit or whether people did so for some other reason. Population increases combined with "start-smoking" and "quit-smoking" rates cloud the picture and make analysis difficult. Usually it is puzzling to measure the effects of regulatory policy. The effect of the government's role in this controversy is no exception to that rule.[2] Nevertheless there has been a drop in per capita consumption and a change in the mix of smokers. In 1964 over 50 percent of the adult male population smoked; by 1985 only 32 percent did; and by 1994, only 26 percent of American men identified themselves as smokers.[3]

At the same time, the rate of smoking remains high among the nation's youth. This is a problem of significant import given that 80 percent of smokers take up the practice before they turn 20 (currently, the average smoker begins smoking at 14 and a half years of age).[4] The Office on Smoking and Health reports that approximately 35 percent of white high school seniors smoked in 1992, a percentage that has remained stable for over 12 years. (Meanwhile, the percentage of black high school seniors who smoke has declined steadily, from 35 percent in 1978 to approximately 10 percent in 1992.) The smoking rate among adolescent women has been a particular concern of health officials; while overall smoking rates for adolescent men have declined marginally over time, the rate for adolescent women has increased sharply to the point where young women now are as likely as young men to take up the smoking habit.[5] Thus the health warnings seem to have made an impact on the adult population over time given the declining percentage of adult smokers and the increasing percentage of those who see smoking as a health risk (see Figure 1-1), while the nation's youngsters who smoke appear to be immune to the message that smoking is hazardous to one's health.

Figure 1–1* Smoking Rates and Perceptions of the Relationship between Smoking and Lung Cancer

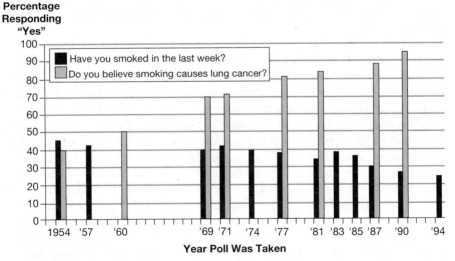

Note: Only one of the two questions was asked in years where only one bar is indicated (1957, 1960, 1974, 1983, 1985, 1994).
*Data through 1990: George Gallup, Jr. *The Gallup Poll: Public Opinion 1990* (Wilmington, Del.: Scholarly Resources, Inc., 1991), pp. 79–92. 1994 data from "Tobacco: Does It Have a Future?" *Business Week*, July 4, 1994, p. 25.

There has been a much clearer relationship between the intro-duction and requirement of health warnings and major changes in to-bacco politics. The quiet, gentlemanly folkways of tobacco politics grew turbulent when it appeared in 1964 that the government might be successful in its efforts to warn smokers about possible health haz-ards. The traditional procedures for resolving conflicts between to-bacco producers and the government quickly changed. Health warn-ings in advertising and changes in consumption are the widely visible results of a political process involving administrative agencies, Con-gress, the courts, organized health and tobacco interests, and the public. These institutions and actors are involved in a continuing con-troversy involving both politics and science. The processes used to separate fact from fiction and to determine which policy should be adopted by government are common to policy making in the United States; as such the cigarette labeling controversy is a piece of modern political Americana.

The processes from which emerged the temporary and changing policies in the smoking and health controversy are also characteristic of consumer or public interest politics as it developed and expanded in the 1960s. Public interest politics uses the policy-making powers of legislatures, bureaucracies, and the courts in patterns of conflict inducing strategies. These strategies confirm the observation that the institutions of government operate, alone and in concert, in ways which ill fit traditional separation-of-powers notions of how the policy process works.

The politics of cigarette labeling demonstrates how institutions with separate responsibilities in the framework of the Constitution co-operate, conflict, and form temporary alliances to achieve policy goals. Further, the controversy illustrates the central role of the bureaucracy as policy initiator and policy maker in modern society. While policy-making powers are shared among the three traditional constitutional divisions of government—the legislative, the executive, and the judi-cial—one of these institutions is usually more powerful in the policy-making process than the other, depending on the nature of the issue. Frequently, when the issue involves matters of technical complexity and powerful special interest opposition, the bureaucracy plays the leading role, but there is no fixed distribution of power. And even though one institution might play a leading role, it is clear that the policy process cannot function with much in the way of dispatch or efficiency when one of the institutions encounters concentrated op-position from another. The Federal Trade Commission (FTC) discov-ered the truth of this statement when it encountered a Congress hos-tile to its proposals for cigarette health warnings.

TOBACCO SUBSYSTEM

What has come to be the normal relationship among the institutions of national government was typified by traditional, or pre-1964, tobacco politics. Policy was made in a spirit of friendly and quiet cooperation between small segments of Congress, the bureaucracy, and the interest group community. The coalition of these fragments is referred to in social science literature as a subsystem. The term *subsystem* describes a structure dependent upon a larger political entity but one that functions with a high degree of autonomy. A committee of Congress could be called a subsystem of the larger legislative system, just as an agency might be referred to as a subsystem of the bureaucracy. The tobacco subsystem is different from these in that it is a more encompassing policy subsystem. It cuts across institutional lines and includes within it all groups and individuals who are making and influencing government decisions concerning cigarettes and tobacco.[6]

The tobacco subsystem included the paid representatives of tobacco growers, marketing organizations, and cigarette manufacturers; congressmen representing tobacco constituencies; the leading members of four subcommittees in Congress—two appropriations subcommittees and two substantive legislative committees in each house—that handle tobacco legislation and related appropriations; and certain officials within the Department of Agriculture who were involved with the various tobacco programs of that department. This was a small group of people well known to each other and knowledgeable about all aspects of the tobacco industry and its relationship with the government.

As long as no one objected too loudly, the important and complex tobacco programs, like price supports and export promotion, were conducted without interference from those not included in this subsystem. There are hundreds of similar subsystems functioning in Washington that quietly and efficiently bridge the gap created by the constitutional separation of powers.

When a change in the prevailing power configuration is desired, but those in the subsystem are unwilling to accommodate such demands, outsiders seeking the change attempt to mobilize the latent antagonisms inherent in institutions whose authority and responsibility are defined within a framework of constitutionally separated powers. Policy subsystems tend to reduce or eliminate conflict by concentrating economic and political power in the hands of a few individuals who tend to have overlapping interests. Dissidents interested in altering the status quo can do so most effectively by moving outside the established subsystem, thereby broadening the scope of conflict and increasing the chances that some of the dissidents' interests are served through government action.[7]

Those who seek to change a policy controlled by a subsystem often use the policy-making powers of one institution of government to provoke a response and further action from another. A different committee of Congress or an agency of the bureaucracy might be persuaded to concern itself with the issue, which heretofore had been within the guarded domain of the subsystem. Perhaps an interest group or a powerful individual encourages other groups to use their political powers to challenge those who in the past had succeeded in keeping the conflict within manageable bounds. One agency of the bureaucracy might challenge the jurisdiction of another. All of these actions could receive further impetus by direct appeals to public opinion. Conflict is thus created and expanded as more and different actors are induced to challenge the decision makers in the subsystem.

Once control begins to pass from the traditional decision makers, it is difficult to predict what new directions policy will take. The only safe prediction is that there will be a struggle and a challenge to those who were in charge. While the struggle goes on—it can last for years—it is difficult to say *who* controls *what* in the policy area affected. It becomes easier to bring about change while the subsystem is in a state of disarray. Eventually things settle down and a new subsystem emerges. Often it is different in terms of size and membership from the one that existed when the controversy started. The success of the challenge can sometimes be measured by the permanence of any realignment that might occur within a subsystem.

The small group that comprised the tobacco subsystem before 1964 is minuscule in comparison to the cast of characters involved in tobacco politics in the 1990s. The chief additions are, of course, health-related organizations. Groups like the American Cancer Society and the American Medical Association now lobby for a total ban on cigarette advertising. Citizens' lobbying groups fight the tobacco price support system. State and municipal governments also have been added to the fold, due to their efforts to pass antismoking ordinances in public places.

In addition to the increased number and influence of private pressure groups, the smoking issue has appeared on the agendas of an increasing number of federal agencies (and thus, their congressional oversight committees). The Federal Aviation Administration decides if citizens can smoke on airplanes, while the Interstate Commerce Commission does the same for the nation's commercial buses and trains. The General Services Administration banned smoking in all 6,800 federal buildings in 1986, and in 1994, the Department of Defense banned smoking in all the thousands of common work areas it controls worldwide. Meanwhile, the Advisory Council of the National Institute on Drug Abuse has called for a total advertising ban on tobacco products, arguing that tobacco is an addictive substance. More recently, the Food and Drug Administration (FDA) has toyed with the notion of regulating the sale and distribution of tobacco on the same grounds. The Veterans Administration has prohibited smoking in its hospitals. Even the U.S. Fire Administration has gotten into the act by calling for development of a self-extinguishing cigarette, citing statistics that in one year, alone, home fires started by cigarettes killed or injured over 5,000 people and cost $305 million in damages.

TOBACCO POWER
AND GOVERNMENT REGULATION

Any challenge to the tobacco subsystem was fraught at the outset with serious difficulties. Long before the health warning was threatened by the Federal Trade Commission, tobacco power had established itself as an important force in American politics. The tobacco coalition directly includes a clientele of millions who smoke.

More importantly, with revenues of $48 billion a year, tobacco companies are big economic players in state and local economies. In addition to their own financial clout, these companies account—either directly or indirectly—for millions of dollars more in advertising and other related economic activity. Tobacco companies employ nearly 47,000 workers and provide $2.8 billion in crop income for over 100,000 farmers in 16 states. (Two thirds of the tobacco crop is produced in just two states: North Carolina and Kentucky.) The industry as a whole accounts for nearly 2 percent of the nation's GNP and helps raise over $12 billion in taxes for federal, state, and local treasuries every year.[8]

The beneficiaries of this multibillion dollar industry include manufacturers, advertising agencies, farmers, shopkeepers, and tax collectors. These stake holders work hard to discourage any government activity that might in turn discourage the smoker. And smokers, themselves, dislike being told, particularly by politicians, that their pleasures could be injurious to their health. Consequently, health-oriented politicians are likely to devote their time to more popular activities.

The beneficiaries of tobacco also include the entertainment and news media, from which Americans receive much of their information about smoking and health. The FTC reported that in 1983 tobacco companies spent $2.6 billion on advertising.[9] In the nation's 20 largest magazines, tobacco ads made up 10 to 20 percent of all advertising income. This fact caused antismoking advocates to question whether newspapers and magazines could be unbiased in their reporting of the smoking and health issue. In a study cited in the *New England Journal of Medicine*, magazines accepting tobacco ads ran from 12 to 63 times as many stories on health issues like stress and nutrition than on smoking, although smoking was generally considered the nation's number one health problem.[10]

Tobacco interests also find support in American traditions. Tobacco was an early American crop—so important to our early economy it was used for a time as currency. Furthermore, attempts to regulate business enterprise are generally received by most Americans without enthusiasm and frequently with considerable derision. It is surprising, therefore, that more often than not there is strong support from business and industry for regulation. If one were to examine the support for most of the economic regulation on the books of state and national government, one would find it rooted in business. Fair competition guarantees; antitrust laws; banking and currency regulations; and airline, trucking, banking, and financial market regulations have been supported over the years by business and its representatives.[11] There is little reason for business opposition to these regulations because they either support business generally or some segments of it at the expense of other segments.[12] Banking and currency regulations organize the marketplace; antitrust rule making tends to pit big business against small; trucking regulation is supported by the large, established carriers and opposed by the smaller ones and potential entrants into the market.

Regulation of environmental or health matters, or regulation of advertising for public health reasons, is another thing. In the past there were a few moves by government to regulate industry in a comprehensive, across-the-board fashion. No part of industry could see any advantage in such initiatives. When this happens, business politics change. Common ground, or at least broader grounds, for opposition surfaces in the business community. Part of the tactic used to oppose these government regulatory actions is to call up the basic American cultural values, which ride against big government and regulation and for free enterprise.

The business schizophrenia in reacting to government regulation was nowhere more clearly seen than in the smoking and health area. Since 1933 tobacco producers have benefited from federal regulatory programs. The U.S. Department of Agriculture operates a price support program and marketing quota rules, which carry with them mandatory limits on production. Although the costs of these activities to government are relatively small,[13] the regulations certainly have been good for the industry (keeping prices up and supply down). For the proponents of these tobacco regulations to turn around and fight consumer-health regulation on the grounds that government regulation is unwarranted interference by Big Brother and bad for the economy is the kind of argument that makes rational people wince.

The beneficiaries of the multibillion-dollar tobacco industry work hard to discourage reductions in the tobacco regulatory programs which benefit the industry, while arguing forcefully against big government and government intervention in the economy. The only possible explanation for this perfidious behavior was offered by Senator Jesse Helms (R-North Carolina). Reacting to proposals to eliminate the tobacco program in the early weeks of the Reagan administration, the Senator said, "In North Carolina, tobacco isn't a commodity, it's a religion."[14] As recently as 1985, Congress voted to retain the price support program for tobacco.

Making the cigarette research findings of scientists available to the public through government action is a difficult task when tobacco is so large economically and so important to the national ethic. In the early 1960s, federal regulatory activity in environmental and advertising areas had been limited. Health regulation had been confined to food, drugs, and dangerous substances—a list which the tobacco interests made certain was never allowed to include tobacco.[15] The legions of tobacco supporters did all they could to assure that smokers heeded the titillation of full-color advertisements rather than the dark foreboding of the scientific community. Scientists, and those interested in bringing to the public information that would discourage smoking, had unsuccessfully challenged the pro-tobacco forces for many years. There was little to give them encouragement as the decade of the 1960s began.

NICOTIANA: THE BEGINNINGS
OF THE CONTROVERSY

The health scientists' troubles began when a Frenchman introduced the native American plant, tobacco, to the world. Jean Nicot, the French ambassador to Portugal, wrote to a friend in 1560 that an American herb he had acquired had marvelous curative powers. Consumption of tobacco quickly gained popularity and Nicot earned a place for himself in history. His name became the base for the scientific term for tobacco, *Nicotiana.*

Shortly after Nicot made his discovery, skepticism of the marvelous curative powers of tobacco began to develop. Some condemned smoking as a foul, smelly habit that rendered social intercourse distasteful. More serious criticism developed in the 1850s when scientific evidence began to appear that supported the skeptics who questioned the medicinal value of cigarettes.

A British medical journal, *The Lancet,* published an article on March 14, 1857, that proved to have an element of timelessness about it. The scientists' indictment, which could well be the same today, read:

> Tobacco is said to act on the mind by producing inactivity thereof; inability to think, drowsiness; irritability. . . . On the respiratory organs, it acts by causing consumption, haemoptysis, and inflammatory condition of the mucous membrane of the larynx, trachea, and bronchae, ulceration of the larynx; short irritable cough; hurried breathing. The circulating organs are affected by irritable heart circulation.[16]

These rather alarming charges against smoking received little public notice. There were relatively few smokers and chewers of tobacco in those days, so the medical disclosures were not received as a threat to the public health. Smoking was neither easy nor feminine because one had to roll his own or smoke a pipe or cigar. The introduction of the cigarette and the advertising that accompanied it in the early 1900s helped to remove these barriers.

The cigarette became popular very quickly, and smoking came to be a mark of social distinction. Spurred by advertising, which made cigarette smoking seem like good sense, and even healthful, sales soared.[17] Per capita annual consumption of cigarettes for people over 18 years old grew from 49 cigarettes in 1900 to a high of 4,345 by 1963. This is more than 11 cigarettes per day for every American over the age of 18.

Smoking was not always legal or socially acceptable, however. By 1890, small groups of social reformers had convinced legislators in 26 states to enact laws prohibiting the sale of cigarettes to minors.[18] Around the turn of the twentieth century, the Anti-Cigarette League was becoming more organized and effective in pushing for bans on the sale of cigarettes to residents of all ages. By 1909, 15 states had done just that.[19] Meanwhile, excise taxes were raised high enough in two other states—Tennessee and West Virginia—that prohibition was the indirect result.

The successes of these grass-roots prohibitionists were short-lived, however. By 1918 cigarettes had become identified with the war effort as a symbol of courage and dignity. Citizens' groups organized to send cigarettes to soldiers, and General John J. Pershing was quoted as saying, "You ask me what we need to win this war. I answer tobacco as much as bullets."[20] Manufacturers and merchants organized to repeal existing prohibitions during the 1920s as the temperance movement declined and the political emancipation of women made smoking more socially acceptable for them. These developments spelled doom for the anti-cigarette movement and by 1930, every single prohibitionist law enacted in the preceding decades had been repealed.[21] Those interested in advancing the cause of cigarette smoking, including tobacco growers, cigarette manufacturers, retailers, advertisers, and even smokers themselves, enjoyed wide social acceptance and even public sector encouragement for the next quarter century. Members of the tobacco subsystem had, in the end, prevailed.

A CHALLENGE TO THE SUBSYSTEM

Beginning in the early 1950s, the question of what the government should do about warning the cigarette consumer began surfacing on the agenda of one governmental institution or another. Those who opposed a warning were able to keep it a low priority item until the mid-1960s. The tobacco interests were successful in keeping the issue within the confines of a few agencies and within the offices and committee rooms of a few key congressmen. No one could gather enough support to bring about any change in the status quo. Those who favored a cigarette health warning had to devise some method to involve other agencies and different members of Congress, to interest them in working for the adoption of legislation that would limit cigarette consumption. Until early in the 1960s, the health interests were unsuccessful in doing this.

The strategy of the cigarette interests was to play off various agencies against each other or against Congress to prevent the smoking and health controversy from expanding. This style of tobacco politics resulted in little government regulation of tobacco advertising or sales. The strategy was successful as long as there was little public support for a government policy to reduce cigarette consumption. As scientific evidence began to document the link between smoking and ill health, pressure for regulation grew, but the tobacco subsystem proved impenetrable to these demands. Tobacco was more firmly entrenched and more richly supported than most other consumer products. One journalist succinctly described the dilemma of the health groups: "If tobacco were spinach the government would have outlawed it years ago, and no one would have given a damn."[22] There were, however, many who cared about the fate of tobacco.

In 1964, the government proposed that a health warning be given in advertising as well as on cigarette packages. Such a statement in advertising, in all likelihood, would have been more effective than the package warning alone. This threat to advertising encouraged others to join the tobacco people in opposition. The American Newspaper Publishers Association, the Advertising Federation of America, the Association of National Advertisers, the Radio Advertising Bureau, and the National Association of Broadcasters, all fearing that advertising restrictions would mean a loss of revenues, aligned themselves with the tobacco interests. This coalition strengthened the position of those who supported the business-as-usual tobacco–government decision-making structure.

Because the tobacco interests exerted considerable influence within the traditional legislative system through congressmen serving on committees or subcommittees immediately involved in tobacco politics, there was little hope for the successful initiation of new policy within Congress. To effect a change in public policy, other avenues of policy making had to be used. Through the collaboration of a few members of Congress and two agencies of the bureaucracy that were not part of the tobacco subsystem, a new coalition was formed to combat the tobacco interests. Congress was generally unfriendly to consumer legislation, since consumers rarely generated pressures or did favors on a scale to match the organized interest groups. As consumer groups organized in the late 1960s, congressional resistance to consumer legislation lessened. When the controversy began, however, the fate of the cigarette health warning, like other consumer measures, depended heavily on the power of administrative agencies to make public policy.

ADMINISTRATIVE POLICY MAKING

Over the years, Congress has found it necessary to grant or delegate policy-making powers to administrative agencies because insurmountable obstacles face Congress in writing legislation with sufficient detail and foresight to meet all of the situations that might arise under that legislation. Recognizing this difficulty, Congress leaves it to the agencies to initiate policies and promulgate rules and regulations to implement the broad programs created by legislation.

Frequently Congress gives only the sketchiest guidelines to the bureaucracy, often requiring an agency to run a program in "the public interest" or in "the public interest, convenience, and necessity."[23] These guidelines give agencies considerable freedom in administrative rule making. The power that agencies have been delegated over the past several decades has made them an important force in the public policy process; some have even called them a fourth branch of government. Agency policy, made in the form of rules, regulations, and interpretations of the way a law is to be applied, accounts for most of the policy output of government today. The largest number of policies that directly affect and govern people and property are made by administrative agencies through powers delegated by Congress.

Agency policy-making powers result in regulations having the effect of law—no different from the end product of the congressional legislative process or the decisions of courts of law. In fact, agencies are capable of adopting regulations under delegated authority that Congress itself might not have adopted.[24] This is often the case when strong lobbies prevent elected members of legislatures from responding to public demands. For example, while Congress was struggling to strengthen gun control legislation in the wake of the murder of Senator Robert F. Kennedy, the Post Office Department used its delegated authority to discourage the shipment of all guns through the mails. The National Rifle Association had succeeded for years in keeping Congress inactive, but it was taken by surprise by the swift action of the Postmaster General.[25]

The issuance of a requirement that there be a health warning in cigarette advertising and on packages was also the work of an administrative agency in the face of anticipated congressional inaction. The Federal Trade Commission first proposed the rule requiring a health warning and later felt the full wrath of congressional disapproval. Congress would not have done what the commission did. The commission rule called for a warning in advertising and on packages. Congress wanted neither, but the commission's action forced Congress to accept first half, then all of the ruling. Congress accepted the label on packages reluctantly and coupled it with a severe rebuke to the FTC. This rebuke of the FTC is a clear example of how Congress can control the authority it delegates to administrative agencies. More important than the initial actions of the FTC or the congressional rebuke that followed them is the fact that the commission started a process that eventually brought about substantial policy change. In this instance, agency policy-making powers broke the stalemate perpetuated by subsystem politics and opened the way for a series of changes in policy affecting cigarette smoking and public health.

The importance of the bureaucracy as a policy-making institution raises some basic questions for democratic government. This is not the place to discuss in detail the complicated and elusive ideals of democracy. Any definition, however, would include at least these elements: A democratic government provides means through which citizens can participate in policy making, and it also provides machinery citizens can use to hold the government accountable for the decisions it makes. An independent judiciary and frequent elections based on a wide franchise help to ensure that these conditions will be met. When policy-making powers are concentrated within agencies of preponderantly nonelected, nonpartisan bureaucrats, the effectiveness of both of the above may be lessened. It is difficult, although far from impossible, to build both accountability and participation into the policy-making process when administrative agencies are the chief policy makers.[26]

In the cigarette labeling controversy, the legality and propriety of allowing the FTC to require and enforce a health warning on cigarettes were questioned. The commission was accused of acting unconstitutionally, in isolation from any checks generated by a system of constitutionally separated powers. Although one should not assume that the powers of administrative agencies are always "natural and good," as one student of politics recently warned,[27] the dangers of excessive and arbitrary use of those powers are reduced when the agency acts as a part of a system in which power is widely dispersed. During the course of the controversy, it became clear that the FTC was not acting in isolation. On the contrary, there were checks on the commission's powers through its interaction and conflict with other agencies, the public, interest groups, the courts, and eventually Congress. This indicates that interests broader than those represented solely by a single bureaucracy were represented in the policy-making process. It was the existence of agency powers that gave the impetus for policy change and innovation in this case. Power concentrated in the hands of possessive congressional committees was forced out into the open where it had to be shared because bureaucratic agencies had the authority to act.

BUREAUCRATS AND MEMBERS
OF CONGRESS

The cigarette labeling controversy demonstrates for those worried about the potential abuses of unchecked power in bureaucratic agencies that limits to agency power exist in a pluralistic system of separated powers. In the labeling fight, as in other areas of domestic policy making, the bureaucracy found it difficult to start anything without at least the acquiescence and usually the outright support of some members of Congress and portions of the interested public. Congressmen, bureaucrats, and pressure groups each have at least one political resource the other needs. The bureaucracy has expertise and knowledge derived from continued experience. Congressmen control the money and are closer to the political power bureaucrats lack. Pressure groups often are the catalytic agents and possess the power to unite congressmen and bureaucrats for action.

These rather fundamental relationships are often overlooked by those who argue that bureaucratic policy-making power is excessive in that it is responsible for originating most major legislation. In a strict technical sense this might be true. Yet, more often than not, an idea for a new piece of legislation, or at least its impetus, comes from within the halls of Congress instead of the monotonous corridors of the bureaucracy. A member of Congress finds it easy to give voice to a new idea. He or she can do it alone or with the assistance of his or her personal staff. An idea planted in the ear of one of the staff can be put into formal legislative language by other congressional staff offices in a few days.[28] The member then drops the bill in the hopper and, if really interested in pressing for action, might make a speech on the floor or take other steps to gain support.

Thousands of bills are introduced each year, but only a few become law. The low productivity rate is a reflection of the inability of most members to successfully guide legislation through Congress.[29] Power in Congress is concentrated in a few hands. Committee chairmen hold nearly complete control over the bills that come within their committees' jurisdictions. If a member wants to enact a bill, he or she needs the support of the appropriate chairman. It is often difficult to enlist this support from within Congress. Consequently, the eager member faced with a disinterested committee chairman must look outside Congress for help to enact a bill. The member has the option of turning to the bureaucracy for expertise and, perhaps, presidential support, and to a pressure group for necessary public support.

The bureaucrats' problems are nearly the opposite of the problems experienced by members of Congress. Most bureaucrats find it difficult to initiate change, particularly if that change is substantial and unwanted by the leaders of a powerful subsystem. Bureaucrats may find it difficult to access a public forum for advancing their views. Bureaucrats may also find that their ideas have to be cleared by bureaucratic committees in- and outside their respective agencies before they are advanced in public. For example, typically, the Office of Management and Budget has to clear the new policy to make certain it conforms with the President's program. All of this is complicated; it takes time, and issues tend to die because of these difficult procedures. A member of Congress has access to the public, the White House, and the Cabinet. Drawing on these assets, he or she can assist the agency by shortening the bureaucrats' clearance process and by removing some opposition. There is a system of mutual dependencies even at the stage of policy initiation, and these dependencies are observable right through the implementation stage.

Tobacco politics would have continued as it had for years if those favoring change had relied solely on Congress or solely on the bureaucracy to initiate that change. Instead, members of Congress and

Figure 1-2   The "Traditional" Tobacco Subsystem

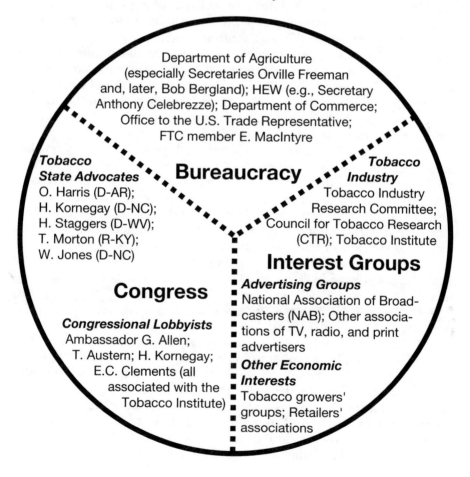

Department of Agriculture (especially Secretaries Orville Freeman and, later, Bob Bergland); HEW (e.g., Secretary Anthony Celebrezze); Department of Commerce; Office to the U.S. Trade Representative; FTC member E. MacIntyre

Bureaucracy

Tobacco State Advocates
O. Harris (D-AR);
H. Kornegay (D-NC);
H. Staggers (D-WV);
T. Morton (R-KY);
W. Jones (D-NC)

Tobacco Industry
Tobacco Industry Research Committee; Council for Tobacco Research (CTR); Tobacco Institute

Interest Groups

Advertising Groups
National Association of Broadcasters (NAB); Other associations of TV, radio, and print advertisers

Other Economic Interests
Tobacco growers' groups; Retailers' associations

Congress

Congressional Lobbyists
Ambassador G. Allen;
T. Austern; H. Kornegay;
E.C. Clements (all associated with the Tobacco Institute)

bureaucrats in league with some interest groups called on each other for help. The bureaucracy had a long, although mixed, history of concern with the content of cigarette advertising and the dangers of smoking to health. In its employ were scientists and economists who had devoted a large portion of their professional careers to these issues. At least one agency in the bureaucracy, the Federal Trade Commission, had been ready to implement a health warning for several years but lacked the power or support to do so. To realize their goals, bureaucrats had to act in league with other bureaucrats, members of Congress, and special interest representatives (see Figure 1-2). Once the coalition of tobacco dissidents was formed and active, the "traditional" tobacco subsystem began to quake.

NOTES

1. The Public Health Cigarette Smoking Act of 1969, passed in 1970, altered the package warning to read: "Warning: The Surgeon General Has Determined That Cigarette Smoking Is Dangerous to Your Health."

2. An analysis of the impact of the health warnings has been done by the Federal Trade Commission. See Richard A. Ippolito, R. Dennis Murphy, and Donald Sant, *Staff Report on Consumer Responses to Cigarette Health Information* (Washington, D.C.: U.S. Federal Trade Commission, August, 1979).

3. Data on the sales and consumption of cigarettes are from the U.S. Internal Revenue Service, as determined by the taxes levied when cigarettes leave manufacturers' warehouses for the consumer market. Per capita figures combine Revenue Service data with Census Bureau estimates of population growth. Since part of the period under discussion is between the national census periods, the population figures are necessarily estimates. The National Center for Health Statistics, U.S. Public Health Service, took national surveys in 1964 and 1965, 1970, 1974, 1978, 1979, 1980, and 1985. The drop in numbers of smokers in the U.S. is taken from the results of those surveys and the Adult-Youth Survey of 1970 and 1975, conducted by the National Clearinghouse for Smoking and Health (now the Office of Smoking and Health), U.S. Public Health Service. Figures for 1994 come from "Should Cigarettes Be Outlawed?" *U.S. News & World Report,* April 18, 1994, p. 35.

4. "Should Cigarettes Be Outlawed?" *U.S. News & World Report,* April 18, 1994, p. 38.

5. Data cited here come from the Surgeon General's 1994 report on smoking and health, the twenty-third in a series that began in 1964. It focuses exclusively on the issue of adolescent smoking, which the report terms to be a problem of epidemic proportions. U.S. Department of Health and Human Services, *Preventing Tobacco Use Among Young People: A Report of the Surgeon General* (Atlanta, Georgia: U.S. Department of Health and Human Services, Public Health Service, Centers for Disease Control and Prevention, National Center for Chronic Disease Prevention and Health Promotion, Office of Smoking and Health, 1994).

6. Subsystems have also been described as "subgovernments," "whirlpools," and "iron triangles." In the words of B. Guy Peters, the underlying phenomenon is the same in each case: "Each functional area tends to be governed as if it existed apart from the remainder of government, and frequently the powers and legitimacy of government are used for the advancement of individual or group interests in society rather than from the broader public interest." See *American Public Policy; Promise and Performance,* 3rd

ed. (Chatham, N.J.: Chatham House Publishers, 1993), p. 23. For the classic statements on the subject, see J. Leiper Freeman, *The Political Process: Executive Bureau-Legislative Committee Relations* (New York: Random House, 1965), and Theodore J. Lowi, *The End of Liberalism: The Second Republic of the United States*, 2nd ed. (New York: W. W. Norton, 1979).

7. For theoretical accounts of conflict theories of change, see E.E. Schattschneider, *The Semi-Sovereign People* (New York: Holt, Rinehart & Winston, 1960); Georg Simmel, *Conflict and the Web of Group-Affiliations* (New York: Free Press, 1955); and Lewis Coser, *The Functions of Social Conflict* (New York: Free Press, 1956).

8. *USA Today*, June 9, 1994, p. 1.

9. Ibid. More recent data peg annual advertising and promotional spending by the tobacco industry at about $4 billion.

10. Kenneth E. Warner, "Cigarette Advertising and Media Coverage of Smoking and Health," *New England Journal of Medicine*, February 7, 1985, pp. 384–388.

11. Alfred D. Chandler, Jr., has written a very informative essay on the development of federal regulation in the United States. He shows how much of our early economic regulation was supported by small business and farmers. See "Government Versus Business: An American Phenomenon," in *Business and Public Policy*, ed. John T. Dunlop (Cambridge, Mass.: Harvard University Press, 1980).

12. This point is elaborated on in Chapter 3 of A. Lee Fritschler and Bernard H. Ross, *Business Regulation and Government Decision-Making* (Boston: Little, Brown, 1980).

13. Since 1982, the price supports themselves have been financed by a special assessment paid by the growers and tobacco companies. Still, the U.S. Department of Agriculture estimates that the federal government spent approximately $56 million in 1988 to administer the price support program and provide a variety of research and marketing information to the tobacco growers. See General Accounting Office, *Trade and Health Issues: Dichotomy Between Tobacco Export Policy and Anti-smoking Initiatives* (GAO/NSIAD-90-190, May 15, 1990), p. 39.

14. Helen Dewar, "Spending Cuts Just Fine—in Other Districts," *Washington Post*, February 5, 1981, p. B1.

15. Legislation that created the FDA was passed only after Congress bowed to the interests of members of tobacco states by amending the act to explicitly exclude tobacco products from FDA regulation.

16. Quoted in a speech by Franklin B. Dryden, Assistant to the President, Tobacco Institute Inc., before the 21st Tobacco Workers Conference, January 17–20, 1967, Williamsburg, Virginia (mimeo).

17. The advertisement that showed a plump woman of 1920s vintage reaching for a Lucky instead of a sweet conveyed an important message to young ladies in various stages of obesity. This ad is credited with making smoking acceptable to women. Medical doctors, athletes, and movie stars, tempted by large fees, gladly signed testimonials that implied that their good health and looks and, in the case of the doctors, those of their patients, were in no way compromised by smoking.

18. Ronald J. Troyer and Gerald E. Markle, *Cigarettes: The Battle over Smoking* (New Brunswick, N.J.: Rutgers University Press, 1983), pp. 33–34.

19. Ibid., p. 34. The affected states were Arkansas, Illinois, Indiana, Iowa, Kansas, Michigan, Minnesota, Missouri, Nebraska, New Hampshire, North Dakota, Oklahoma, South Dakota, Washington, and Wisconsin.

20. Ibid., quoted on p. 40.

21. Ibid., pp. 123–124.

22. D.S. Greenberg, "Cigarettes and Cancer: Pressure Grows for the Government to Respond to a Health Hazard," *Science*, May 18, 1962, p. 838.

23. The term *bureaucracy* is meant to include all the employees of a government agency—from political levels through the clerical staff.

24. Similarly, an executive agency might administer an act in such a way as to transform the original legislative intent of Congress into another kind of substantive policy. See David S. McLellan and Donald Clare, "Public Law 480: The Metamorphosis of a Law," *Eagleton Institute Cases in Practical Politics* (New York: McGraw-Hill, 1965).

25. The regulation requires that all packages containing guns be marked "firearms" and local police notified of their arrival before they leave the post office for delivery. *Washington Post,* June 18, 1968. See 33 *Federal Register,* pp. 8667 and 8678 (1968).

26. See William W. Boyer, *Bureaucracy on Trial: Policy Making by Government Agencies* (Indianapolis: Bobbs-Merrill, 1964), and Peter Woll, *American Bureaucracy* (New York: W. W. Norton, 1967) on this point and for a general discussion of agency policy-making powers. See also Francis Edward Rourke, *Bureaucracy, Politics, and Public Policy,* 3rd ed. (Boston: Little, Brown, 1985); and A. Lee Fritschler and Bernard H. Ross, *How Washington Works: The Executive's Guide to Government* (Cambridge, Mass.: Ballinger, 1986).

27. Theodore J. Lowi, *The End of Liberalism: The Second Republic of the United States,* 2nd ed. (New York: W.W. Norton, 1979), pp. 124–126.

28. In addition to legislative draftsmen who work within offices and committee counsels of some members of Congress, each house of Congress has an Office of the Legislative Counsel. This office will, upon presentation of only vague and minimal ideas, draft a bill for a member of Congress.

29. Often members introduce bills for constituents as a favor. Members generally don't expect to see these bills enacted; usually they are introduced with the understanding that they will be ignored.

Chapter

2

Smoking and Administrative Politics

Tobacco, divine, rare, superexcellent tobacco, which goes far beyond all their panaceas, potable gold, and philosopher's stones, a sovereign remedy to all diseases. . . . But, as it is commonly abused by most men, which take it as tinkers do ale, 'tis the plague, a mischief, a violent purger of goods, lands, health, hellish, devilish, and damned tobacco, the ruin and overthrow of body and soul.

Robert Burton (1577–1640)

When medical research began to establish a positive relationship between illness and smoking early in the 1900s, the cigarette controversy began to move slowly toward the center of the political arena. At the dawn of the century the abolitionist forces that existed were motivated by the view that smoking was an anti-social, immoral activity, while the effects of smoking on health had generated controversy only in the medical community. The cigarette health issue did not begin to concern the public or the government until the 1950s. The normal difficulties of transferring matters of scientific importance to the lay public were exacerbated by the efforts of the cigarette manufacturers to allay any fears smokers might have been experiencing as a result of conflict in the medical field. When unfavorable research findings were released, the manufacturers found ways to discredit and obliterate them in the public consciousness through more glamorous advertisements and intensified lobbying. Each major medical discovery and government response was followed by a reaction of the manufacturers or their advertisers. An examination of the chronology in Appendix I reveals this pattern of action and reaction in tobacco politics.[1]

Results of the first major health study were released in 1939. They received little public consideration, but what little attention they did get began to teach cigarette makers how to cope with future health scares. The early health studies failed to gain much credence because they dealt only with the medical *records* of human beings and not with human beings themselves. These studies were prepared from data contained in personal medical and mortality records of large groups of people. Over the years the significance of the studies has grown. The studies indicate that more cigarette smokers contract lung cancer than nonsmokers. Furthermore, they demonstrate that symptoms like chronic cough, sputum production, breathlessness, chest illness, and decreased lung function are found more often in smokers than in nonsmokers.

RESEARCH UNCOVERS
A HEALTH HAZARD

As frightening as the results of the earlier studies were, they failed to make the impact on the public that the post-1954 studies did. These studies dealt with smokers and nonsmokers, were conducted in laboratories and hospitals, and included autopsies. The results of the first of these studies, by E. Cuyler Hammond and Daniel Horn, concluded firmly that smoking causes lung cancer.[2] Later research discovered major and disturbing changes in the cellular structure of smokers' lungs. The statistics were startling; they revealed that 93.2 percent of smokers had abnormal lung cells, whereas only 1.2 percent of the lungs of nonsmokers contained evidence of abnormality. The Public Health Service analyzed seven population studies ten years after the first study was released. It was found that among 1,123,000 men, the mortality ratio of smokers to nonsmokers was 1.7 to 1 or nearly 70 percent higher for smokers than for nonsmokers.[3] Hundreds of studies have been conducted since 1954, nearly all of them expanding the catalog of chronic diseases attributable to cigarette smoking. Besides cancer of a wide variety of organs, the list now includes heart diseases and diseases of the respiratory system, as well as pregnancy problems. Drs. Hammond and Horn have written that the death rate from all causes for male smokers between the ages of 45 and 64 is twice as high as that for nonsmokers.

Research conducted after 1954 gave public health groups the impetus to mobilize their educational and lobbying activities. The Public Health Cancer Association and the American Cancer Society adopted resolutions acknowledging support of the 1954 studies and agreeing that there is a positive relationship between smoking and lung cancer. A report issued simultaneously by the British Ministry of Health came to the same conclusion. Four public health groups in 1957 joined to study the accumulating scientific evidence. The conclusion of their survey, released on March 6 of that year, stated:

> The sum total of scientific evidence established beyond reasonable doubt that cigarette smoking is a causative factor in the rapidly increasing incidence of human epidermoid carcinoma of the lung. *The evidence of a cause-effect relationship is adequate for the initiation of public health measures.* [Emphasis added][4]

INDUSTRY'S RESPONSE

The tobacco industry did not take this, or any of the subsequent studies that pointed to the health hazards of smoking, without attempting to challenge the veracity of the damaging claims. To the contrary, the tobacco industry has always been quick to point out the major shortcomings of scientific research on cigarette smoking. Most importantly, tobacco groups and their allies point out that most of the unfavorable cigarette findings that have been reported over the years have relied on statistical inference (i.e., post hoc examination of clinical records rather than scientifically controlled experiments) to establish a link between smoking and disease. While correlations show that those who smoke contract a variety of respiratory and related diseases at greater rates than those that do not, tobacco groups have suggested that, perhaps, the tendency to smoke and the tendency to become ill are both related to a third independent characteristic of smokers. It may be, for example, that smokers are generally more reckless when it comes to life-style choices, while nonsmokers are more self-protective in their life patterns (e.g., by watching their weight and being more attentive to their diet).

Tobacco groups also point out that, thus far, scientists have been unable to determine exactly which (if any) of the thousands of components in cigarette smoke causes disease. It would be unfair to strictly regulate cigarette production and sales, they argue, when it is not clear what—if anything about the product they ply—is harmful.[5]

These criticisms notwithstanding, scientists have become more and more sure-footed about their findings as the data on smoking has accumulated over the years. Today, statistical correlations between smoking and disease are widely accepted in the scientific community as valid evidence of a direct causal relationship between the two. Furthermore, the absence of specific information on those ingredients in cigarettes that cause diseases is no longer considered a valid criticism of the relationship between smoking and ill health. The comments made by Surgeon General William H. Stewart at the World Conference on Smoking over a quarter century ago sum up well the current scientific consensus:

> The proposition that cigarette smoking is hazardous to human health long ago passed the realm of possibility. It has now gone beyond the probable, to the point of demonstrable fact. . . . The sentence with which all of us are familiar—"Caution: Cigarette Smoking May Be Hazardous to Your Health"—is inadequate as a description of the present state of our knowledge. Cigarette smoking *is* hazardous to health. . . . This is no longer a matter of opinion nor an evangelical slogan. It is a flat scientific fact.[6]

Today, the task that seems most immediate to the largest portion of the health community involves communicating to the general public the enormous magnitude of the smoking problem, in terms of both individual health as well as national welfare. Death from smoking-related diseases has reached epidemic proportions in the 40 years since serious clinical research on the relationship between smoking and disease began in earnest. It is estimated that, today, at least one of every six deaths in the United States can be attributed to smoking. Tobacco causes more deaths every year than alcohol and drug abuse, infectious disease, toxic agents, firearms, and automobile accidents *combined*. The death toll in just one year, 1992, was estimated to be 434,000, greater than the total number of America's battlefield casualties during all four years of World War II (see Figure 2-1).[7] The over-40-million American smokers constitute a large portion of the national population. Their care, cure, and skill replacements in economic terms alone is estimated by the Congressional Office of Technology Assessment to be approximately $68 billion.[8]

BIRTH OF A LOBBY

Beginning in the early 1950s, the tobacco supporters found it expedient to go on the offense, combine forces, and attempt to counter the increasing amount of data running against their product. The first visible sign of significant change was the creation of the Tobacco Indus-

Figure 2-1* American Death Tolls from Major Wars and Annual Tolls for Leading Causes of Death in America

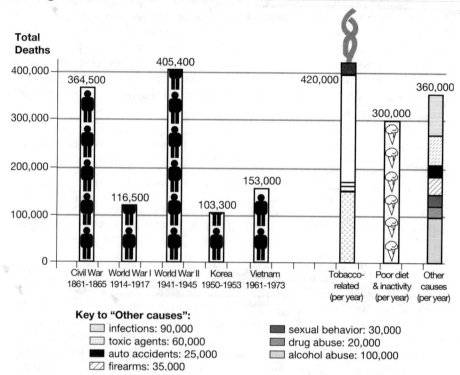

Key to "Other causes":
- ☐ infections: 90,000
- ▨ toxic agents: 60,000
- ■ auto accidents: 25,000
- ▨ firearms: 35,000

- ■ sexual behavior: 30,000
- ■ drug abuse: 20,000
- ☐ alcohol abuse: 100,000

*Data on per annum causes of death come from a recent report published by the National Cancer Institute, Robert L. Rabin and Stephen D. Sugarman, eds., *Smoking Policy: Law, Politics, and Culture* (New York: Oxford University Press, 1993), p. 11. Data on battle casualties comes from *Information Please Almanac: Atlas and Yearbook 1987*, 40th ed. (Boston: Houghton Mifflin, 1987).

try Research Committee (now called the Council for Tobacco Research—U.S.A.). Its purpose is to distribute funds for scientific research for studies on the use of tobacco and its effect on health. In its first twenty-five years of operation it awarded 744 grants totaling $64 million to 413 scientists at 258 hospitals, laboratories, research organizations, and medical schools. There have been 1,882 reports published acknowledging council support.[9]

The creation of this research organization was an indication that there would be intensified opposition from the tobacco interests on the health issue. Whenever criticism of smoking grew, the tobacco interests responded with more research or more public relations expenditures. Formation of the Tobacco Institute, Inc., a lobbying and public relations group formed in 1958, was a further indication of the industry's will to contain the possible adverse political effects of the health studies. In 1964, cigarette producers set up still another organization called the Cigarette Advertising Code, Inc. This was a self-policing organization to assure fairness and accuracy in competitive advertising.

The most important of these organizations as far as the cigarette labeling controversy is concerned was the Tobacco Institute. Fourteen of the major tobacco producers formed the institute, and the presidents of the companies sit on its board. It is financed by contributions from these large corporations, which contribute according to their share of the market.

In its promotional literature, the institute notes that it is concerned with the historical role of tobacco, its place in the economy, and public understanding of the tobacco industry. To these ends, it publishes a monthly tabloid, *The Tobacco Observer.* The real genius of the institute rests with the executives it hires. Former Ambassador George V. Allen was director of the institute at one time. A well-known and highly regarded career diplomat, Ambassador Allen brought considerable prestige to the organization. When the ambassador returned to government service as director of the Foreign Service Institute in 1966, the institute was successful in hiring former Senator Earle C. Clements as their director. For two years prior to that, the former senator had been a lobbyist for the six major cigarette companies.

Clements brought a very impressive set of credentials to the Tobacco Institute, including a public service record of long standing and a political record that few could equal. Previously, he had been Kentucky's governor and represented that state in the House and the Senate. With the loss of his Senate seat, he eventually returned to Kentucky where he became state highway commissioner. As an alumnus of Congress he still had floor privileges, though he was never known to have used them during the debates on the labeling bill. Indebted to political interests in Kentucky, his services as a lobbyist for all the deep-South tobacco interests were not difficult to obtain.

Politically, Clements was as close to the Johnson administration as anyone could possibly have been. In 1951, as the junior senator from Kentucky, Clements was placed on the powerful Senate Democratic Policy Committee at the urging of Lyndon Johnson when the death of Virgil Chapman, senior senator from Kentucky, left a seat open. Clements reciprocated in 1953 by endorsing Johnson for the position of minority leader, giving the impression, since Clements had established himself as a liberal, that the conservative Johnson was acceptable to all quarters of the party. Under Johnson's leadership, the Senate Democrats accepted Clements as minority whip and later as majority whip. During Johnson's absence because of a heart attack in 1955, Clements was entrusted with the rank and power of acting majority leader. A year later Majority Leader Johnson, knowing full well the consequences for Clements, asked him to vote in the affirmative on medical insurance legislation, a vote that contributed to his defeat in Kentucky.[10] Again Johnson came to the rescue of his old friend and secured for him the position of executive director of the Senate Democratic Campaign Fund. One of Clements's last activities for Lyndon Johnson came in 1960 when, as an advance man for Johnson, he attempted to gather delegate support for the majority leader after it became clear that Senator Hubert Humphrey's campaign for President had collapsed. In addition to this long personal involvement with Johnson, Clements claimed a rather unique tie to the White House. His daughter, Bess Abell, served as Lady Bird Johnson's social secretary. As a Johnson crony and working with the best-known law partner of the firm of Arnold, Fortas and Porter—Abe Fortas, a Johnson confidant and later a Supreme Court Justice and one-time nominee for the Chief Justice position—Clements helped plan and execute a careful and forceful campaign to save the tobacco industry from any governmental action that might be harmful to its sales.

The government action that the cigarette manufacturers anticipated as early as 1954 did not begin to materialize until the mid-1960s. The slowness of the government's response to the smoking studies of the 1950s was due, in part, to the successful efforts of the Tobacco Institute and, in part, to the relative weakness of the public health interest groups. The institute had enough economic and political power to make certain that government activity would be unproductive. The size and economic strength of the tobacco industry was bolstered politically by the size and strength of the advertising industry. It was in the cigarette selling business to the extent of $312 million a year in 1967. Cigarette promotions earned 8 percent of the total advertising revenue for television, 2.7 percent for radio, 2.3 percent for newspapers, and 3.3 percent for magazines. These figures show the importance of cigarettes to the mass media.

The disorganized array of health groups had neither the leadership nor the financial means to coalesce into an effective lobbying organization. They were overwhelmed by the giant tobacco industry and its supporters from the early 1950s onward.

CONGRESS REBUFFS HEALTH
PROPONENTS

Members of Congress from tobacco states were in powerful positions in the early 1960s. In the Senate nearly one fourth of the committees were chaired by members from the six leading tobacco states. Of the twenty-one committees in the House, tobacco state congressmen chaired seven.[11] Given the power distribution in Congress, the members from these states could exert extraordinary influence on matters that would come before their committees. As committee chairmen they could demand the support of their colleagues in return for legislative favors covering the broad spectrum of congressional action. Chairmen could use this power skillfully to indefinitely delay consideration of measures that might adversely affect their constituents. The tobacco state members used their power to protect the tobacco industry.

Certain members of Congress had worked for years to introduce legislation that would have either restricted the sale of cigarettes or conveyed health warnings to the public. More than 15 bills were introduced in the House and Senate by various lawmakers between 1962 and 1964 alone. None of these were considered seriously. The absence of public support for these health measures, combined with the opposition of the tobacco congressmen, prevented such proposals from receiving serious consideration.

The outcome of the first set of committee hearings on smoking and health, held in 1957, was indicative of just how potent the opposition of tobacco-state congressmen could be. The hearings were conducted by John A. Blatnik (D.-Minnesota) who was chairman of the Legal and Monetary Affairs Subcommittee of the House Government Operations Committee. The purpose of those hearings was to define or redefine the responsibility of the Federal Trade Commission for enforcing standards of truthfulness in advertising claims relating to the effectiveness of cigarette filters. Blatnik confessed during the hearings that his physician had warned him about his smoking habit but, despite the warning, he continued to smoke cigarettes and enjoy them. His personal testimonial on the enjoyment of smoking, however, did not assuage the anger of the tobacco interests over the content of the subcommittee's report. The report concluded, "The cigarette manufacturers have deceived the American public through their advertising of cigarettes." The subcommittee found that an individual was not safer if he or she elected to smoke filter tip cigarettes. Filters were not as effective as the manufacturers claimed; furthermore, lower-grade tobacco can be used in filter cigarettes and lower-grade leaves contain more tars and nicotine. Shortly after the report was issued, Blatnik's subcommittee was dissolved and he lost his chairmanship. The subcommittee was revived, but without Blatnik as a member. His loss was attributed to the power of the tobacco lobby.[12]

SMOKERS SUE MANUFACTURERS

When policy activism is thwarted in one branch of a separated-powers system, that activism often surfaces in another form, in another branch of that system. So it was in the case of smoking and politics. When it was clear that the friends of tobacco could successfully prevent meaningful congressional action on the health issue, the anti-smoking interests began concentrating their efforts elsewhere. One place they turned to was the judiciary.

Cigarette manufacturers have been subjected to judicial proceedings by lung cancer victims or their survivors on several occasions. The availability of scientific data that linked smoking and lung cancer spurred cancer victims or their heirs to sue, but many of the cases were initiated in the late 1940s and early 1950s, when the studies were not as definitive as they were later. The arguments against the manufacturers rested in most instances on the theory that cigarette producers acted in violation of their responsibility to supply a product of merchantable quality. Attorneys for the smokers argued that manufacturers had an obligation to make sure that cigarettes were healthful, and that manufacturers had implied such assurance in promotional activities. Throughout the 1950s and early 1960s, manufacturers of cigarettes were protected against suit, according to the courts, because they had no way to foresee the harm their product might do to a consumer.[13] This left open the question of what responsibility a producer might have when medical studies more clearly, or even absolutely, showed that smoking causes diseases. Then, of course, the harm could be foreseen.

One of the cases, brought by Edward L. Green of Miami in 1957, caused considerable difficulty to the cigarette companies. Mr. Green began smoking Lucky Strikes when he was 16 years old in 1925. After smoking three packages a day, he discovered in 1956 that he had contracted lung cancer. He commenced an action against the American Tobacco Company in 1957 that was continued by his son in 1958 after the elder Mr. Green's death and resulted in a jury verdict for the company. A United States Court of Appeals affirmed the judgment.[14]

Although the company won on the first round, Mr. Green's heirs succeeded in having the same court of appeals direct a new trial. This time the court directed a new jury to consider the question of whether the American Tobacco Company's cigarettes were reasonably fit for general public consumption. The new jury found that cigarettes were reasonably safe and wholesome, and Mr. Green's heirs were denied at that time any part of the $1.5 million they sought.[15]

The medical evidence introduced at the trial did have some impact on the jury. The foreman of the jury at Mr. Green's trial was a pack-a-day smoker who, after listening to the medical evidence, gave up smoking halfway through the trial. He explained afterward that if the judge had asked the jury members to decide whether or not cigarettes were safe, they would have said no. The judge had instead asked them to decide if cigarettes were reasonably safe and wholesome for human consumption. The key word was *reasonably.* The jury apparently decided that if it took cigarettes 20 to 30 years to affect Mr. Green, they were reasonably safe.

The decision was appealed three years later because of subsequent Florida court decisions concerning liability. This time, in light of the new decisions, the court decided in favor of Mr. Green. The decision read in part:

> We are now left in no substantial doubt that under Florida law the decedent was entitled to rely on the implied assurance that the Lucky Strike cigarettes were wholesome and fit for the purpose intended and that under the facts found by the jury his personal representative and widow are entitled to hold the manufacturers absolutely liable for the injuries already found by a prior jury to have been sustained by him.[16]

This decision, favorable to the descendants of lung cancer victims, did not stand, however. The full court of appeals reversed the decision in April 1969; and held that the American Tobacco Company was not liable for Mr. Green's death from lung cancer.[17]

The judiciary has been even more sympathetic to the tobacco companies since 1965, when warning labels started appearing on packs of cigarettes. Before that time, the cigarette companies were successful in arguing that there was insufficient evidence to conclude that cigarettes were harmful. After that time, the manufacturers could claim that consumers had been fairly warned that health hazards may exist, making it nearly impossible for anyone to sue successfully for breach of warranty. One now smokes at one's own risk, it seems, for time and again the courts have found that the health warning label relieves the manufacturers of responsibility under the law of liability.

In 1988, there were about 135 liability cases pending against tobacco companies by smokers or their families.[18] In one case—*Gal-*

braith v. *R.J. Reynolds Industries*—nationally known trial attorney Melvin Belli claimed that his client, Mr. Galbraith, was addicted to tobacco, so health warnings on labels were useless. In another highly publicized case, *Marsee* v. *U.S. Tobacco*, a woman argued that her son died of oral cancer because he used snuff. Juries in both of these cases ruled in favor of the tobacco companies. In a third important case, *Cipallone* v. *Liggett Group*, a U.S. circuit court of appeals ruled that tobacco companies have limited immunity from liability in such cases because of the warning labels. On January 12, 1987, the Supreme Court upheld this finding by declining to review the case.[19] As of 1995, the tobacco industry has preserved its perfect record in liability suits by smokers who have died or become ill from diseases associated with tobacco; not one penny has been paid out by tobacco companies in punitive damages to date.[20]

BUREAUCRATIC CONFLICT

While the courts and Congress experienced procedural and political difficulties with the cigarette health issue that were peculiar to those institutions, the bureaucracy was experiencing some of its own. A gigantic, complex operation, the federal bureaucracy employs about two and one-half million people in hundreds of agencies. One agency or another has had some interest in cigarettes since the turn of the century. There has, however, been little agreement among them on what the government position was, or what it should be, concerning smoking and health. The cigarette issue divided the bureaucracy rather sharply, pointing out the inescapable fact that although the bureaucracy is huge, it is anything but monolithic in its views. On cigarettes, agencies were on both ends of the policy spectrum. Some were attempting to boost cigarette and tobacco sales, while others—the FTC, for example—were planning programs designed to reduce cigarette consumption.

The United States Department of Agriculture's (USDA) interest in tobacco is related to its mission as the protector of farmers and the promoter of their products. According to then-Senator Maurine Neuberger (D.-Oregon), officials of the department's Tobacco Division once disparagingly referred to the cigarette health crusade as a big smokescreen. The department administers price support programs for tobacco and endeavors to promote with assistance and encouragement from the office of the U.S. Trade Representative, the sales of U.S. tobacco abroad. At the height of the smoking and health controversy, the Department of Agriculture was distributing an expensive sales promotion film that it had paid to have produced. The film stressed the virtues of cigarette smoking, and it was available at no charge to any nation that wanted to consider importing U.S. tobacco products.

Former Secretary of Agriculture Orville Freeman found himself in a tight spot when reporters questioned him about the continuation of tobacco price supports in view of recent smoking and health revelations. In what could be a political classic, the secretary responded that the government could in good conscience continue price supports and, indeed, must continue the price support program for tobacco. If the program were discontinued, he argued, tobacco prices would fall and cigarettes would cost less. The price reduction would then result in more people smoking and this, after all, would be contrary to the spirit of the health studies.

Later the Department of Agriculture took an official position against the inclusion of a health warning on packages or in advertising. Acting to protect its constituent tobacco producers, the department wrote:

> Much more explicit identifications of the constituents of tobacco smoke and more complete understanding of their role as related to health must be sought and achieved. Only this will provide an adequate basis for deciding whether or not such stringent provisions as those in [the bill, which required only the health warning on packages] are warranted.[21]

The views of the Department of Agriculture found little support in the Federal Trade Commission. While there were people in the commission concerned with cigarette health questions, it was the commission's jurisdiction over unfair and deceptive trade practices that brought about their earliest regulation of cigarette manufacturers. Since the early 1930s, the commission had brought approximately 20 actions against cigarette companies for false or misleading advertising. Many of these actions involved what the commission considered misleading health claims. The manufacturers of Chesterfields were prohibited, for example, from claiming their product had "no adverse effect upon the nose, throat or accessory organs."[22] Another producer was proscribed from claiming that Kools would keep one's head clear in the winter or any other time, give extra protection, or provide an excellent safeguard during cold months.[23]

The commission broadened its attack on cigarette advertising in September 1955 when it adopted some advertising guides. It prohibited, among other things, stating or implying in advertising that there is medical approval of cigarette smoking in general or smoking any brand of cigarette in particular.

After the guides were issued, the Federal Trade Commission attempted to monitor cigarette advertising. Monitoring ads and moving to prohibit some of them did not satisfy the commission's goals, however. In the light of the increasing scientific data that questioned the healthfulness of cigarette consumption, the actions of the commission looked puny and insignificant. The commission knew that consumption of cigarettes was increasing rapidly, particularly among younger age groups.[24] It attributed this increase to advertising that portrayed smoking in an attractive way, particularly on television. Advertisements quite naturally dwell only on whatever satisfactions there might be in smoking. They associate smoking with individuals or groups worthy of emulation, especially by the young. Smoking is portrayed as being fun, romantic, and even sexy.

To the FTC's consternation, these advertisements did not violate any law. They did not even violate the intent of the 1955 advertising guidelines. It became clear to the commission that a positive health warning was needed; otherwise any health message could be overcome by the subtleties of modern advertising. To adopt a new policy requiring a warning would necessitate overcoming not only the tobacco interests in and out of Congress, but also could be expected to involve doing battle in the courts, where the right of the FTC to take such bold policy-making steps would surely be questioned by the tobacco industry. Opposition from other bureaucratic agencies that were sympathetic to tobacco interests could be expected as well.[25]

One of the bureaucracies opposing the health warning idea was, surprisingly enough, the large Department of Health, Education and Welfare (HEW; in 1980 it became the Department of Health and Human Services [HHS]), the parent organization for both the Food and Drug Administration (FDA) and the Public Health Service (PHS). Just as siblings frequently are quite different from each other and from their parents, the agencies of health, education and welfare have held remarkably divergent views. From the top, then-Secretary Anthony Celebrezze indicated that he thought the government should play no significant role in advising the public of the supposed hazards of cigarette smoking. In mid-1964, Celebrezze wrote to the chairman of the House Interstate and Foreign Commerce Committee that the department advised rejection of all those cigarette control bills then pending. He argued that the bills might be helpful in developing legislation that the department would submit, but they were, for reasons, not explained, unacceptable to the department. HEW never submitted any legislation on cigarettes and health. Senator Neuberger, a staunch congressional advocate of the antismoking position in this period, referred to the action of that department in straightforward terms: "It's fair to infer that they [members of HEW] don't want anything at all."[26]

The hesitancy displayed in the secretary's office was not an accurate index of the feelings on the smoking and health issue in other parts of the department, however. The Public Health Service had undertaken some research in 1957 and from that time showed some desire to act. When the PHS was prodded to move by the President in 1964, the agency's quick response was an indication of the extent to which its leadership was anxious to take some action. After the head of the PHS, Surgeon General Luther L. Terry, had publicly adopted a position that favored a health warning, he was sent to Congress to testify on the labeling requirement bill. He was obliged to state the position of the secretary of HEW, however, and consequently made it appear that the PHS did not strongly favor the bill. This unnecessary opposition helped to split the bureaucracy at a crucial time; it also helped to insure that meaningful antismoking action would either not be taken or at least be substantially delayed.

The Food and Drug Administration, the agency that the Surgeon General suggested as the proper regulator of warning requirements, had demonstrated even less interest in the smoking and health issue than its sister agency, the PHS. The FDA's reluctance was due, according to Senator Neuberger's book, *Smoke Screen: Tobacco and the Public Welfare,* to a late-Victorian episode in congressional politics. She claims that the item "tobacco" appeared in the 1890 edition of the *U.S. Pharmacopoeia,* an official listing of drugs published by the government. It did not appear in the 1905 or later editions, according to the senator, because the removal of tobacco from the *Pharmacopoeia* was the price that had to be paid to get the support of tobacco state legislators for the Food and Drug Act of 1906. The elimination of the word *tobacco* automatically removed the leaf from FDA supervision.

The FDA was given what appeared to be another opportunity to concern itself with cigarette smoking when the Hazardous Substances Labeling Act was passed in 1960. It empowered the FDA to control the sale of substances which, among other things, had the capacity to produce illness through inhalation. Secretary Celebrezze suggested in a letter to the Senate that the act could be interpreted to cover cigarettes as "hazardous substances." In what had become characteristic behavior of HEW, however, the secretary went on to argue that it would be better to wait and let Congress amend the act to make it more explicit and thereby avoid controversy.[27] Subsequently, Congress rejected such an amendment.

The reluctance of the FDA could be traced to still other factors. During the early 1960s, the agency was having serious problems of its own. It suffered through some devastating investigations conducted by the late Senator Estes Kefauver (D.-Tennessee). The hearings dealt with the pricing practices, safety, and monopoly aspects of the drug industry. One of the alarming revelations to emerge from the hearings was the extent to which the FDA was dominated and supported by that sector of the business community it was supposed to regulate—drug manufacturers and distributors.[28] In what might have been simple reflex action, the FDA found it easier to keep quiet and follow Secretary Celebrezze's lead to continue to protect its good standing in the business community. The FDA found it expedient to ignore the cigarette health issue even though scientific indictments mounted in the early 1960s and other agencies began to take some action.

The cigarette and health controversy showed very clearly that agencies represent interests, often very specialized ones. Agency views can be compromised or made to accommodate one another; this is the special role of the president and the White House staff. However, presidents are not eager to become involved in controversies between agencies, especially when these controversies have deep, political roots and the differences seem unreconcilable.

The disparity of views and the bickering between agencies existed up to and through the congressional hearings in 1965. President Johnson made no attempt to coordinate agency programs although he had the administrative mechanism to do so. One of the functions of the Bureau of the Budget (now called the Office of Management and Budget) was to make certain that all agency programs coincided with the President's program. All agency letters sent to Congress, whether favoring or opposing the health warning idea, had to have been cleared by the bureau. The final paragraph of each letter contained these words (or a slight variation of them): "The Bureau of the Budget has advised us it has no objection to the submission of this report from the standpoint of the administration's program."

With the White House publicly silent, the bureaucracy divided among itself, and Congress in the grips of inaction, there appeared to be very little hope for enacting the requirement of a health warning. The tobacco subsystem had been successful in containing the controversy.

At this early stage, the policy-making process resembles a large warehouse of ideas and proposals, with agencies and Congress represented by separate cubicles of various size and importance. Events and participants in the political system might be successful in shifting proposals from one storage cubicle to another, but seldom does this movement result in taking a proposal from the warehouse to a position in the decision-making process where it might be favorably acted upon. Lacking the power to move a proposal results, frequently, in the warehouse becoming a graveyard. The antismoking forces had to find some way to rescue the health warning from the certain oblivion of the political warehouse, where it was already beginning to show signs of atrophy and approaching death.

NOTES

1. For example, 14 major studies linking smoking and disease were completed during the watershed years between 1950 and 1954. On January 3, 1954, cigarette manufacturers set up the Council for Tobacco Research (originally called the Tobacco Industry Research Committee) to better control the type and interpretation of scientific information that was being generated. A few years later, in 1957, Senator Wallace Bennett (R.-Utah) introduced legislation requiring that cigarette packs carry a warning label. That same year, Richard Neuberger (D.-Oregon) introduced legislation that would eliminate crop price supports for tobacco farmers. In 1958, the major U.S. cigarette manufacturers responded by establishing the Tobacco Institute, an entity designed to consolidate the manufacturers' public relations and lobbying efforts.

2. E. Cuyler Hammond and Daniel Horn, "The Relationship Between Human Smoking Habits and Death Rates: A Follow-Up Study of 187,766 Men," *Journal of the American Medical Association,* August 7, 1954.

3. U.S. Department of Health, Education and Welfare, *Smoking and Health: Report of the Advisory Committee to the Surgeon General of the Public Health Service,* Public Health Service Document No. 1103 (Washington, D.C.: U.S. Government Printing Office, 1964), p. 28.

4. The four groups were the American Cancer Society, the National Cancer Institute, the American Heart Association, and the National Heart Institute.

5. A well-written summary of the tobacco industry's position by Robert C. Hockett, associate scientific director of the Tobacco Industry Research Committee, appears in the April 1964 issue of the *Yale Scientific Magazine.* This position is also evident in recent studies and publications sponsored by the industry. The January 1979 Tobacco Institute study "Smoking and Health 1964–1979 The Continuing Controversy" points out that linking smoking to cancer and other diseases may be unfounded because of conflicting evidence. A 1984 Tobacco Institute publication, "The Cigarette Controversy: Why More Research Is Needed," updates the arguments. For a less scientific, more personal accounting of the tobacco industry responses to the mounting evidence in the smoking and health controversy, see Roger Rosenblatt, "How Do Tobacco Executives Live with Themselves?" *The New York Times Magazine,* March 20, 1994.

6. Quoted in Warren G. Magnuson and Jean Carper, *The Dark Side of the Market Place* (Englewood Cliffs, N.J.: Prentice Hall, 1968), p. 188.

7. Robert L. Rabin and Stephen D. Sugarman, eds., *Smoking Policy: Law, Politics, and Culture* (New York: Oxford University Press, 1993), p. 3.

8. John Carey, "It's Time for the Regulators to Stop Blowing Smoke," *Business Week,* March 14, 1994, p. 34.

9. In addition to the $64 million expended by the council, the six major cigarette producers contributed $15 million between 1964 and 1973 to the American Medical Association Education and Research Foundation to support a comprehensive program of research on tobacco and health. The initial award came at the time the Federal Trade Commission announced that it was considering a health warning requirement. The American Medical Association did not actively support the FTC's proposal.

10. See Rowland Evans and Robert Novak, *Lyndon B. Johnson: The Exercise of Power* (New York: NAL, 1966), p. 159ff.

11. Maurine B. Neuberger, *Smoke Screen: Tobacco and the Public Welfare* (Englewood Cliffs, N.J.: Prentice Hall, 1963), p. 110.

12. Abolishing a subcommittee of the Government Operations Committee for punitive reasons has happened more than once. The Subcommittee on Foreign Operations and Government Information was threatened with abolition by the chairman of the full committee, William L. Dawson (D.-Illinois), in the spring of 1968 because of its criticism of United States aid programs and the progress of land reform in Vietnam. *The Congressional Quarterly* staff reported that informal sources indicated the order was a case of the hawks about to devour the subcommittee. (*Congressional Quarterly Weekly Report*, No. 17, April 26, 1968, p. 914).

13. See Richard A. Wegman, "Cigarettes and Health: A Legal Analysis," 51 *Cornell Law Quarterly*, 678 (1966), for a detailed analysis of many of the suits brought against cigarette manufacturers.

14. *Green* v. *American Tobacco Co.*, 304 F. 2d 70 (5th Cir. 1962).

15. Referred to in *Green* v. *American Tobacco Co.*, 391 F. 2d 101 (5th Cir. 1968).

16. Ibid., p. 106.

17. *Green* v. *American Tobacco Co.*, 409 F. 2d 1166 (5th Cir. 1969).

18. *Investors Daily*, November 26, 1985, p. 3.

19. *Marsee* v. *U.S. Tobacco*, WDOB 639 F. Supp. 466; *Cipallone* v. *Liggett Group, Inc.*, 593 F. Supp. 1146 Rev. 798 181.

20. For an historical treatment of tobacco tort liability, see Robert L. Rabin, "Institutional and Historical Perspectives on Tobacco Tort Liability," and for an up-to-date treatment of the tort liability of cigarette manufacturers, see Gary T. Schwartz, "Tobacco Liability in the Courts." Both articles appear as chapters in Rabin and Sugarman, eds., *Smoking Policy: Law, Politics, and Culture.*

21. Letter to Senator Warren G. Magnuson, printed in *Cigarette Labeling and Advertising, Hearings Before The Committee on Commerce, United States Senate*, 89th Congress, 1st Session, 1965, p. 28.

22. *Liggett and Myers Tobacco Co.*, 55 Federal Trade Commission 354 (1958).

23. *Brown and Williamson Tobacco Corporation*, 34 Federal Trade Commission 1689 (1942).

24. A study done by the Bureau of the Census for the Public Health Service in 1956 highlighted the trend toward higher consumption in lower age groups. See: Haenszell, Shimkin, and Millers, *Tobacco Smoking Patterns in the U.S.*, Public Health Monograph No. 45 (1956).

25. The impact of television advertising on smokers and potential smokers was pointed out in a Federal Trade Commission survey released in 1967. The commission noted the sponsorship of television programs during one week in January of that year. Eighty-seven programs were sponsored in whole or in part by six major cigarette manufacturers. Nearly 1.5 billion viewers watched these programs. (A person who watched 10 of the 60 programs was counted as 10 viewers.) Approximately 322.7 million were under the age of 21.

26. Dan Cordtz, "Congress Likely to Vote a Mild Law Requiring Warnings on Packages," *The Wall Street Journal*, March 22, 1965, p. 1.

27. *Cigarette Labeling and Advertising Hearings*, 89th Congress, 1st Session, p. 22.

28. For an excellent analysis of the Kefauver drug hearings, see Richard Harris, *The Real Voice* (New York: Macmillan, 1964).

Chapter

3

The Advisory Committee and New Policy Directions

Tobacco is an evil weed.
The Devil himself sowed the seed.
It stains your teeth,
And scents your clothes
And makes a chimney of your nose!

Anonymous children's rhyme, 19th century

Moving an issue from obscurity to the top of the government's agenda is a difficult task; there are no guidebooks or manuals detailing the steps in this process. Those who want to initiate change in policy have come to recognize that their cause will succeed only with hard work, careful strategy, and large portions of luck. In consumer affairs, the obstacles to change are nearly overwhelming; they range from the powerful inertia of tradition to forceful opposition from important individuals and groups who see some challenge to their fortunes in whatever policy change is contemplated. Those who oppose government action to protect consumers are better organized and better financed than consumer groups. Lacking the necessary political resources—organization and money—consumer supporters are forced to put together large coalitions of marginal interest groups and work diligently to capture public support.

The decade of the 1960s has been called the Decade of the Consumer by some because of the amount of consumer legislation passed by Congress.[1] Although more legislation was passed than in other periods, its usefulness was somewhat questionable. Cigarette legislation passed in 1965 was of dubious value to the public; it contained a mild health warning requirement for packages but prohibited government agencies from imposing other health rules on cigarette advertising or labeling. But the content of the legislation was not the whole story. Once the characteristics of the policy subsystem began to change, the possibilities increased for significant alteration in the policies for which that subsystem had been exclusively responsible.

The public health interests followed a pattern that has been used recently with considerable success by consumer advocates. They located an agency willing to take action that was unpopular with powerful economic interests and powerfully placed members of Congress. Once the agency acted, the economic interests were forced to react. The reaction brought other agencies, interest groups, and members of Congress into the policy arena. The substance of the initial bureaucratic and congressional actions of the mid-1960s was not as important as the fact that action was taken. The fact that the action compelled future policy to be made in an arena broader than the subsystem that normally controlled smoking and health politics was also significant.

Public support might have been favorable toward the health groups, but it was not well organized or forcefully articulated. Surveys taken by the government in 1964 and 1966 showed between 70 and 75 percent of the public agreeing with the statement, "Cigarette smoking is enough of a health hazard for something to be done about it."[2] A newspaper poll in 1967, two years after the passage of the first cigarette act, revealed that congressmen favored, two-to-one, a stronger health warning on packages and a requirement that the warning appear in all advertising. More than majority support is sometimes necessary to overcome the power of strongly entrenched interests, however. One of the congressmen surveyed commented, "Let's face it. . . . When you combine the money and power of the tobacco and liquor interests with advertising agencies, newspapers, radio, and television . . . there is too much political muscle involved to expect much accomplishment."[3]

Gaining mass support to overcome the resistance built into policy subsystems is difficult. At certain times in consumer history, a dramatic event or the work of a single individual has provided the impetus necessary to stimulate a change in policy. Upton Sinclair's book, *The Jungle,* on the stenches of the meat-packing industry at the turn of the century, and Ralph Nader's forceful volume, *Unsafe at Any*

Speed, accusing the automobile industry of irresponsibility in the safety field, are examples of this. The Kefauver drug control legislation was floundering until Frances Kelsey, M.D., shook the government's conscience with data demonstrating that a sleep-inducing drug called thalidomide, when taken by pregnant women, caused severe, ghastly deformities in babies. Air travel safety systems were expanded and improved after two commercial airplanes collided over the Grand Canyon, killing 128 persons. Although the smoking issue was to have its highly visible public advocate, John F. Banzhaf and his group called ASH (Action on Smoking and Health), Banzhaf did not appear until after the first major breakthrough for the health interests. The cigarette issue came to the government's agenda without the backing of organized public opinion.

SUPPORT FOR A HEALTH WARNING

The events that lead to action on the smoking and health issue were not as dramatic as the events that led to action on other consumer issues. They were characteristic, however, of the manner in which bureaucrats and members of Congress draw on each other's assets to bring an issue into public view. Developing support for a health warning was not easy, but the success of the supporters of the warning is an indication of the political power latent within the bureaucracy. When this power is skillfully marshaled, change can be initiated.

Three related occurrences set the policy-making process in motion. The first of these was a Senate Joint Resolution (SJR 174) introduced by Senator Maurine Neuberger in March 1962, which called for the establishment of a presidential commission on tobacco and health. Congressional reaction was predictable; there was no interest in the resolution. There were no hearings, little discussion, and SJR 174 seemed to face certain death. Senator Neuberger knew from experience that Congress would do little on the smoking issue because of the support the tobacco industry had. Furthermore, if the resolution had passed, it would have only encouraged, not required, the President to establish a study commission. This suggests that the senator was seeking a wider audience than Congress. Her resolution provided the health interests with an opportunity to rally and take the idea to the President or directly to the public. It first appeared that the resolution was not the appropriate vehicle. Senator Neuberger's resolution lay dormant for two months. Had it not been for the efforts of an enterprising reporter, it might have been interred forever in the legislative graveyard.

Spurred by the suggestion in the resolution of a presidential commission, a reporter at one of President Kennedy's major news conferences asked the President what he intended to do about the question
of smoking and health. These live televised news conferences put the
President under considerable pressure to appear calm, knowledgeable, and confident. President Kennedy had earned the reputation of
handling questions at these conferences with skill and poise. Adept in
answering questions, witty, and most important, thoroughly briefed
by his staff on what questions the press might be expected to raise,
he was seldom embarrassed.

Lengthy briefing sessions preceded each press conference, but
the briefing for the conference in May 1962 must not have included
the smoking and health issue. When the President was asked whether
he or his advisers agreed with the findings of an increasing number
of studies that linked smoking and ill health, there was an embar-
rassing pause. Then the response came awkwardly:

> The—that matter is sensitive enough and the stock market is in suffi-
> cient difficulty without my giving you an answer which is not based on
> complete information, which I don't have, and therefore perhaps we
> could—I'd be glad to respond to that question in more detail next
> week. . . .[4]

As a result of the press conference, the issue was moved from
Congress to the President. He was now publicly committed to initiat-
ing some action within the bureaucracy. The pressure of public opinion, combined with pressure from those bureaucrats who saw an
opening they had been waiting for, guaranteed a speedy presidential
response. Soon after the press conference, President Kennedy asked
the Public Health Service to report on what it had been doing in the
field of smoking and health. The agency had done a considerable
amount, although its activities were not well known. Officials of the
PHS were aware of the smoking studies done by medical scientists and
had even done some of their own. In 1957, the PHS had published the
report of a study group that assessed the smoking and health data
available at the time. The report concluded that excessive smoking
was one of the causal factors in lung cancer. Soon after its release, the
report was officially endorsed by the PHS.

When the Kennedy White House expressed interest in the research of the Public Health Service in terms that indicated that the
research findings might be implemented, it was not surprising that
the PHS responded enthusiastically. Only two weeks after the press
conference, Surgeon General Luther Terry announced he would establish a high-level advisory committee to study the impact of smoking on health. The appointment of the committee was the culmination

of the events that gave the health warning issue the momentum it needed to eventually receive serious consideration as national policy.

ADVISORY COMMITTEES
IN THE BUREAUCRACY

Advisory committees have been used by the bureaucracy for a long time. They are designed to bring outside views into bureaucratic policy making, usually at the stage where new policies are being considered. Some advisory committees are made up entirely of experts who provide an agency with special kinds of information it could not expect to get from its own staff. Others, called representative advisory committees, are composed of those who represent some special interest. Representative committees serve at least two useful functions for the agency they advise: They inject some new, outside ideas that might not otherwise find their way into agency policy, and they serve as sounding boards for testing agency proposals.

Both the representative and the expert advisory committees can be used for political purposes. The Surgeon General's Advisory Committee on Smoking and Health was an expert committee. Its purposes, however, were as much political as scientific. The report of a high-level committee of well-known, respected experts was bound to have a significant impact on the public. The forcefulness of that impact could be heightened if selection of committee members, reports of their meetings, and announcement of their findings were handled with political skill and an appreciation for the nature of public opinion. The Surgeon General must have sensed that the Advisory Committee and its recommendations would give the Public Health Service the support it needed to pursue programs designed to reduce the health threat posed by the mass consumption of cigarettes. The events that followed the announcement that a committee would be created proved that at least some physicians and bureaucrats knew the politics of policy making very well.

The first clues to the political dimensions of the Surgeon General's committee appeared early. One was that the committee was to make no new scientific study of its own. Instead, its mandate was to assess the value of existing studies and their conclusions. This had already been done on a small scale by private health groups and earlier by the Public Health Service itself. It was important to the Public Health Service to have a new, outside group review the results of the existing studies. The Advisory Committee was well suited to giving the existing studies new currency in the public eye.

Another clue to the political nature of the committee was the manner in which the 12 (later 10) members were selected. The Surgeon General stated publicly that the group was to include scientific, professional persons concerned with all aspects of smoking and health. The tobacco industry, health groups, professional associations, and federal agencies were called upon to participate in selecting individuals who might serve on the committee.[5]

The names of 150 scientists were presented to those groups involved in the selection process. These groups were to eliminate from consideration individuals for any reason they saw fit and return the list to the Surgeon General. One "blackball" apparently could have eliminated any name from consideration for appointment. From the approved lists the Surgeon General selected the members of the Advisory Committee on Smoking and Health.

The selection process underscores the great pains to which the Surgeon General went to make certain that the report of the committee would not be attacked on the grounds that the membership was stacked against any particular interest. To further protect the committee from such an attack, anyone who had made any public statements on the smoking and health controversy was ineligible to serve. The gentleman named to serve as executive director of the committee was removed shortly after he was appointed. Learning of the appointment, reporters from his home-town newspaper asked for a comment. The response they received was that recent studies definitely suggested that tobacco was a health hazard.[6] The neutral integrity of the committee was thus challenged, and a new executive director was appointed.

Those appointed to the Advisory Committee were among the most distinguished members of their profession. Eight were M.D.'s with specializations in internal medicine, epidemiology, and pharmacology. The nonphysicians were a chemist and a statistician. All were professors at leading medical schools with the exception of Dr. Eugene H. Guthrie, the panel's staff director, who was a 12-year veteran of the Public Health Service. There were three cigarette smokers in the group and two who smoked pipes and cigars on occasion.[7]

THE SURGEON GENERAL'S COMMITTEE AT WORK

The newly formed Advisory Committee on Smoking and Health met for the first time on November 9, 1962. At this meeting the committee agreed on its operating procedures. They agreed first to review the scientific literature on all aspects of the use of tobacco and smoking habits. Other possible contributing factors to ill health such as air pollution, industrial exposure, radiation, and alcohol were also included in the committee's agenda.

The full committee held nine meetings of two to four days' duration during 1963, and there were several meetings of subcommittees. The witnesses who appeared were consultants hired by the committee and representatives of special interest groups, including the tobacco industry. A transcript was kept but not made public. In fact, a great degree of secrecy surrounded all activities of the Advisory Committee. The extraordinary precautions taken to assure there would be no leaks were so out of character for the Public Health Service that tensions were exaggerated for those who already entertained substantial fears about the content of the committee's report. It probably was necessary for the PHS to take precautions to prevent erroneous information from spreading through rumors. The secrecy did serve another function, however. It provided some suspense, and by the time the report was ready to be released, all the major news agencies of the nation focused their attention on the Advisory Committee.[8]

In Washington, even the most tightly sealed conferences emit some information to the press. There was substantial speculation about the committee's meetings taking place deep within the confines of Public Health Service headquarters in Washington's fashionable suburb, Bethesda, Maryland. Virtually none of the speculation gave any comfort to those whose fortunes were dependent upon the sale of tobacco and tobacco products.

THE ADVISORY COMMITTEE'S REPORT

On Saturday, January 11, 1964, the world discovered what had made the tobacco interests uneasy. In a well-prepared, carefully staged news conference, the Surgeon General announced the results of the Advisory Committee's study.[9] The conference was held behind locked doors in the State Department auditorium, the same room used by President Kennedy for his meetings with the press. With the reporters seated and the television cameras in place, the Surgeon General and his committee took seats on the stage. The large "no smoking" signs affixed to the walls on both sides of the raised platform were unintentional indices of the tone of the conference that was to follow. The reporters were given 90 minutes to ask questions and read the published 387-page report. At the end of 90 minutes the doors were opened, the reporters released, and the results of the study were telegraphed around the country and the world.

Selecting a Saturday for the day of the press conference had some significance. It signaled that the report might adversely affect the price of tobacco shares on the nation's stock exchanges.[10] Scheduling the press conference on a Saturday, normally a slow news day, also increased the chances that the report's findings would make headline news in the Sunday morning papers. Politically, this was an extraordinarily savvy move to make considering the fact that bureaucrats, the orchestrators of this event, tend to operate outside of the media limelight. Media neophytes or not, the tack paid off, for Sunday's papers were splashed with headlines about the commission's report, and the news for the tobacco subsystem was not good.[11]

The report included detailed summaries of the studies that the committee had considered. These studies established a positive relationship between cigarette smoking and a host of other diseases. There was scant encouragement in the report for those who smoked cigars and pipes. Although the evidence of the ill effects from these tobacco products was not as devastating as for cigarettes, there was indication that their consumption was related to high mortality ratios for ". . . cancers of the mouth, esophagus, larynx and lung, and for stomach and duodenal ulcers."

At the press conference, the Surgeon General noted that the precise role of smoking in causing chronic diseases was not established by the studies. The Advisory Committee agreed, however, that it was more prudent from the public health viewpoint to accept the cause-and-effect relationship that the data indicated than to wait until the exact relationship had been determined. In short, the members of the committee concluded unanimously that "Cigarette smoking is a health hazard of sufficient importance in the United States to warrant appropriate remedial action."

IMPACT OF THE ADVISORY COMMITTEE'S REPORT

The selection techniques employed by the Surgeon General and the reputation of the Advisory Committee's members assured that there would be little criticism of the committee itself. The Surgeon General held his committee in high esteem, and he worked closely with it. He officially accepted the committee's report within 16 days of its completion, although the Department of Health, Education and Welfare, itself, was less than enthusiastic about the report and its political implications. Immediately after its acceptance, Dr. Terry moved to clean his own house of those products the report had indicted. He ordered a halt to the free distribution of cigarettes in the 16 public hospitals and 50 Indian hospitals under the direction of the Public Health Service; the staff members of those hospitals were ordered to conduct educational programs to discourage cigarette smoking.

A measure of the political success of the Advisory Committee on Smoking and Health experienced was the speed with which other agencies rallied to the antismoking cause. One week after the Advisory Committee's report was issued, the Federal Trade Commission announced that it would issue rules governing the advertising and labeling of cigarettes. The announcement was accompanied by a draft of the proposed rules and an invitation for all interested parties to submit their views to the commission.[12] Hearings were held on the new rule within a month, and six months later an FTC rule requiring package and advertisement warnings was published in the *Federal Register.*

Ultimately, the impact of the Surgeon General's report on the political system was just what the antismoking interests had hoped for: It provided the Federal Trade Commission with an opportunity to make its move. The Advisory Committee, by bringing the issue into focus, gave the subsystem a blow that was to prove fatal. The bureaucracy was given the backing it needed to spring into action. But before the bureaucracy could succeed in implementing its policy, congressional resistance had to be overcome.

Congress was to make it clear that it still had a great deal to say about what policy would be made and how it would be made. As it turned out, the cigarette labeling rule first floated by the FTC in 1964 did not stand, for tobacco interests successfully bullied Congress into passing a watered down version of the FTC rule the following year. Still, it would be hard to imagine any policy being made at all had it not been for the Surgeon General's skillful maneuvering in both framing and highlighting the issue.

NOTES

1. In *The Dark Side of the Market Place: The Plight of the American Consumer* (Englewood Cliffs, N.J.: Prentice Hall, 1968), Senator Warren Magnuson and Jean Carper discuss what, prophetically, they saw as a long and difficult road to more effective protection.

2. U.S. Department of Health and Human Services, Public Health Service, Office on Smoking and Health, *Use of Tobacco* (available at the Technical Information Service, Office on Smoking and Health, Rockville, Maryland), July 1969, pp. 431–432.

3. *Christian Science Monitor,* October 20, 1967. Similarly, Senator Robert Kennedy was once heard to have said, "Cigarettes would have been banned years ago were it not for the tremendous economic power of their producers." Cited in Kenneth

Michael Friedman, *Public Policy and the Smoking-Health Controversy: A Comparative Study* (Lexington, Mass.: Lexington Books, 1975), p. 1.

   4. *The New York Times,* May 24, 1962, p. 16.

   5. Those groups asked to suggest people for the committee were: American Cancer Society; American Medical Association; Tobacco Institute, Inc.; Food and Drug Administration; National Tuberculosis Association; Federal Trade Commission; and the United States Office of Science and Technology.

   6. Maurine B. Neuberger, *Smoke Screen: Tobacco and the Public Welfare* (Englewood Cliffs, N.J.: Prentice Hall, 1963).

   7. Members of the Advisory Committee were Dr. Eugene H. Guthrie, Public Health Service, the committee's staff director; Dr. Stanhope Bayne-Jones, Walter Reed Army Institute of Research; Dr. Walter J. Burdette, University of Utah; William G. Cochran, Harvard University; Dr. Emmanuel Farber, University of Pittsburgh; Dr. Louis F. Fieser, Harvard University; Dr. Jacob Furth, Columbia University; Dr. John B. Hickman, Indiana University; Dr. Charles A. LeMaistre, University of Texas; Dr. Leonard M. Schuman, University of Minnesota; and Dr. Maurice H. Seevers, University of Michigan.

   8. In 1972, Congress enacted two laws which would have made the procedures used by the Surgeon General's committee improper. These were the Federal Advisory Committee Act (5 U.S.C., App. I) and the Government in the Sunshine Act (5 U.S.C. 552b). Under these laws meetings must be in the open and transcripts must be available to the public. Although certain advisory groups and some meetings are exempted, the smoking and health committee would almost certainly not be exempt were it to meet today. Secrecy and the drama it generated were important to the political strategy of the Surgeon General's Advisory Committee. The outcome of its work, or at least the timing of its implementation, would be different under the new requirements. The Advisory Committee's impact would surely have been less significant.

   9. U.S. Department of Health, Education and Welfare, *Smoking and Health: Report of the Advisory Committee to the Surgeon General of the Public Health Service,* Public Health Service Document No. 1103 (Washington, D.C.: U.S. Government Printing Office, 1964).

   10. When the smoking and health issue was first raised in 1954, there were pronounced adverse effects on tobacco shares, and the new report was even more directly critical of smoking than the earlier study. The bold-faced summaries of the committee's work were forceful enough for reasonable people to anticipate an unfavorable reaction in the stock market and in certain other quarters. The summaries read, "Cigarette smoking is causally related to lung cancer in men; the magnitude of the effect of cigarette smoking far outweighs all other factors. The data for women, though less extensive, point in the same direction." *Smoking and Health: Report of the Advisory Committee to the Surgeon General of the Public Health Service,* p. 37.

   11. Ronald J. Troyer and Gerald E. Markle, *Cigarettes: The Battle over Smoking* (New Brunswick, N.J.: Rutgers University Press, 1983), p. 77.

   12. The notice was published in the *Federal Register* on January 22, 1964, four days after the Federal Trade Commission made the announcement, *29 Federal Register,* pp. 530–532 (1964).

Chapter
4

Development of Administrative Policy-Making Powers

Ods [sic] me, I marvel what pleasure or felicity they have in taking their roguish tobacco. It is good for nothing but to choke a man, and fill him full of smoke and embers.

Ben Jonson (1573–1637)

The Federal Trade Commission's announcement of its intention to require a health warning was a reminder to everyone that agencies have the power to make policy. The cigarette interests were not pleased by the announcement, although they had every reason to expect it. A closely held notion in American public life is that regulatory agencies are the captives of those they regulate. The commission's action demonstrated that capture is not the only rule governing agency behavior. Those who were to be regulated knew that Trade Commission policy making would be different in both procedure and outcome from congressional policy making, because agency personnel were much less sympathetic to the tobacco position than were congressmen. Lobbyists make it their business to know where they are likely to receive the most favorable decisions, and those representing business and industry have come to view Congress as being more responsive to them than the bureaucracy.

The strategy of the tobacco supporters was to question Federal

Trade Commission authority to make policy involving a cigarette health warning and thereby ensure that the final policy decision would be made by Congress, not the FTC. Consequently, in their argument against the commission's announcement of its intention to require a health warning, the tobacco interests raised with skill and eloquence some of the most basic questions that have stalked the growth of agency policy-making powers. For example, they asked how, in a democratic form of government, non-elected bureaucrats could be permitted to exercise powers of government that are constitutionally allocated to elected representatives of the people. How could so important a matter, one affecting a large industry and thousands, perhaps millions, of people, be decided by bureaucrats? How were those associated with the tobacco interests to participate in the policy process when the policy makers were not subject to popular control through elections? And, how might they hold the administrative decision makers accountable for their decisions when they had no electoral process to resort to? These questions were then and are now fundamentally important to any system of representative government.

CONGRESSIONAL DELEGATION OF AUTHORITY

The basis of the complaints of the cigarette interests rested in the clear language of Article I of the Constitution—"All legislative powers herein granted shall be vested in a Congress of the United States. . . ." There is nothing in other sections of the document to indicate that legislative or policy-making powers should reside in the bureaucracy. Yet the accumulation of all policy powers in the legislature has never worked well, and from the beginning Congress has been obliged to find ways to share its powers.

Although legislative bodies theoretically could write and enact all the rules that govern society, it is seldom practical for them to do so. For a time, Congress and state legislatures tried it. They grappled with many complex policy issues that experience has now taught them to entrust to administrative agencies. Railroad rates and other matters of a regulatory nature, for example, were once written by legislatures. Yet, from the time the Constitution was adopted, Congress recognized that it could not effectively handle the intricacies of policy making. In 1789, the first Congress delegated to President Washington the authority to set benefits for disabled revolutionary war veterans. Even in those early years it was recognized that there are natural limitations on legislatures, which make them incapable of acting as effective policy makers under certain conditions.

These conditions arise when policy decisions involving complex and technical knowledge are called for. Congress does not have sufficient expertise or the necessary time to devote to the details of much modern policy making. There is no good way to write legislation that is sufficiently clairvoyant to foresee all of the individual cases and circumstances that are bound to arise in the administration of policy in a dynamic, complex society. Under these conditions, policy has to be made incrementally, over extended periods of time. Career experts in the bureaucracy are in a better position to devote continued attention to a particular problem and develop policy standards and guidelines than are members of Congress. If Congress were to enact all the specific rules and regulations necessary for the administration of programs, one of two equally undesirable results would occur: The rules would be too general to serve as effective guidelines for administrators, or they would be too rigid and inflexible, rendering them useless in short order. In delegating policy-making powers to agencies, Congress relieves itself of the burden of detailed work and frees itself to devote time to issues of basic policy.

Under delegated authority, agencies shape, mold, and even change policies set down by Congress in legislation. When Congress authorizes the creation of an agency or a new program, there is usually little reference to the details of implementing the program. Instead of writing an operations manual, which would guide the agency through all situations, Congress usually states simply that a program should be carried out in a "just" or "reasonable" manner. A phrase that sometimes appears in legislation is the mandate that an agency perform "in the public interest, convenience and necessity." The vagueness of such instructions or guidelines allows an agency considerable latitude in making policy as it sees fit.

The official policy-making process might be thought of as taking place in three consecutive stages. The first is legislative, involving Congress and the President, that is, congressional passage and presidential approval of a bill. The remaining two stages are administrative. The second has been alluded to by the late Supreme Court Justice Robert Jackson: "It may clarify the proper administrative function . . . to think of [congressional] legislation as unfinished law which the administrative body must complete before it is ready for application."[1] In this stage the agencies clarify legislation by writing detailed regulations or rules. The third stage occurs when a program is being administered. At that point, policy is made and altered to account for changing conditions. There is a possible fourth stage—review by Congress or the courts. Congress, through its oversight procedures, can change the handiwork of an agency as it changed the Federal Trade Commission policy in the cigarette controversy. By writing new legislation, changing appropriations, or simply threatening to do these things, Congress can make its influence felt. And whether or not Congress acts, judicial review of agency policy making might reverse or substantially alter what an agency has done.

As the problems of society become more complex, Congress tends to rely increasingly on agencies for policy making. American society has already reached a point where administrative agencies are producing more policy than the other two branches of the government combined. One observer, former Commissioner Lee Loevinger of the Federal Communications Commission, has compared the frequency of agency policy making with that of Congress and the courts:

> While the courts handle thousands of cases each year and Congress produces hundreds of laws each year, the administrative agencies handle hundreds of thousands of matters annually. The administrative agencies are engaged in the mass production of law, in contrast to the courts, which are engaged in the handicraft production of law.[2]

One cannot quantify and measure amounts of policy making with precision. Yet it is not unreasonable to conclude that in terms of policy decisions that directly affect persons and property, administrative agencies are today of major importance.[3]

Production of law by agencies could be dangerous for representative government. If there were no way for elected officials or an independent judiciary to control administrative decisions, policy making by an independent bureaucracy would negate traditional theories of representation upon which democratic systems are built. As indicated earlier, such traditional theories imply that means are available for citizens to both participate in policy making and hold government accountable for the decisions it makes.[4] The effectiveness of democratic controls on agency policy making has been questioned for many years, as the history of the Federal Trade Commission and other agencies shows. The protestations of the tobacco lobbyists were a modern revival of all the most difficult questions about agency policy making that had been raised in the past. Yet, the actions of the FTC in the cigarette labeling controversy show that in some circumstances bureaucratic policy making can enhance the representational qualities of government.

Although there are serious theoretical and practical obstacles to the delegation of policy-making authority, agencies have been operating under the umbrella of delegated authority for many years. In only two cases has the Supreme Court held congressional delegations to be unconstitutional.[5] Consequently, many claim there is little question about the legal ability of Congress to delegate. The law on this point seems so firm to one authority on administrative law that he has commented, "Lawyers who try to win cases by arguing that congressional delegations are unconstitutional almost invariably do more harm than good to their clients' interests."[6] Nevertheless, this constitutional issue, as any other, is within the discretion of the Court.

Congressional delegation has two aspects, however. Even if it is rarely possible to argue today that *Congress* has transgressed constitutional limits in delegating its powers to an agency, it is still feasible to argue in an appropriate case that some specific action by the *agency* has exceeded the limits of the power delegated to it. The basic delegation, in other words, may be constitutionally proper, but the agency's particular action may exceed the delegated powers.

An argument like this was made in 1972, when one industrial group, the National Petroleum Refiners Association, achieved a ruling in the U.S. district court which declared that the FTC lacked the statutory authority to issue trade regulation rules. The immediate issue concerned whether or not the commission could issue a rule requiring octane ratings on gasoline pumps. The U.S. court of appeals reversed the district court on June 27, 1973, and upheld the commission's authority to make binding rules. Neither court was asked to say whether Congress could, or could not, delegate the power to make these rules without violating the Constitution. The issue was simply whether Congress *had* delegated that power; the district court thought it had not, but the appellate court disagreed.

The tobacco interests' strategy against the FTC's action was based in part on the claim that Congress had stopped short of providing authority to the commission to issue so-called regulation rules—essentially the same kind of argument later made by the Petroleum Refiners. The Tobacco Institute's position in regard to the FTC is summarized in the following words:

> . . . in terms of policy and discretion, whatever substantive regulation may be believed to be necessary in this area of smoking and health, Congress alone should enact it.
> . . . we respectfully submit that in these proposed Trade Regulation Rules the Commission is not exercising the authority conferred upon it by Congress in the Federal Trade Commission Act. It is plainly legislating.[7]

The tobacco interests must have recognized that their argument contained some elements of risk, in view of what the Supreme Court had been saying for years about the propriety of congressional delegation. If it were thought that they were arguing that any delegation of power to make the rules in question was unconstitutional, their argument might be dismissed in the way suggested by Professor Davis. But if it were realized that what they were arguing was that the FTC had exceeded the limits of the power Congress did give it, their approach was astute in more than one respect. Important segments of public opinion could be expected to rally to the cry that faceless administrators were performing a role that should be, and indeed was, reserved to the elected representatives of the people. The powerful industrial and commercial communities could be expected to be sympathetic to that view. Furthermore, by arguing the delegation issue, they were able to gain the attention of Congress and thus increase the possibility that the controversy would be transferred, eventually, from the commission to Congress.

Questioning the power of Congress to delegate and examining closely the limits of its delegations challenge the concept of administrative policy making and, indeed, the nature of policy process in which powers are shared by several institutions of government. The challenge is obvious when it is argued that a particular delegation is unconstitutional. It is more subtle, but no less real, when the focus is on whether the agency has exceeded the limits of a delegation which is conceded to be proper in itself. This is true because a narrowly legalistic reading of the delegation can go far to cripple the agency's policy-making efforts, while a broader construction, tending toward the conclusion that any powers reasonably needed to achieve the law's objectives are implicitly given to the agency, can greatly facilitate them.

Since the legality and limits of delegation are so important to the administrative system in general, one profits from a closer examination of the causes that have prompted Congress to delegate authority and the basis for judicial approval of such action. The history of the Federal Trade Commission and its early responsibilities in the antitrust field are relevant to an understanding of these subjects.

REGULATORY AUTHORITY DELEGATED
TO FEDERAL TRADE COMMISSION

In the latter part of the nineteenth century, the nation experienced the growth of large industrial enterprises that cornered large shares of the market for various commodities. The notion that one or a few companies should control a market ran counter to the time-honored, laissez-faire ideal of vigorous competition. State regulation proved to be largely ineffective in breaking up or preventing the creation of large monopolies, partially because many of them were national in scope. The federal government entered the "trust-busting" picture with the passage of the Sherman Act in 1890. The Sherman Act required that the government rely for policy development on vague, legislative language and judicial decisions. The act created no administrative agency; no policy-making authority was delegated by Congress. The statements of major purpose in the first two sections alert the reader to the problems of enforcement that were to develop:

> *Section 1* Every contract, combination in the form of trust . . . or conspiracy in restraint of trade or commerce . . . is hereby declared to be illegal. . . .
>
> *Section 2* Every person who shall monopolize, or combine or conspire with any other person or persons, to monopolize . . . shall be deemed guilty of a misdemeanor. . . .

The language of these sections required further definition. Who was to define what constituted "a conspiracy in restraint of trade," for example? There was no answer to this question in the Sherman Act, although by implication the burden fell on the federal courts.

Thirteen years after passage of the act, the Antitrust Division was established within the Department of Justice to investigate and initiate prosecution of those corporations and individuals who violated the Sherman Act. Almost immediately, the division encountered serious difficulty. The wording of the act provided very few guidelines for prosecution, and the division had to develop workable definitions or guidelines from the act's general language. Without delegated policy-making powers from Congress, the division found its job exceedingly difficult and, eventually, close to impossible.

The only technique available for developing standards was the case-by-case method. Alleged violators of the act had to be taken to court. The judges, on the basis of the information presented, decided whether or not the challenged action violated the Sherman Act. This proved to be an unsatisfactory way of developing standards. It was not only slow, awkward, and unpredictable, but it relied on judges who might or might not have been fully aware of the intricacies of corporate finance and economics. The courts were confronted with a wide range of cases; judges could not afford to specialize in these vastly complicated matters. The results were that no hard or firm standards emerged under the Sherman Act. Nearly all questions that could conceivably arise under the act had to be tested in the courts, but it was difficult to rely on precedent because cases differed sufficiently enough from one another to make the formulation of rules of general applicability virtually impossible.

Uncertainty grew as a result of reliance on the courts for interpretation. Neither the government nor the corporate giants knew what might violate the Sherman Act. The pinnacle of uncertainty was reached in 1911 with two Supreme Court decisions, one involving the Standard Oil Company, the other the American Tobacco Company.[8] In these cases, the Court wrote what came to be called the "rule of reason." Basically, the Court said that only *unreasonable* restraints of trade or monopolies were in violation of the Sherman Act. These decisions underscored the frustration of the Court in dealing with antitrust policy. Nothing was clarified; in fact, the situation was made even more difficult because there was another term that begged for definition. What constituted an "unreasonable" restraint of trade? Where would the courts draw the line between what was "reasonable" and what was "unreasonable"?[9]

The experience of the government with the Sherman Act dramatized the need for Congress to delegate policy-making power to an administrative agency. It was clear that reliance on the courts for policy making would result in an inadequate body of law, unpredictable and difficult to enforce. The antitrust situation grew more and more critical. President Taft expressed the fears of many when he stated that judicial involvement in antitrust policy making "might involve our whole judicial system in disaster."[10]

Concerned members of Congress realized that the Sherman Act had to be modified. Some members thought that the modification ought to be in the direction of making the act more explicit. They wanted to spell out in detailed legislation the corporate actions that violated the Sherman Act. This delineation would have eliminated or reduced reliance on the courts for the development of enforcement standards, according to those who favored this approach. Others disagreed. They argued that Congress was not well equipped to write the detailed legislation necessary; furthermore, Senator Newlands of Nevada argued that it would be unwise to attempt to write detailed legislation to clarify the Sherman Act. He said on the floor of the Senate, "If there were 20 bad trade practices today and you were to name them in law and condemn them, there would be others established tomorrow."[11] Continuity and expertise were needed to enforce antitrust policy. The Senator supported the creation of an administrative board that would have both enforcement and policy-making powers. The Interstate Commerce Commission, which had been established in 1887, served as Senator Newlands's model. A commission of this sort, he reasoned, could develop precedents, traditions, and a continuous policy based on orderly experience in enforcement and in the refinement of guidelines. The views of Senator Newlands prevailed, and the Federal Trade Commission was established by Congress in 1914.

The same year the Federal Trade Commission was created, Congress passed the Clayton Act. Passage of this act showed that Congress was not yet willing to give up its prerogative of writing detailed regulations for an agency such as the FTC. In an attempt to refine the Sherman Act by legislating regulations, the Clayton Act detailed those actions of corporations or individuals that were prohibited. Thus, for example, the Clayton Act prohibits price discrimination, if the purpose of such discrimination is to lessen competition or create a monopoly. This congressional attempt to be more explicit did not withstand the tests of time and experience, however. The provisions of the Clayton Act were still too broad and ill defined to provide enlightened guidance for effective enforcement. The courts would have remained the principal policy maker in the antitrust field had Congress not created the Federal Trade Commission, for neither the Clayton Act nor the Sherman Act ended the need for interpretation by the courts. It eventually fell, at least in part, to the Federal Trade Commission to interpret and enforce the provisions of the Clayton Act, thereby reducing some of the burden on the courts.

The process of experimentation with antitrust policy making at the turn of the century has been repeated in other areas of public policy. Whenever standards have had to be developed for the administration of new and continuing programs, Congress has increasingly found it practical to empower bureaucratic agencies to do the task. Since agencies are better equipped to carry out the task of filling out the skeletal programs that Congress legislates, they have, over the years, received increased policy-making responsibilities.

THE SUPREME COURT ON DELEGATION

From the earliest days of our constitutional history, Congress has found it necessary to delegate certain of its powers to bureaucratic agencies. Yet, the Supreme Court held unconstitutional delegations in only the two cases previously cited, both of which were decided in 1935. One suspects that the decisions in these cases were more closely allied to the Court's skepticism of New Deal programs than to genuine concern about violation of the separation of powers doctrine. For years prior to 1935, the Court had upheld delegation after delegation. While doing so, the justices inserted into their opinions statements on the inviolability of the separation thesis. In one of the earliest cases involving this question, the Court wrote a reaffirmation of the separation principle while upholding the delegation itself:

> . . . it is essential to the successful working of this system that the persons entrusted with power in any one of these branches (executive, legislative and judicial) shall not be permitted to encroach upon the pow-

ers confided to the others, but that each by the law of its creation be limited to the exercise of the powers appropriate to its own department and no other. . . .[12]

A few years later, in 1892, the Court upheld powers delegated to the President to change import duties. In doing so, the majority declared, "That Congress cannot delegate legislative power to the President is a principle universally recognized as vital to the integrity and maintenance of the system of government ordained by the Constitution."[13] Having made this point, the Court satisfied itself that the power to change import duties was not legislative power.

The doctrine of separation came into conflict with the demands of modern policy making long ago. The Court, through semantic flights of fancy, seemed content to satisfy itself with strong statements about the theoretical impossibility of delegation, while in the same decisions upholding the impossible. The Court began to take a less ambiguous approach in the 1930s when it held that, under certain circumstances, Congress might find it necessary to delegate authority. Still, these powers were to be limited by congressional standards. "Congress cannot delegate any part of its legislative power except under the limitation of a prescribed standard," wrote the justices in 1931.[14]

The question of standards did not erect any important barriers to delegation. Acceptable standards were as vague and ill defined, as such statements as "the public interest" and "fair and equitable allocation." Within a few years, the Court came very close to admitting that, in certain circumstances, no standard at all was necessary. In a 1947 decision, the Court wrote that it might have been desirable to have written explicit standards in the Home Owners Act of 1933, but it acknowledged that the existence of standards in this field perhaps was not really crucial. In such a highly developed and professionalized field as corporate management the Court reasoned, "experience and many precedents have crystallized into well-known and generally acceptable standards."[15] Therefore, Congress did not have to write standards into the legislation in this case.

At various times, certain portions of the Federal Trade Commission Act were tested on the grounds that they were unconstitutional delegations. A court of appeals held that similar delegations had been upheld in the past and found no reason to hold these unconstitutional.[16]

The policy-making powers of regulatory commissions such as the Federal Trade Commission have caused some special problems of control. Congress, anxious to keep the commissions under surveillance, was reluctant to give the President as much influence over them as he had over the executive departments. Consequently, the commissions were assigned to a kind of no man's land between the executive agencies and Congress. Their unusual status led to the use of the term *independent* in describing their relationship to both Congress and the chief executive.

The history of the commissions has been one of debate and political struggle between those who argue that the President should have more power over commissions and those who wish to strengthen congressional control. The presidential backers argue that the President is responsible for seeing that the law is faithfully executed and that independent commissions make this responsibility difficult, if not impossible, to carry out. Others cite the broad delegated powers enjoyed by the commissions and argue that Congress, as the source of these powers, should keep close watch over their use. Over the past 50 years, the presidential power advocates seem to have won a few victories, but the residency of the commissions in their no man's land remains unaffected. The institutional location of the independent commissions does result in differences in the way they are managed as well as differences in the way policy issues and goals are selected and decided. Often, disagreement over policies leads to calls for organizational reform which would put a commission more clearly within the orbit of either the President or Congress. However, throughout U.S. history the independents seem to relate more closely to Congress than the President. One would surmise this to be true because those agencies are doing the work Congress once did.[17]

William L. Cary, former chairman of the Securities and Exchange Commission, disagrees somewhat. He claims there is often little difference between an executive agency and a regulatory commission in terms of its relationship to the President or Congress. He says that some executive agencies, like the Army Corps of Engineers, are closer to Congress than to the President even though scrutiny of an organization chart would seem to reveal the opposite. However, influence over the commissions depends to a considerable extent on personalities within the congressional–interest groups–executive branch subsystem and the nature of the issue involved. Cary reflected the frustration of those caught between Congress and the President when he wrote, after his retirement:

> Government regulatory commissions are often referred to as "independent" agencies, but this cannot be taken at face value by anyone who has ever had any experience in Washington. In fact, government regulatory agencies are stepchildren whose custody is contested by both

Congress and the Executive, but without very much affection from either one.[18]

CHANGE IN EMPHASIS AT THE
FEDERAL TRADE COMMISSION

Congressional and presidential concern over government antitrust policy failed to lead to vigorous action by the Federal Trade Commission. Immediately after its establishment, the FTC encountered difficulties in enforcing those laws within its jurisdiction. The major problem which faced the FTC in its early years was the narrow interpretation that the Supreme Court gave to its enabling legislation. A member and one-time chairman of the commission wrote that in the first ten years the Supreme Court emasculated the commission's powers.[19] He thought the commission had made serious and thoughtful attempts to determine what it could and should prevent. The courts were not impressed with this thoughtfulness, and the FTC's powers were seriously limited in four cases decided soon after it had been established by Congress.[20]

The courts also narrowly defined the Federal Trade Commission's jurisdiction over unfair trade practices. When the commission acted to prevent misleading advertising for an obesity cure called Marvola, the Supreme Court objected. The FTC directed the producers of this substance to include in their advertising the statement that Marvola could not be safely taken without the supervision of a competent physician. After reviewing medical testimony, the Court held that the question of safety was one of opinion and not one of fact. The Court said that since the advertisers testified that they honestly believed their product to be safe, the FTC would have to prove with scientific evidence that the product was harmful before it could act. Any question about the safety of a product, therefore, was resolved in favor of the producer. In an earlier case, the Court had weakened even more substantially the powers of the commission. According to the Court, the FTC's jurisdiction over unfair trade practices was limited to instances where a party injured or impaired the business of a competitor.[21] This left the commission without the power to move against a company that injured consumers through harmful or deceptive practices. Consumer protection was wrested, almost in its entirety, from the FTC by this decision; the consumer had no grounds upon which he could bring a complaint.

However, by 1938, sufficient momentum had been generated in Congress to expand the jurisdiction of the Federal Trade Commission.

to include consumer protection. The Wheeler-Lea Act of that year specifically empowered the commission to deal with "unfair or deceptive acts or practices in commerce." It contained provisions extending the commission's powers to dealing with false advertising of foods, drugs, devices, and cosmetics. With the Wheeler-Lea Act, the FTC began to devote most of its energies to the elimination of deception, particularly deception in advertising. Its antitrust activity subsided precipitously.

When the Surgeon General's report appeared in 1964, the Federal Trade Commission had had a substantial amount of experience with misleading advertising, including cigarette advertising. It had refined its regulatory techniques considerably over the years. A court decision had even upheld the commission's right to demand positive disclosure of information where the effect of nondisclosure was to deceive a substantial segment of the purchasing public.[22]

Yet even with this experience and the necessary legal authority, all was not well with the Federal Trade Commission and its regulation of cigarette advertising. The commission had succeeded in issuing a ban on cigarette advertisements that made or inferred claims about the supposed health benefits of smoking in 1955. And in 1960, the FTC banned advertising claims regarding the relative health benefits of smoking filtered cigarettes. All the while, cigarette consumption was rising rapidly. Policing advertisements had apparently not resulted in conveying to the public the health dangers involved in cigarette smoking. The commission was coming around to the view that in the face of all the adverse health reports, it was cigarette advertising alone that accounted for the rise in sales. Some of the commissioners had concluded that the public was being deceived into thinking that the consequences of smoking were social status and popularity rather than ill health. They felt that FTC actions against cigarette ads were not productive and, at the same time, that the commission should be able to use its powers over deceptive trade practices to stop whatever parts of advertisements were misleading the public.

Ironically, the root of the Federal Trade Commission's problem was substantially the same as the government's under the Sherman Act over half a century earlier. It was a procedural difficulty as much as anything else. The commission was attempting to regulate cigarette advertising on a case-by-case basis. Each time the commission ruled a particular advertisement deceptive, the industry came up with a variation that could squeak by under the rule of the previous case. This was proving to be an endless and fruitless process. The commission needed to write general regulations for the whole industry; the case method, whether employed by an agency or by the courts, was proving to be too cumbersome a method of developing regulatory policy.

In 1963, the commission moved to solve its problems by incorporating in its rules a procedure that could be used to write enforceable regulations for a whole category of industries. The chairman of the FTC saw the adoption of rule-making procedures as the only way to make the commission an effective regulator. The Surgeon General's report gave the commission the impetus and the substantive information it needed to use its new rule-making procedure in the field of cigarette advertising. This new procedure was set into motion one week after the Surgeon General released his report on smoking and health.[23]

NOTES

1. *Federal Trade Commission* v. *Ruberoid,* 343 US 470 (1952).

2. Lee Loevinger, "The Administrative Agency as a Paradigm of Government—A Survey of the Administrative Process," *Indiana Law Journal,* 40, no. 3 (Spring 1965), 305. Justice Jackson noted the rise of administrative powers in a now famous dissent, "The rise of administrative bodies probably has been the most significant legal trend of the last century and perhaps more values today are affected by their decisions than by those of all the courts. . . . They also have begun to have important consequences on personal rights. They have become a veritable fourth branch of Government, which has deranged our three branch legal theories much as the concept of a fourth dimension unsettles our three-dimensional thinking." *Federal Trade Commission* v. *Ruberoid.*

3. The Administrative Conference of the United States claims there are more than 30 departments and agencies that have power to make decisions affecting individual rights. Each year the conference develops recommendations to Congress and the President for improvements in agency procedures that affect the rights of private persons and business interests through administrative investigation, adjudication, licensing, rule making, rate making, claims determination, and other proceedings.

4. See pp. 12–14.

5. *Panama Refining Company* v. *Ryan,* 293 US 388 (1935); and *Schechter Poultry Corporation* v. *United States,* 295 US 495 (1935).

6. Kenneth Culp Davis, *Administrative Law and Government* (St. Paul: West, 1960), p. 55.

7. From the statement on behalf of the Tobacco Institute, Inc. submitted to the Federal Trade Commission, p. 6 (mimeo).

8. *Standard Oil Company* v. *United States,* 221 US 1 (1911); and *American Tobacco Company* v. *United States,* 221 US 106 (1911).

9. See Gerard C. Henderson, *The FTC: A Study in Administrative Law and Procedure* (New Haven: Yale University Press, 1924), for a thoughtful discussion of the enforcement problem.

10. *Congressional Record,* 61st Congress, 2nd Session, p. 382, quoted in Henderson, *The FTC,* p. 16.

11. *Congressional Record,* Senate, June 13, 1914, 63rd Congress, 2nd Session, p. 11084.

12. *Kilbourne* v. *Thompson,* 103 US 168 (1881).

13. *Field* v. *Clark*, 143 US 649 (1892).

14. *United States* v. *Chicago, Minneapolis and St. Paul Railroad Company*, 282 US 311, 324 (1931).

15. *Fahey* v. *Mallonee*, 332 US 245, 250 (1947).

16. *Sears, Roebuck and Company* v. *Federal Trade Commission*, 258 Fed. 307 (CCA 7 1918).

17. See Robert A. Katzmann, *Regulatory Bureaucracy: The Federal Trade Commission and Antitrust Policy* (Cambridge, Mass.: MIT Press, 1980) for an interesting discussion of management and goal setting in independent regulatory commissions.

18. William L. Cary, *Politics and the Regulatory Agencies* (New York: McGraw-Hill, 1967), p. 4.

19. Nelson B. Gaskill, *The Regulation of Competition* (New York: Harper and Brothers, 1936).

20. *Federal Trade Commission* v. *Warren, Jones and Gratz*, 253 US 421 (1920); *Federal Trade Commission* v. *Curtis Publishing Company*, 260 US 568 (1923); *Federal Trade Commission* v. *Klesner*, 230 US 19 (1929); *Federal Trade Commission* v. *Raladam*, 233 US 643 (1931).

21. *Silver* v. *Federal Trade Commission*, 292 F. 752 (1923).

22. *P. Lorillard Company* v. *Federal Trade Commission*, 136 F. 2d 52.58 (4th Cir. 1950).

23. According to the Federal Trade Commission's manual, which was amended in 1962 to cover this new rule-making procedure, trade regulation rules may "cover all applications of a particular statutory provision, may be nationwide in effect, or may be limited to particular areas or industries or to particular products or geographical areas. . . ." Trade regulation rules give the FTC the capability of issuing formal rules or guides to govern the conduct of large categories of producers. Further, it was stipulated that once the rules were issued, any violation of them could be used to initiate adjudicatory proceedings.

Chapter
5

Procedures Used in
Administrative Policy Making

And a woman is only a woman, but a good cigar is a Smoke.

Rudyard Kipling (1865–1936)

Although the agencies of government are pictured in organization charts as arms of the executive, they derive their power from acts of Congress. Two types of power are granted by Congress: rule making and adjudicatory authority. Although the two powers are often indistinguishable because of functional overlap and mutual support, adjudicatory authority is frequently referred to as quasi-judicial in nature, while rule making is characterized as quasi-legislative or sublegislative. As a practical method of distinguishing these powers from each other, one may think of adjudicatory actions as being used to perform judicial or courtlike activities, while rule-making activities serve to develop policies in a manner comparable to that used by legislatures.

Since judicial decisions frequently have the same effect as legislative acts, it is sometimes difficult to distinguish between rule-making and adjudicatory powers. Courts engage in rule making and adjudication simultaneously, as Supreme Court decisions in school desegregation and reapportionment have dramatically illustrated. When the Court gives detailed interpretation to one of the generalized commands of the Constitution, it might be compared to an agency making detailed rules under a statute. Legislative and judicial policy making differ partly because of the way a decision is made and partly because of the scope or applicability of the decision itself. Rule making is characterized by its general applicability. Rules formulated by agencies uniformly affect all within a given category, such as all cigarette producers. In contrast, adjudicatory action is based on a specific case involving an individual, a partnership, or a corporation. The end result of an adjudicatory proceeding is a determination whether or not those named in the suit have violated a law or rule, or perhaps whether the parties in question qualify for a license of some kind. Once the adjudicatory decision is made, a precedent is established that may apply to others similarly situated. Consequently, adjudication—as well as rule making—can have a broad impact on society or general policy.

The difference between these two types of power is of more than passing interest.[1] Each has its own procedural advantages and disadvantages. When an agency acts in its adjudicatory capacity, it must use procedures that are more formal and more carefully developed than those employed under its rule-making functions. Adjudicatory procedures in agencies are very similar to the procedures and practices used in a courtroom. Rule-making procedures, on the other hand, are usually much less formal. In some cases, agency rule-making procedures are less formal than those used to govern university senate meetings. At times they are similar to the procedures, or absence of procedures, used by moderators of roundtable discussions. The different degree of formality of the procedures is largely determined by the expected impact of the rule under consideration. In agency rule making, it is incumbent upon the agency itself to determine which issues require formal rule-making procedures and which do not. The more formal procedures require that the public be notified and be given the opportunity to be heard. They are patterned after those used when congressional committees hold public hearings and call witnesses to testify.

ADJUDICATION AND RULE MAKING AT THE FEDERAL TRADE COMMISSION

The Federal Trade Commission now uses both adjudicatory and rule-making powers to enforce and implement the laws within its jurisdiction, although for many years it used rule-making powers only in certain very narrowly defined areas, such as the labeling of fur products.

Figure 5–1   Federal Trade Commission Powers

I. Formal Powers
Procedurally cumbersome, but relatively easy to enforce

A. Adjudicatory (quasi-judicial)
1. **What:** independent administrative law judges preside over court-like proceedings
2. **Benefits:** regular, predictable procedures with many protections, ability to appeal
3. **Drawbacks:** case-by-case, court-of-law-like decision-making process; fine for specific cases, but hard to regulate general behavior
4. **Example:** 1942 cease-and-desist order regarding Penn Tobacco Company's claim that its Julep brand of cigarettes was a remedy for coughs

B. Rule-making (quasi-legislative)
1. **What:** commissioners and staffers preside over proceedings (very much like congressional hearings, quite informal compared to adjudicatory procedures)
2. **Benefits:** easier to control industry with class-based decisions
3. **Drawbacks:** concern for arbitrary use of agency powers
4. **Example:** FTC Trade Reg. Rule on Cigarette Labeling and Advertising (1964)

II. Informal Powers
Less costly and complex, but difficult to enforce

A. Advisory Opinion
1. **What:** commissioners make a nonbinding ruling on a hypothetical case
2. **Benefits:** popular; gives industry chance to meet agency standards before the fact
3. **Drawbacks:** decisions are nonbinding on government; industry may be misled
4. **Example:** FTC's 1993 advisory opinion that gasohol should be considered "automotive gasoline" for purposes of octane-posting requirements

B. Trade Practices Conference
1. **What:** broad-based arbitration of voluntary codes or trade practice rules between agency and parties from affected industry
2. **Benefits:** builds a consensus that both the agency and the industry can live with
3. **Drawbacks:** bargaining required of both sides to the conflict

4. Example: FTC's 1955 advertising guidelines prohibiting claims about the tar and nicotine content of various brands (ending the "tar derby")

C. Consent Order

1. What: mutual agreement between agency and industry; no admission of guilt

2. Benefits: may be the most expeditious course; in lieu of adjudicatory proceeding

3. Drawbacks: no official record of malfeasance

4. Example: 1972; six cigarette companies agree (at behest of FTC) to include "clear and conspicuous" health warnings on all cigarette advertisements

The adjudicatory procedure that the commission frequently uses may be initiated through a complaint filed by those who consider themselves aggrieved by a violation of one of the laws within the commission's jurisdiction. The complaint is followed by a formal hearing, usually before an administrative law judge, designed to assure the accused party of many of the same protections provided for defendants in court. If the examiner decides there has been a violation, he or she can recommend that a cease-and-desist order be issued. The defendant then has the opportunity to appeal, to the commissioners themselves. Should that attempt fail, defendants are permitted to make an appeal to a United States court of appeals, which may render a decision that can then be appealed to the U.S. Supreme Court. As a result of its ruling, the commission has the power to levy fines up to $5,000 per day if the offense continues.

Although adjudicatory and rule-making procedures are the most powerful devices at the command of the commission, they are not the most frequently used. Rule making was utilized very sparingly until the commission rewrote its own operating procedures in 1963, and adjudicatory proceedings are initiated in cases of blatant industrial violations, and then only when everything else has failed. Most of the Federal Trade Commission's efforts over the years have been directed toward gaining voluntary compliance or informal agreement. This practice is comparable to settling matters out of court and has the same virtues: expediency, less complexity, and lower costs; but it is also fraught with disadvantages. No formal record is made to guide others and neither party in the dispute is protected by the rights and practices of legal proceedings.

The Federal Trade Commission uses three techniques to secure voluntary compliance with the law. One device is the advisory opinion. In the federal judicial system, unlike those of other countries and some of the states, the courts will not tell an inquiring party hypothetically whether or not something it plans to do might be illegal. Courts will decide only actual cases and controversies at law. However, the bureaucracy is not so limited. Given the complexities of modern government, and of modern business planning, it is fortunate that the bureaucracy is free to tell an interested party how it might view some proposed action. Industry frequently requests opinions from the Federal Trade Commission, and the commissioners respond but note that their opinions are only advisory and not binding on the government. The advisory opinion is a useful device and it is so popular that it accounts for a large part of the growth of quasi-judicial functions of agencies.

When the Federal Trade Commission wants to reach a broad spectrum of the corporate world, it resorts to another informal device called the Trade Practices Conference. The commission invites industry to these conferences to discuss with the commissioners their regulatory problems and, it is hoped, all leave the conference with their problems solved. Occasionally, voluntary codes or voluntary trade practice rules come out of these meetings.

The third kind of informal procedure leads to what are known as consent orders. These are voluntary agreements reached by the commission and a party about to enter, or in the course of, an adjudicatory proceeding. In the case of the consent order, the Federal Trade Commission has some leverage to exert over an accused business or corporation. By signing a consent order, the parties involved in the proceeding agree to stop whatever they were doing that the commission thought suspect, and the commission agrees to drop the proceedings. Signing the consent order is not an admission of guilt. The pressure that the commission can apply to sign an order—especially to a small company, which might find it could ill afford the time or cash required to fight the commission or the publicity that would result—has made the consent order procedure one that receives much criticism.

The informal procedures and adjudicatory procedures are a languid regulatory stick for the commission. General rule making is, in many ways, a much more potent device, but there have been powerful pressures on the commission not to use this procedure. And, of course, there was some question—articulated by industrial groups such as the cigarette producers—as to whether the legal authority to exercise general rule-making powers was delegated to the Federal Trade Commission.

THE FEDERAL TRADE COMMISSION'S
EXPERIENCE WITH CIGARETTE
REGULATION

The limited effectiveness of the commission's policy-making procedures is evident in the FTC's record on cigarette advertising regulation. The commission had invoked its adjudicatory powers in individual cases of deceptive advertising involving cigarette producers approximately 25 times between 1938 and 1968. But each of these decisions applied only to the parties cited in the particular case. Others who might have been engaged in the same deceptive act, or one closely related, were not immediately affected by the commission's decision involving their less fortunate brethren. It is possible for those not named as a party to the case to continue the "illegal" practice until the Federal Trade Commission moves against them. This can take months or even years. Furthermore, only activities or practices complained of in the suit can be prohibited by the decision; slight variations from that practice even by the same parties must be dealt with by separate decisions.

In the case of cigarette advertising, the commission found itself putting out brush fires of deception while the inferno raged on. There was no way for the commission to state authoritatively a general policy of what constituted deception in cigarette ads for all advertisers. The procedures employed in adjudicatory actions narrowly define the scope of admissible evidence. Discussion of the ramifications of an industrywide problem is difficult under such circumstances. Then too, the commission's action against cigarette producers only provided requirements about what *could not* be done, but not about what *had* to be done. That is, the Federal Trade Commission could not require that a health warning appear on all packages through its adjudicatory procedures. The only way it could have approached this requirement would involve convening a trade practice conference in which a voluntary agreement to this effect was hammered out. Failing that, the FTC would have to deal with cigarette companies one at a time. In each instance, the FTC would have had to prove that such a positive disclosure was necessary.

One of the early cases involving cigarette advertising points up the problems with the commission's adjudicatory procedures. The manufacturers of a now extinct brand called Julep cigarettes claimed in their advertisements that their product was a remedy for coughs. Even in the early 1940s, this strained the credulity of the commission, and the Julep makers were forced to stop making the claim.[2] Yet within a short period, other makers advertised similar health claims. One producer proclaimed that there was not a cough in a carload of their cigarettes. That same manufacturer later announced that more doctors smoked their cigarettes than any other brand. Now, according to the FTC, other manufacturers use subtle techniques to achieve the same purpose, as when they imply that a filter protects the smoker. Some examples of such innuendoes are, "the flavor of the world's finest tobaccos through the Kent filter" and "white filter flavor" (L & M).[3]

Since it was impossible to fight the health inferences and subtleties in cigarette ads through adjudicatory procedures, the best way to eliminate deception, according to the Federal Trade Commission, was to require that a positive health warning statement appear in each advertisement. Rule-making authority was necessary before that requirement could be made. Commissioner Philip Elman summed up the FTC's frustration with adjudicatory procedures in the field of cigarette advertising and defended the effectiveness of rule-making procedures. When the tobacco interests challenged the commission's authority to use rule-making procedures, Commissioner Elman responded:

> Suppose there is a product in general use throughout the United States. . . . And suppose scientific research should conclusively establish that that product induced sterility. Would you say that under the Federal Trade Commission Act the only way in which this Commission could proceed to carry out its responsibilities of preventing deception . . . is to issue a complaint and a cease and desist order against each of the thousands and thousands of manufacturers? Or has Congress allowed us an alternative method of proceeding . . . ?[4]

The Federal Trade Commission did not rely on adjudicatory procedures alone but also attempted, without success, to deal with misleading cigarette advertising by informal means. In 1955, as a result of a Trade Practices Conference, the commission issued a set of cigarette advertising guidelines. These were used in an attempt to have cigarette manufacturers voluntarily refrain from advertising the levels of tar and nicotine contained in their cigarettes. The guidelines did bring an end to the "tar derby" when the manufacturers agreed to discontinue advertisements containing confusing and ambiguous claims about the tar and nicotine content of their products.[5] But other parts of the voluntary guidelines worked unsuccessfully because the FTC was powerless to enforce them.

Ultimately, it would become clear to individuals, both inside the FTC and outside, that case-by-case quasi-judicial rulings and voluntary trade practice agreements, while helpful in specific instances, would be inadequate to the broader task of effectively warning the public of the health hazards of smoking. To accomplish that end, quasi-legislative rule-making procedures would have to be developed and adopted for commission use. These rule-making powers are not always granted to agencies by Congress in any specific, formal way. Instead, agencies often must nurture these procedures into existence themselves. So it was with the FTC.

THE FEDERAL TRADE COMMISSION ADOPTS RULE-MAKING PROCEDURES

In April 1962, Senator Maurine Neuberger wrote a letter to Paul Rand Dixon, the newly appointed chairman of the Federal Trade Commission, suggesting that any cigarette advertisement that failed to carry a health warning was inherently deceptive. She asked why the FTC could not adopt this position officially and subsequently require that all cigarette advertising carry a health warning. The answer to Senator Neuberger's inquiry was that the commission had never adopted the necessary rule-making procedures to do what she suggested. None of the informal or adjudicatory procedures that the FTC had been using could have accomplished what the senator was suggesting.

Senator Neuberger's letter found a responsive ear within the commission, however. When Chairman Dixon came to the Federal Trade Commission in 1961, he began almost immediately to push for the use of general rule-making powers. He saw the incorporation of rule making as an important means to strengthen what was a rather ineffective regulatory process. Plans for the adoption of rule-making procedures were already in the works when the chairman answered Senator Neuberger's letter. His response hinted openly that the only major obstacle to the adoption of the Neuberger suggestion was the gathering of substantial evidence establishing a direct relationship between smoking and ill health:

> If the Commission is able to secure competent probative scientific evidence including that furnished by the Public Health Service, that a causal relationship exists between cigarette smoking and lung cancer, heart ailments, etc., it is likely that an order of the Commission, based on such evidence, which required an affirmative disclosure of the possible hazards to health from smoking cigarettes, would be upheld in the appellate courts.[6]

One might have guessed, as the cigarette people did, that the Federal Trade Commission was preparing itself for the report of the Surgeon General's Advisory Committee. The FTC announced the adoption of general rule-making procedures in June 1962, at about the same time the Surgeon General set up his Advisory Committee.

Although the adoption of rule-making procedures was probably coincidental to the cigarette controversy, the commission busied itself issuing trade regulation rules (the official name given the end product of the new rule-making procedure) for uncontroversial products as if it might have been practicing for its cigarette rule. The first rule was issued in mid-1963 while the Surgeon General's committee was preparing its report. It concerned the standards for size of sleeping bags. A few months later another rule was issued concerning the use of the term *leakproof* or *guaranteed leakproof* in advertising dry cell batteries. Another prohibited misbranding leather belts. None of the three trade regulation rules stirred much controversy; they were promulgated practically without popular reaction. The fourth rule-making attempt was, however, destined to stir more public reaction than the Federal Trade Commission had anticipated or desired.

The Federal Trade Commission followed the progress of the Surgeon General's Advisory Committee by appointing a liaison who attended most of the open meetings of the committee. Several months before the Surgeon General was to issue the report, the Federal Trade Commission organized within its staff a special task force on cigarettes, consisting of physicians, economists, and attorneys. When the report was issued, the commission was ready to move. Within one week the Federal Trade Commission issued a notice that it planned to begin a rule-making proceeding that would lead to the issuing of a requirement that cigarette ads and packages carry a warning label describing the health hazards of smoking.

The cigarette makers, committed to resisting such a requirement, were determined to prove that the FTC had no authority to write such rules. If they could succeed, they would have had a double victory: The cigarette rule would have been quashed, and the commission would have remained a weakened watchdog of the public interest, confined to either its informal or its case method of regulation.

NOTES

1. For a detailed discussion of the differences between rule making and adjudication see David L. Shapiro, "The Choice of Rulemaking or Adjudication in the Development of Administrative Policy," 73 *Harvard Law Review* 921 (1965).

2. *Penn Tobacco Company*, 34 F.T.C. 1636 (1942).

3. *Report to Congress*, Federal Trade Commission, June 30, 1968, p. 20 (mimeo).

4. "Hearings before the F.T.C. on Cigarette Labeling and Advertising," Vol. VII, March 16, 1964, p. 61 (typewritten).

5. In 1966, in light of growing public and congressional interest in the possible health implications of tar and nicotine, the Federal Trade Commission reversed itself and notified cigarette manufacturers that they were at liberty to advertise tar and nicotine levels, provided they made no health claims with respect to them. A year later, after standardized measurement techniques had been agreed upon, the commission announced the opening of a smoking laboratory to measure these levels.

6. Quoted in Maurine B. Neuberger, *Smoke Screen: Tobacco and the Public Welfare* (Englewood Cliffs, N.J.: Prentice Hall, 1963), p. 58.

Chapter
6

The Rule-Making Hearings

No pleasure can exceed
the smoking of the weed

Phrase from nineteenth-century advertisement

Witnesses and spectators at Federal Trade Commission hearings sit in a large, impressive, wood-paneled room that resembles both a congressional hearing room and a courtroom. The focal point of the chamber is a raised bench, behind which are velvet draperies that serve as a backdrop for the elegantly upholstered swivel chairs of the five commissioners. There are counsel tables in front of the bench, a small table for the official recorder, and a lectern on which witnesses may rest their notes and elbows. A railing separates the hard wooden spectator pews from the seats of the staff and those who are participating in the hearing.

Ordinarily, the commissioners rely upon the Division of Trade Regulation Rules, an office within the FTC, to write the draft rule and arrange for and conduct preliminary hearings in this venerable setting. Typically, after the record has been made, the commissioners examine it and decide either to vote on the proposed rule or call a second round of hearings over which they may preside, either individually or as a group. The cigarette labeling rule was no ordinary rule, however. The commissioners decided to handle this matter themselves and they prepared for it carefully.

On March 16, 1964, the commissioners took their seats in front of the long, blue velvet draperies to begin three consecutive days of hearings on the cigarette label and advertising rule. The proposed rule, which had been circulated well in advance of the hearing, contained two major sections. The first was the requirement that a health warning appear in all advertising and on cigarette packages. Drafts of two warning statements, either of which would have satisfied the Federal Trade Commission, were also in the first section:

1. CAUTION—CIGARETTE SMOKING IS A HEALTH HAZARD: The Surgeon General's Advisory Committee has found that "cigarette smoking contributes to mortality from specific diseases and to the overall death rate."

2. CAUTION: Cigarette smoking is dangerous to health. It may cause death from cancer and other diseases.

A second section of the rule attempted to reach the more subtle implications of cigarette advertising by banning "words, pictures, symbols, sounds, devices or demonstrations, or any combination thereof that would lead the public to believe cigarette smoking promotes good health or physical well-being."

The FTC was to find itself overruled by Congress on half of its proposal. The label was to be required only on packages, not in advertising. The ban on radio and television ads came later, and when it came it was by an act of Congress, not the FTC or the FCC. The requirement for inclusion of the health warning in all printed advertising also came later. It was the result of a voluntary agreement between the commission and the manufacturers; the result of a consent order arrived at in 1972 when a congressional ban on commission action against forcing such a requirement was expiring.

CIGARETTE HEARINGS AT THE FEDERAL TRADE COMMISSION

Hearings themselves serve some useful and important purposes. However, one of these purposes does not seem to be changing the viewpoints of any of the participants. The hearings do provide an opportunity to make a public record on the issue and to communicate views among those involved in a controversy. Such a hearing is likely to facilitate subsequent enforcement and public acceptance of the agency action. In some highly complex technical matters, agency hearings provide useful, factual information that the staff has not been able to find elsewhere. With the considerable amount of time that went into the preparation of the cigarette labeling case, however, there was little factual information that the commissioners did not have at their disposal. Backed by the scientific evidence of the Surgeon General's report and the detailed legal work of their counsel's office, the commissioners seemed fairly certain as to what the outcome of the hearings would be. Chairman Paul Rand Dixon had some doubts about the wisdom of confronting the powerful cigarette industry while the Federal Trade Commission's new rule-making procedures might be vulnerable. He was anxious to expand the use of the rule-making device in commission activities, but as an experienced chief investigator for a congressional committee during the Kefauver drug investigation, he was politically sensitive to the pitfalls of consumer regulation.

Three commissioners—John Reilly, Mary Gardiner Jones, and Phillip Elman—were in favor of the rule as the Federal Trade Commission had drafted it. Commissioner Reilly took no part in the questioning at the hearings, but the active participation of Commissioner Elman apparently strengthened his support of the FTC's proposed rule. The tobacco interests' challenge to the commission's power to issue the ruling irked Elman. His interest in establishing the authority of the commission to act in the cigarette case seemed to grow stronger with the intensity of the tobacco interests' challenge.

Commissioner Everett A. MacIntyre, who had been with the Federal Trade Commission about 25 years, was not a strong supporter of the rule, yet he was not active in opposition to it. Regarded as the commission's expert on administrative law, he was cautious about infringing upon the powers of other agencies, particularly the Federal Communications Commission and its jurisdiction over radio and television advertising. Commissioner MacIntyre was more reluctant than the others to undertake any action that could have proved injurious to the tobacco economy, and after the other commissioners had adopted the proposed rule, he issued a separate statement of disagreement. (Some attributed this reluctance to the fact that he was a native of North Carolina, the leading tobacco-producing state in the country.) He wrote that the wording of the health warning in both advertising and on packages should be left to negotiations that would follow further developments in the smoking and health field. He also suggested delaying the effective date six months to give all parties more adequate opportunity to work out an effective solution. Indeed, Commissioner MacIntyre opposed the imposition of additional regulations on cigarette manufacturers in all of the Federal Trade Commission's reports to Congress during his tenure.

WITNESSES

The commissioners heard the testimony of 29 witnesses during three days of hearings. The unpublished record, available to the public at commission headquarters, is 538 pages long.[1] It would have been difficult for any observer to detect differences between what they were watching at the Federal Trade Commission and what they might have watched had they traveled a few hundred yards down Pennsylvania Avenue to the Capitol. Chairman Dixon opened the proceedings by inviting each witness to read or submit his statement for the record, and then the witness was asked to answer questions from the commissioners. Some witnesses were asked no questions at all. The atmosphere of the hearing room was light and friendly toward those who testified in favor of the commission's proposal. But when those who came to question the wisdom of the commission rose to testify, tension crept into the air. At times opponents were questioned closely, providing some of the same electric drama television viewers have come to expect in more recent decades after witnessing impeachment proceedings regarding the Watergate scandal in the 1973–1974 timeframe, investigatory hearings associated with the Iran-contra affair in 1987, and the Supreme Court confirmation hearings of Judge Clarence Thomas in 1991.

The order of appearance of witnesses at a hearing is a clue as to how those conducting the hearings are disposed toward the issue involved. Sympathetic witnesses are scheduled during prime time, which is generally early in each day, with the "prime" of the prime being early in the first day. These are the hours when interest is highest and the press is most alert to what is said. The whole tone of the hearings, at least in the public eye, can be governed by what happens first.

It was no accident that the Assistant Surgeon General of the Public Health Service was scheduled to appear first. He was followed by Senator Neuberger. Thus, the Federal Trade Commission began its hearings with two very strong statements in favor of its proposed rule. The third witness was from the Tobacco Institute, and he was followed by two university research scientists who favored the proposed rule.

The second day of the hearings saw marketing experts, scientists, representatives of advertising, and tobacco growers' associations testify. The third and final day was somewhat more unusual. It was politi-

cian's day at the commission. Governors of tobacco states or their representatives and four members of the North Carolina congressional
delegation testified. The appearance of congressmen before an administrative agency is an interesting reversal of roles. It is not unusual
for a member of Congress to intervene with agencies on behalf of a
constituent, but it is unusual for members to testify at an agency
hearing, especially when trying to prevent the agency from acting. The
appearance of this large a number of elected officials underscores the
importance of agency policy-making activities. The commissioners listened patiently and courteously to the elected officials before them.
There was little questioning, although some commissioners expressed
skepticism that the proposed rule would bring as much economic and
social damage as the witnesses claimed it would. Nevertheless, the
commissioners understood that elected officials from the tobacco
states really had no choice but to testify and vigorously protest a proposal such as this one, which so directly affected their constituents.
The congressmen present similarly knew that they were not going to
change the commissioners' views simply by testifying against the proposed rule. Instead, they hoped with the cigarette manufacturers to
have the issue transferred from the commission to Congress. By the
time the Federal Trade Commission announced that it was scheduling hearings, those who opposed the health warning requirement
knew that congressional action would be one of the most effective
ways, if not the only way, of halting the commission's proposal.

POSITION OF THE INDUSTRY

One tactic in the strategy to move the controversy to Congress required cigarette manufacturers to publicly ignore and downgrade the
importance of the Federal Trade Commission by electing not to per-
sonally appear at its hearings. Instead, a lawyer from the prestigious
Washington firm of Covington and Burling was retained by the Tobacco Institute to represent manufacturers at the hearings. The
lawyer, H. Thomas Austern, chose to ignore the merits of the smoking
and health controversy and instead concentrated on the position that
the commission did not have general rule-making powers. He insisted
that the absence of these powers in the Federal Trade Commission legislation meant that the issue of a health warning requirement would
have to be settled by Congress; furthermore, according to Mr. Austern,
the issue was of too much importance to be decided by an administrative agency. The elected representatives of the people should decide
this, he said. Mr. Austern warned the commissioners that if they

adopted the proposed rule, the Tobacco Institute would take the Federal Trade Commission to court to demonstrate that rule-making powers were not delegated by Congress.

With this defense decided upon, the attorney for the Tobacco Institute was faced with the task of developing the legal arguments necessary to show that the commission was acting where it lacked the authority to do so. The major thrust of his argument was that if the members of Congress had intended that the commission formulate general rules under the Federal Trade Commission Act of 1914, they would have said so in the act itself. Austern pointed to other acts administered by the commission in which the delegation of rule-making authority was made explicit. Section 8 of the Fur Product Labeling Act of 1945, for example, contains this statement: "The Commission is authorized and directed to prescribe rules and regulations governing the manner and form of disclosing information required by this Act. . . ."

The commission's arguments, which are discussed more fully below, were that the delegation of rule-making powers was both implicit and explicit in the act. Furthermore, since 1914, judicial interpretation and scholarly opinions of agency authority had pointed to the existence of this authority under the statute that created the Federal Trade Commission. The Tobacco Institute remained adamant in its position throughout the hearings, as was expected. Its opposition, although not well founded in prevailing opinions of the law, served to cast doubt on the commission's authority. Strong tobacco opposition also made it clear that, should the commission promulgate its proposed rule, there would be months of uncertainty as the issue was fought out in Congress, the courts, or both. Most lawyers would not have defended the Tobacco Institute's position if the debate had been strictly academic; the law on administrative rule making is quite clear and favorable to agency powers. Mr. Austern, however, was not engaging in an academic debate. His presentation served the useful purpose for which it was designed. The commissioners knew now, if they had not known before, that their rule was due to be reviewed by the U.S. Congress, an institution where the commissioners were not as likely to receive a sympathetic hearing as they had become accustomed to receiving in the judiciary over the years.

THE COMMISSIONERS RESPOND

As the commissioners listened to Mr. Austern's testimony, it was evident that they were becoming increasingly irritated. Perhaps it was the realization that the powerful tobacco interests might succeed in altering or nullifying their new rule-making procedure by persuading Congress to enact a law specifically removing their rule-making power. Or perhaps they were wearied by the thought of protracted argument in Congress and the courts on the cigarette labeling issue itself. At any rate, the commissioners were lawyers and they were not receptive to criticism of their action based on their alleged misinterpretation of the Federal Trade Commission's legal mandate.

The patience of the commissioners had worn thin by the second day of the hearings. Anxious to consider the substantive issues involved in the enforcement of their proposed rule, they were tired of defending their authority to act. When Gilbert H. Weil, a representative of the Association of National Advertisers, took up the Tobacco Institute's argument, he elicited this spirited response from Commissioner Elman:

> Lawyers apparently feel that all law is divided into either substantive or procedural, or legislative, executive, and judicial, and, therefore they have to talk in those terms. And a lot of lawyers apparently have not read what the Supreme Court and what other students of the administrative process have written on the nature of administrative rulemaking. I suggest you lawyers read these cases and come to us with a more realistic approach to the real problem that we have here—instead of talking about fantasies and fictions.[2]

The commissioner's displeasure could not mask the fact that during the first 50 years of the Federal Trade Commission's existence, no substantive rules had been written except in a few instances where they had been expressly authorized by laws such as the Fur Products Labeling Act of 1945. Whether the commissioners liked it or not, the opponents of the cigarette rule did have historical justification for expressing their doubt about the validity of the Federal Trade Commission's new procedure. Non-use gave cigarette manufacturers some support for their argument that general rule-making powers were not delegated by Congress.

Mr. Austern began his testimony before the commission by attempting to establish what the intent of Congress had been in creating the Federal Trade Commission in 1914. Discussing selected segments of floor debate that preceded the passage of the act and quoting Congressman F. C. Stevens of Minnesota, one of the five House members who managed the debate. Austern focused on a passage in the debate that seemed to limit the legislative authority of the proposed commission.[3]

The trouble with relying on floor debate to establish congressional intent is that the clear language of the legislation itself and judicial interpretation of that language take precedence over what happened on the floor of Congress. Frequently, remarks that arise in debate are not well thought out. Furthermore, in a lengthy record of debate, one often uncovers statements that support contradictory positions.[4]

Many of the arguments developed in testimony by the Tobacco Institute had been anticipated by the commission. A lengthy document written by the Federal Trade Commission staff contained a detailed history of the smoking controversy, including 24 pages of careful argument supporting the FTC's defense of its rule-making authority. The arguments set forth in this document were used to answer the tobacco interests' position at the hearings.

THE FEDERAL TRADE COMMISSION'S DEFENSE OF ITS ACTION

The FTC defended its rule-making procedures and authority through three separate, but closely related, arguments. One was that the rule-making authority had been delegated by Congress both implicitly and explicitly in the Act of 1914. The second argument drew on Supreme Court opinions that had encouraged administrative agencies to rely more heavily on rule making rather than adjudicatory procedures. And the third claimed that the commission was not really doing anything very new through its trade regulation rule procedure.

The commission, in support of its first argument, stated that Congress delegated to it the power to prevent unfair methods of competition and deceptive or unfair trade practices. This delegation is contained in section 5(a)(6) of the act: "the Commission is hereby empowered and directed to prevent persons, partnerships, or corporations . . . from using unfair methods of competition in commerce and unfair or deceptive acts or practices in commerce." The delegation of expressed powers to *prevent* those activities listed indicates that the Federal Trade Commission was to be more than a judicial agency acting in a remedial capacity through quasi-judicial procedures alone. Also, the act gives the commission extensive powers to investigate and inquire. These functions underscored the expectation that the commission was to take affirmative action by exercising rule-making authority.

Another section of the Federal Trade Commission Act empowers the commission "to make rules and regulations for the purpose of carrying out the provisions of this Act." The Federal Trade Commission claimed that this section embraced the trade regulation rule procedure, even though the section was unnecessary because the basic mandate of the commission could not be fulfilled without rule-making powers. The commissioners wrote, "It is implicit in the basic purpose and design of the Trade Commission Act as a whole, to establish an administrative agency for the prevention of unfair trade practices, that the commission should not be confined to quasi-judicial proceedings."[5]

The logic of the forgoing arguments involving the propriety of rule making as a device for carrying out the purposes of the act was the most persuasive element of the commission's defense of its action on the smoking issue. It was buttressed by the fact that the Supreme Court had accepted this logic numerous times in cases concerning the rule-making authority of agencies. The Federal Trade Commission referred to a 1947 decision involving one of its sister agencies, the Securities and Exchange Commission. In that case the Court wrote, "the choice made between proceeding by a general rule or by individual, *ad hoc* litigation is one that lies primarily in the informed discretion of the administrative agency."[6]

The third of the commission's arguments in support of its new rule-making procedure was not as persuasive as the others. It claimed that although the old trade practices rules, which came out of trade practices conferences, were usually advisory in nature, they did at times form the basis for formal enforcement proceedings. The "difference between trade practices and trade regulation rules is one of degree, not of kind." The commission argued further, "The trade regulation rule procedure is not a sudden innovation, but a natural outgrowth of the trade practices rule procedure. It is thus the culmination of more than 40 years of Commission rule-making."

One response to this last argument is to ask, why adopt new procedures if the old ones are nearly the same or almost as good? The answer would have to be that there is a significant difference between what could be accomplished under the trade regulation rules and what could be done with the older, more informal, trade practices rules. The commission nearly refuted its own argument when, in a later section of its report, it explained how the new trade regulation rules could be used in adjudication:

> In . . . adjudicatory proceeding(s) the Commission could not use the trade practice rule to resolve any disputed issue of fact, or to dispense with the introduction of evidence required to make out a *prima facie* case. . . . However, in the case of a trade regulation rule, accompanied by and based upon determinations of fact made in accordance with statutory rulemaking procedures, the Commission could, in subsequent adjudicatory proceeding, rely not only on the propositions of law con-

tained in the rule, but also on the underlying factual matters determined.[7]

In other words, the new rule-making procedure was much more powerful than the old one. It was enforceable and could be used as the rule of law to be applied in subsequent agency adjudications; the informal trade practices rules were much more limited. The commission, in its explanation of how the new rules could be used in agency adjudicatory proceedings, was making the point the tobacco interests had already recognized; their understanding of this point accounts, in part, for their opposition to the Federal Trade Commission's proposal.

PROMULGATION OF RULES

The official record remained "open" for two months after the Federal Trade Commission's cigarette hearings so those who desired to add additional statements to the official record could do so. After the record was closed, the commission issued its trade regulation rule on June 22, 1964. It was published in the *Federal Register* less than two weeks later. The commission also published a small announcement of the rule and a summary statement of its background and purpose, which was mailed to hundreds of people who had expressed some interest in this proceeding.

Publication of the trade regulation rule in the *Federal Register* marks the formal or official promulgation of the rule by the commission. Some months after it appears in the *Register,* it is published in cumulative volumes called the *Code of Federal Regulations.* All of the permanent rules and regulations made by administrative agencies are published in the *Code* and organized according to titles and subject matter. This repository of administrative law is similar in form to the volumes that contain the laws enacted by Congress, the *United States Code.*[8]

The rule that the commission adopted was nearly the same as the initial proposal. It stated that it would consider it an unfair or deceptive trade practice if manufacturers failed to disclose on packages, boxes, and cartons—as well as in advertisements—that cigarette smoking is dangerous to health and may cause death from cancer and other diseases. (See Appendix II for the full text of the rule.) The only significant departure from the FTC's original position had to do with the wording of the warning itself, which it left to the cigarette companies to compose.

TOBACCO INTERESTS OBJECT
TO THE RULE

The cigarette ruling was to take effect on January 1, 1965, about six months after the Federal Trade Commission published it in the *Register*.[9] In the period between the commission's hearings and January 1, the cigarette interests mobilized in earnest. Within a month after the conclusion of the hearings, the industry announced the creation of a voluntary code.[10] This voluntary code was intended to signify to Congress and the public that the industry was interested in regulating itself, and that the action of the Federal Trade Commission was an unnecessary obstacle to self-regulation.[11]

Friends and foes of tobacco interests in Congress reacted nearly as swiftly to the Federal Trade Commission's newly promulgated rule as the cigarette manufacturers, themselves, did. After the announcement, members introduced 31 bills in the House and 4 in the Senate. All of the Senate bills were intended to support the FTC and strengthen government regulatory powers over cigarette producers. The House, which often responds more quickly to the pressures of special interests, found itself with 6 bills designed to strip the Federal Trade Commission of some of its powers to regulate cigarette advertising. The remaining 25 House bills were designed either to set up government research programs on smoking and health or to strengthen the Federal Trade Commission.

The introduction of more bills favorable to the FTC's rule than opposed to it was not an indication of congressional support of the commission. Instead, congressional reaction, overall, was overwhelmingly negative, and it quickly became apparent from speeches on the floor and newspaper accounts that the Federal Trade Commission's action would not stand unchallenged. It is not unusual for bills to be introduced to reverse decisions of administrative agencies; however, most die without the formality of committee action. The cigarette interests had too much political muscle to allow the quiet death of the bills challenging the Federal Trade Commission. The first public indication of tobacco power in Congress came from Congressman Oren Harris (D.-Arkansas). Harris, then chairman of the House Interstate and Foreign Commerce Committee, requested that Chairman Dixon of the Federal Trade Commission delay implementation of the rule until the 89th Congress, which would convene in January 1965, had an opportunity to study it. Congress, according to Harris, feared prolonged litigation over the rule and thought that legislation was needed to clarify the situation. Harris's arguments were the same as those made by Mr. Austern at the commission hearings.

Commissioners at the FTC need not have been worried about losing a court battle to the tobacco companies. This was the case because the tobacco threat—voiced numerous times in the FTC hearings and in press releases—was hollow in the sense that the tobacco companies' case was weak and most certainly would be decided by the courts in favor of the commission. At the same time, the commissioners knew an appeal to the courts could take two to three years to resolve; this could have meant postponing implementation of the rule for at least that long. The postponement itself would have been no small victory for the cigarette manufacturers. Consequently Chairman Dixon chose to yield to congressional pressure and agreed to postpone the effective date (January 1, 1965) of the FTC rule. Subsequently, congressional hearings were scheduled to begin in March in the Senate and April in the House.

As lines were being drawn for the cigarette battle in the ensuing months, it became clear that, although support for the tobacco interests remained strong, the tobacco subsystem was showing signs of weakness. The cigarette manufacturers had in the past been able to rely on Congress to kill any serious attempt by government agencies to interfere with their business. Now circumstances were different. The antismoking forces had the Surgeon General's report and a ruling by the Federal Trade Commission to bolster their position. Furthermore, a rather impressive number of senators and representatives had begun to associate themselves with the commission's action. A prelude to the difficulties that the tobacco interests were to face had arisen unexpectedly shortly before the FTC hearings in the spring of 1964. An amendment was attached to a crop support bill in the Senate that would have abolished the tobacco support and acreage control programs. It was defeated, handily, by a vote of 63 to 26, but this frontal assault shook the tobacco men, and the amendment took them by surprise. This was the first floor test of cigarette sentiment since the Surgeon General's report. It showed the tobacco lobbyists that they would have to work diligently to keep the sympathy they were accustomed to finding in Congress. To that end, the industry mobilized a very impressive lobbying team, a team that was at work well before the 89th Congress convened in January 1965.

NOTES

1. Federal Trade Commission, *Hearings on Trade Regulation Rule on Cigarette Labeling and Advertising*, D. 215-8-7, March 17, 1964 (typewritten).

2. Ibid., p. 190.

3. In the debate a colleague asked if the new agency would, in any sense, exercise legislative functions such as those exercised by the Interstate Commerce Commission. Mr. Stevens answered, "We desired clearly to exclude that authority from the

power of the Commission." The Tobacco Institute pointed to this statement as evidence that the Federal Trade Commission was not meant to have rule-making powers. See *Congressional Record*, 63rd 2nd p. 11084 (June 13, 1914).

4. Senator Newlands, a sponsor of the Federal Trade Commission Act in the Senate, made it clear in the debate, for example, that he expected the commission to use discretionary rule-making power. He argued that it would be up to the proposed Federal Trade Commission to affix meaning to the term *unfair competition*. And he went on to indicate his reliance on the Interstate Commerce Commission as a model for the Federal Trade Commission. If the Interstate Commerce Commission could successfully determine rate structures and other regulatory matters through its rule-making procedures, it could be assumed that the Federal Trade Commission could perform a similar function for the matters within its jurisdiction.

5. *Trade Regulation Rule for the Prevention of Unfair or Deceptive Advertising and Labeling of Cigarettes in Relation to the Health Hazards of Smoking and Accompanying Statement of Basis and Purpose of Rule*, Federal Trade Commission document (n.d.), p. 141.

6. *Securities and Exchange Commission* v. *Chenery Corporation*, 332 US 194, 203 (1947).

7. The three quotes are from the Federal Trade Commission document, *Trade Regulation Rule for the Prevention of Unfair or Deceptive Advertising*, pp. 143, 144, and 246.

8. Before 1948 there was no codification of the rules of administrative agencies that appeared in the *Federal Register.* The *Code of Federal Regulations*, which is the responsibility of the National Archives, has brought some order to the chaos that previously existed. Now it is possible for legal researchers to work systematically with administrative rules and regulations in much the same way they work with congressional enactments.

9. The package warning label was required to appear on January 1, 1965, and the advertising warning six months later, July 1, 1965.

10. Nine major producers were signatories to the code: American Tobacco, R. J. Reynolds, Brown & Williamson, Larus and Brother, Liggett & Myers, P. Lorillard, Phillip Morris, Stephano Brothers, and U.S. Tobacco. By 1968, code membership had dropped to six. For various reasons, P. Lorillard, American Tobacco, and Stephano Brothers quit the organization, which removed about one third of total cigarette advertising revenues from code supervision.

11. This attempt at self-regulation was somewhat duplicative of the code administered by the National Association of Broadcasters (NAB), especially after the revision of the National Association of Broadcasters code during the summer of 1967.

Chapter
7

Congressional Power and Agency Policy Making

What a blessing this smoking is! perhaps the greatest that we owe to the discovery of America.

Sir Arthur Helps (1813–1875)

When he was Senate minority leader, Everett McKinley Dirksen spoke lyrically of the place of Congress in the governmental system at a meeting of the American Political Science Association. In his engaging manner, he directed the thoughts of his audience to Article One, Section Eight of the Constitution, which says, "Congress shall have the *power.* . . ." Looking heavenward, the senator said wistfully, "I *love* those words."

Among the implications of the senator's comment is the suggestion that Congress has the strength to control the powers it delegates to administrative agencies. Although this view might accord with the formal constitutional distribution of powers, it inaccurately describes the realities of contemporary politics. Congressmen might dream of a parliamentary Camelot where they control, direct, or perhaps substantially influence all of the actions of the 2.9 million civilians who work in the bureaucracy, but the hard facts of the modern policy process often shatter that dream.

CONGRESSIONAL OVERSIGHT

Article One, Section Eight has not been repealed, and Congress does have the power to oversee the activities of administrative agencies. These agencies exist because Congress created them; they make policy because Congress delegates the authority for them to do so and appropriates funds for their continuing operation. Yet Congress has considerable difficulty controlling, in meaningful, constructive ways, the agencies it creates. Just as parents have some difficulty controlling their children, Congress often finds its administrative offspring uncontrollable. Congress can harass, it can block temporarily, but it has difficulty sustaining its influence over the long term. As in the parent–child relationship, the causes of family or governmental conflicts are found in the characteristics and attitudes of the parent, Congress, the children, agencies, and society at large. Agencies are more nimble and persistent than their cumbersome congressional parent. And they have the advantage of expertise derived from the ability to concentrate on a limited group of related issues until they understand the issues and their ramifications better than anyone else.

The complex problems of modern society also tend to strengthen agencies in their relations with Congress. In foreign affairs, for example, Congress has been virtually removed from meaningful policy participation; leadership resides increasingly and securely in the executive and its agencies. A similar situation exists in the domestic sphere. Congress as an institution has more in its purview than the activities of any single agency. Even if it could become more specialized to compete with bureaucratic expertise, it would be hard pressed to find time to keep up with the voluminous productivity of the agencies. So Congress, or its component parts, has to choose the issues it wants to concentrate upon and carefully prepare itself to question the agencies on these issues. A great deal of congressional time and thought goes into making decisions regarding which policies are to be scrutinized.

Congressional oversight of agency operations in nearly all cases is the responsibility of the committees or subcommittees within an agency's policy subsystem. Formal oversight can occur in annual appropriation hearings, hearings on proposed legislation, or occasional investigations.[1] The quality of oversight varies from subsystem to subsystem; some agencies are subjected to detailed scrutiny of expenditures down to the number of new file cabinets ordered; others receive more general and enlightened policy guidance. The fact that subcommittees are generally responsible for oversight means that from the agency's point of view a few congressmen are more important than

Congress as a whole. All agencies, then, operate with the knowledge that their overseeing committees and, particularly, the leaders of these committees can wreak havoc upon their programs. This knowledge frequently leads to overcautious agency administration that is more concerned about responding to the wishes of a few members of Congress than to what might be the general, though unarticulated, desire of Congress or the nation as a whole.

Overdependence on small numbers of important congressmen can lead to unethical and even illegal interference in agency matters by powerful members of Congress on behalf of a constituent. Individual member intervention in agency affairs or informal oversight could be quite innocent in appearance. Yet even an innocent congressional query could have unsavory overtones. What if a member queries the chairman of a regulatory commission about progress in awarding a certain license? This might be a perfectly innocuous question, but it could lead to an unfair advantage for that congressman's constituent in a situation where there was competition for that license.[2] In short, it is difficult to generalize about the nature, quality, and ethics of congressional oversight. One suspects that it is weak both in terms of general policy guidance and influence on the millions of policy decisions that bureaucrats make. On the other hand, it can be devastating to an agency that out of ignorance or hubris defies the wishes of its small, but powerful and important, congressional constituency.

THE FEDERAL TRADE COMMISSION'S OVERSIGHT STRUGGLE

In view of most congressional oversight, the actions of Congress against the Federal Trade Commission's attempts to require health warnings for cigarette smokers were unusual both in their form and severity. Congress passed a bill in 1965 that reduced in very specific terms a small portion of the FTC's powers. Oversight legislation of a punitive nature is frequently introduced by an irate member, but it seldom is passed or even given serious committee consideration. Normally, reprimands of agencies are informal, handled by committees through threatened action or by an actual reduction of an agency's budget. Either of these occurrences may take place without introduction of legislation or without public hearings.

Open controversy between Congress and an agency is almost always avoided, an indication that those within a subsystem know each other's attitudes and positions fairly well before an agency tries something new. But in the mid-1960s, the pressure exerted on the Federal

Trade Commission by the health interests and the Surgeon General's report encouraged the commission to take an action that was to invoke the full wrath of Congress. The threat of a warning being required on cigarette packages and in all advertising was more than Congress was prepared to accept. It appeared that no one in the FTC had bothered to check its proposed cigarette rule in advance with the appropriate members of Congress. Perhaps the rule had not been cleared with the Hill because of the newness of the rule-making procedure and the commission's inexperience with it.

The resulting congressional reprimand of the Federal Trade Commission was unexpectedly severe in its intensity. It involved lengthy hearings in both houses of Congress on the substance and wisdom of the FTC action. The legislation that emerged from those hearings specifically negated the commission's rule and temporarily took away its rule-making powers relating to cigarette advertising.[3] In addition, the commission was prohibited from requiring or even considering the requirement of a health warning in cigarette advertising for four years. The jurisdiction of the commission under the 1914 act was not changed; its new, controversial trade regulation rule procedure was left intact except as it applied to cigarette regulation. The pinpoint accuracy of the congressional oversight was so unusual that old-timers on Capitol Hill could not remember when or if it had ever happened that way before.

At the same time, the FTC's health warning requirement did pass muster with Congress, and became part of the statutory law with passage of the Cigarette Labeling and Advertising Act (CLAA) of 1965. The FTC may have been stung by the volume of criticism directed its way, but it did walk away from the battle with half of what it was originally after. The FTC lost on the advertisement warning issue but won on the package warning requirement, even if the warning itself was a watered-down version of what the commissioners had had in mind.

NO VICTORY FOR HEALTH

Congress was not acting alone when it moved against the Federal Trade Commission on the cigarette and health issue. It was assisted by the skills, rhetorical and organizational, of the Tobacco Institute and the allies recruited by the institute. The lobbying effort mounted by this group was brilliantly conceived; it indicated that the cigarette manufacturers had the good sense to adapt their approach to the changing tides of public demand in the health field. The manufacturers saw the beginning of a breakdown in the tobacco subsystem, and they had the political acumen and sensibility to shift their tactics to cope with it. They turned what could have been a substantial threat to the steady expansion of cigarette sales into a limited victory. As a result, ironically, the Cigarette Labeling and Advertising Act passed by Congress in 1965 was more of a victory for cigarettes than it was for health.

The cigarette manufacturers realized that public demands for action in response to the research on smoking and health were much stronger than they had been in the past. The health forces had been strengthened by the Surgeon General's 1964 report, *Smoking and Health.* And it was becoming increasingly clear that the cigarette manufacturers would no longer be able to bury or ignore the criticisms of the health people as they had in the past. The industry's attempts to find a safer cigarette and to mitigate the adverse findings of health research by counter, pro-cigarette research had resulted in very little data favorable to smoking. Consequently, promises for even more research, voluntary advertising codes, and a less dangerous cigarette could no longer be used to stay the momentum that the antismoking people had been able to build. Armed with the Federal Trade Commission rule, the Surgeon General's report, and some public support, the health groups had many things going for them in 1965. The carefully constructed walls of tobacco defense were beginning to crack.

The political assets of the health people in Washington were enhanced by the successes some of their colleagues were having with state and local governments. Cigarette package warnings had been proposed for New York City by the city health commissioner. Similar suggestions were being considered by New York, Massachusetts, and other states. The governor of California had created a cigarette smoking advisory committee, and in several jurisdictions pressure was growing to enforce laws already on the books that banned cigarette sales to minors. Indeed, one month before President Johnson signed the Cigarette Labeling and Advertising Act (on July 27, 1965), Governor Nelson A. Rockefeller of New York signed into law a requirement that all cigarette packages sold in his state carry a health warning. If there was anything the cigarette companies wanted less than federal regulation, it was state requirements that health warnings appear. This could have meant as many different labels as there were states, creating an obvious marketing problem.

In the face of mounting concern over cigarette smoking as a health hazard, there was genius in the Cigarette Labeling and Advertising bill from the industry point of view. The bill contained just enough regulation to pass as a health measure; and while the bill required a health warning, it also contained provisions to dismantle an important part of the work of the Federal Trade Commission. Its most significant provision in these terms was the section that temporarily eliminated the FTC's rule-making power in the cigarette advertising field.

The bill as originally introduced permanently banned such Federal Trade Commission action. When the bill was passed, Congress had reduced the length of the ban to four years or until July 1, 1969. Another important provision of the bill prohibited other federal agencies, for example, the Federal Communications Commission, from taking any action regarding health warnings in advertising in that same time period. State and local action was also blocked or preempted by congressional action. Foreclosing the possibility of state and local regulation was a major attraction of the bill for the cigarette manufacturers.

Despite the inclusion of these provisions, the bill was written in terms of protecting public health. The text of the act begins by declaring that it was the intention of Congress to establish a federal program to inform the public of the possible health hazards of smoking. To this end Congress appropriated $2 million shortly after the labeling act was passed, to establish the National Clearinghouse for Smoking and Health. This agency, which is part of the Public Health Service, was directed to carry out educational campaigns and collect data on smoking and health research in the United States. (The successor agency, now located in the Department of Health and Human Services, is called the Office on Smoking and Health.) In a sense, this was the only significant provision of the bill for the health interests. The package labeling requirement was thought by most to be rather insignificant as long as no warning had to appear in advertising. As the controversy over the bill developed in Congress, it became clear that the tobacco interests thought they had little to fear from the labeling requirement. On the contrary, a suitably discrete package warning was very much in the interests of the tobacco manufacturers. With all the emerging data on the health consequences of smoking, manufacturers began to view a mild warning as shielding them from liability claims down the road (which, indeed, it did) while having only a marginal long-term impact on sales.

As the final votes neared, there was virtually no opposition to the bill from the cigarette manufacturers. Rather, they seemed to be supporting it. The bill passed the Senate by a vote of 72 to 5, with most of the tobacco state senators voting for it. Senators who argued that what was being sold as a public health measure was little more than a boon to the cigarette interests voted against it.[4] Even those who often raised objections to bills that granted the national government regulatory powers instead of allowing the states to have them were quiet on the labeling bill. There were no recorded southern or conservative objections to that part of the bill that prohibited the states from adopting similar or related regulatory legislation.

The House adopted the bill by voice vote under circumstances that were designed to limit debate and dissension. The bill was brought to the floor and passed on a Tuesday afternoon when there were only a few members present. The chief opponent of the bill, Representative John Moss (D.-California), had been informed earlier that the vote would come on the following Thursday. When the vote was taken, he was in a commercial aircraft over the Atlantic flying back from Europe. This switch in scheduling violated the gentleman's agreement that governs such matters in Congress. Congressman Richard Bolling (D.-Missouri) spoke of the questionable tactics of bringing the labeling bill to the floor early:

> . . . the Committee [Interstate and Foreign Commerce] was able to get through this House of Representatives a piece of legislation which it agreed upon, when the only person who opposed the legislation strongly enough to sign a minority report was known to be away and unable to return. . . .[5]

The committee chairman, Mr. Harris, denied having any knowledge that his dissenting committee member was out of the country. This episode and other earlier signs discouraged Moss and his liberal colleagues from protesting loudly or fighting with any enthusiasm against the labeling bill in the House. The liberal Democratic Study Group, sensing the overwhelming support for the cigarette manufacturers, decided against organizing any opposition to the bill.[6]

The House was considerably more pro-cigarette than the Senate. Realization of this factor by all parties shifted the scene of the most intense activity to the Senate, and especially the Senate Commerce Committee. The Senate could be expected to go along with that committee's very powerful and popular chairman, Warren Magnuson (D.-Washington). The strength of the tobacco interests in the House, as opposed to the Senate, could be seen in the conference that followed the passage of the bill in each chamber. The House had passed a permanent ban on the Federal Trade Commission's involvement in cigarette advertising; the Senate conferees forced their House counterparts to accept a maximum four-year limit. In the bargaining, the House refused to accept the Senate provision that the printed warning appear on the front of cigarette packages; instead, the conferees agreed to leave the decision concerning where the warning would appear up to the manufacturers.

In the end, the passage of the Cigarette Labeling and Advertising Act was a victory for cigarette manufacturers and their allies. The unwary might find that reading of events difficult to accept; yet this interpretation can be supported. First, the CLAA negated the more sweeping FTC trade regulation rule and specifically restricted the FTC from making decisions on the advertising issue for four years. Second, the warning label requirement was watered down, and the states were preempted from enacting more onerous warning laws. Third, the warning label took the wind out of the health lobby's sails, while shielding the manufacturers from product liability suits. Given the mood of the country and the shifting nature of tobacco politics at the time, the manufacturers could have hardly asked for more. As one observer commented: "In fact . . . the bill is not, as its sponsors suggested, an example of congressional initiative to protect public health; it is an unashamed act to protect private industry from government regulation."[7]

STRATEGY FOR SUCCESS

How did the cigarette manufacturers manage to win such an impressive victory? What led to their success in persuading Congress to do what the Federal Trade Commission could not be persuaded to do? These enviable accomplishments were designed and executed under the able leadership of former Senator Earle C. Clements of Kentucky.

Senator Clements's experience on the Hill provided him with both the knowledge of congressional operations and the personal support from members he needed to be effective. His one-time executive directorship of the Senate Democratic Campaign Fund enabled him to draw on the assets of old political favors. Aside from his power in Congress, the former senator was one of the few men who could keep President Johnson out of the controversy. Mr. Johnson had as good, if not better, a record on consumer legislation than any President in memory. Yet he made no public attempt to support the Federal Trade Commission in its struggle on the Hill. He was uncharacteristically silent during the whole affair, from the announcement of the congressional hearings through the bill signing formality.

Senator Clements was hired by the six largest cigarette manufacturers in 1964. Reinforcing the strategy to downgrade the Federal Trade Commission's rule-making authority, Clements was at work in Congress well before the commission adopted its rule. The first thing he had to do was coordinate the thinking and strategies of the cigarette manufacturers and their allies. He knew that success could very well depend on how quickly and firmly he could forge a united front among the manufacturers, tobacco state congressmen, growers, advertisers, and other friends of the cigarette business.

Clements rightly sensed that this time the cigarette companies were going to be forced to give up something; the protestations of the health groups were too strong to be ignored. He decided to persuade his employers to accept the label on packages in return for a ban against a similar requirement in advertising and a ban against state action requiring health warnings. This strategy, which seems so sensible in light of its success, did not seem as sensible when the former senator began his work.

Shortly after Senator Clements arrived in Washington, he scheduled regular weekly meetings with the Tobacco Institute's attorneys, public relations firms, and friends. The public relations firm of Hill and Knowlton had been on retainer to the institute since its inception. While not registered as lobbyists, Hill and Knowlton represented the Washington interests of firms estimated at that time to account for more than 10 percent of the gross national product.[8] At these meetings detailed plans were worked out for the Federal Trade Commission hearings, for congressional lobbying, and for a possible appeal to the courts should all else fail. Once it was decided that Congress should be the prime target, it was obvious that the Senate Commerce Committee held the key to victory.

Senator Clements knew that both houses could be expected to follow the dictates of their committees. Generally, the whole body affirms the work of its committees; moreover, floor revolts are even less likely than usual against the commerce committees because of their important jurisdictions. Members are not anxious to jeopardize a favorable relationship with these committees by failing to heed their recommendations.

The Interstate and Foreign Commerce Committee was, at the time, a rather conservative force in the House, and southerners held key positions in 1965. The chairman, Oren Harris, represented a rural area in Arkansas, and the second ranking member, Harley Staggers, was from a similar area of West Virginia. Seven other members of the 33-member committee were from tobacco regions, including Congressman Horace R. Kornegay of North Carolina, who was a vociferous advocate for the tobacco companies. Kornegay decided not to run for Congress in 1968. Instead he assumed the post of vice-president and counsel of the Tobacco Institute in January 1969, and later became chairman of the institute.

The Senate Commerce Committee was more consumer-oriented than its House counterpart. It was beginning to develop and report out bills on a series of consumer matters unrelated to cigarettes except for their common purposes of strengthening protection of the public from business abuses. The membership of the committee was closely divided over the cigarette issue, making the chairman, Senator Magnuson, of crucial importance to both the smoking and the health forces. He was careful to avoid committing himself to either group at an early date.

Senator Neuberger worked strenuously to rally support for the health forces among her colleagues on the committee. Her work was destined to be unproductive because she faced a united Republican opposition under the leadership of Thurston Morton, the popular senator from Kentucky. Meanwhile, Senators Vance Hartke of Indiana and Ross Bass of Tennessee, both Democrats, were unsympathetic to the pleas of their colleague. Senator Bass had a sizable tobacco constituency, and Senator Hartke was indebted to Earle Clements for his aid as director of the Senate Democratic Campaign Fund. Hartke was subject to no strong pressures from his constituency on either side of the smoking issue, so he displayed some loyalty to those who had been loyal to him. The six Republicans and two Democrats united in opposition to Senator Neuberger, plus some wavering Democrats unenthusiastic about the health position, made the Oregon lawmaker's attempt to give congressional approval to the Federal Trade Commission ruling impossible. It became clear as the hearings began that the Federal Trade Commission action would be either reversed or substantially modified in the Senate Commerce Committee. The health groups could not rally the necessary political support to prevent Congress from changing the FTC's rule.

The antismoking forces were not nearly as well organized or as well financed as the cigarette interests. Lobbyist David Cohen of the Americans for Democratic Action characterized the contest between the tobacco people and the health people as similar to a match between the Green Bay Packers and a high school football team. The tobacco state congressmen had powerful reasons to reverse the Federal Trade Commission action, namely, their constituents' support. On the other hand, there were few if any "health" congressmen. Those members who did champion the health cause had no substantial constituent interest to back them up.

In the absence of support from special interest constituencies, congressmen find it difficult to vote for regulatory measures that are unpopular across the whole business and industrial spectrum. Consequently, they find it relatively easy to vote funds for health research but difficult to vote for programs that would end or reduce those hazards that are identified in the health research they sponsored, as indicated in this statement:

The lawmakers enthusiastically vote hundreds of millions of dollars—more, usually, than is requested—for health research, for when it is simply a matter of research, what congressman is against health? However, when the officials go to Capitol Hill with proposals to put research findings into effect—to curb air pollution or discourage smoking—they are skunks at the lawn party. For on these issues there are large economic issues at stake.[9]

THE HEALTH LOBBY

The efforts of health organizations outside of Congress were no more successful than they were inside. Those who might have benefited from the cigarette legislation were confirmed or prospective smokers, and neither group was particularly interested in creating any government program geared to pointing out the group's foolishness. The public health interest groups have very small constituencies, usually coalitions of the various professionals in fields related to medicine and health. These people find it difficult to devote the time and resources necessary to put their complex, technical reasoning before the public and convince them of its validity. Instead, their activities are confined primarily to research and fund raising. Consequently, these groups, the American Cancer Society, the American Heart Association, the National Tuberculosis Association, and others, confined most of their activities to the hearing rooms.[10]

The health- and consumer-oriented agencies in government were weak in the face of organized congressional opposition. The Federal Trade Commission, for example, had little clout with committees on the Hill because it had virtually no support from its constituents, the industries it regulated. Without good congressional connections or an active clientele group, the commission was in a poor position to do battle with Congress.[11] Paul Rand Dixon, chairman of the FTC, had little desire to stir up more controversy in Congress than the commission had done already with the adoption of the rule. He testified on behalf of the commission, but there is little evidence of any meaningful activity on his part outside of the hearing room. There are good reasons for commissioners to confine most of their activities to the commission hearing room.

Members of regulatory commissions wear two hats. They sit as judges as they listen to cases brought before them under the formal procedures of the Administrative Procedure Act. And, they perform as policy makers as they decide which issues to pursue and how to pursue them. These two roles are incorporated in one individual nowhere in government except in the persons of appointed commissioners of the independent agencies.[12] It is difficult to keep the two roles separate, as one might easily imagine. Should the roles become closely intertwined, a commissioner runs the risk of being disqualified from voting on a case on the grounds that the judicial dictum against prejudgment has been violated.

Meanwhile, the Public Health Service was ill equipped to lead a legislative struggle to protect the sanctity of its *Smoking and Health* report. The Public Health Service has a large annual budget it likes to preserve; furthermore, it has never demonstrated much competence in lobbying for substantive legislation, and its parent organization, the Department of Health, Education and Welfare, had declared at an earlier date that it would not wholeheartedly support the action of the Federal Trade Commission.

The health groups acted as if they knew there was little hope for legislation supporting the ruling of the Federal Trade Commission. They too sensed the opposition in the House and devoted very little time to attempting to overcome what was insurmountable opposition. Instead, they devoted most of their time to the Senate, but given the House opposition, they knew their efforts in the upper chamber held little promise of bringing a strong piece of legislation out of Congress.

The health groups made some concerted attempts to take their case directly to the public. To facilitate their campaign, they formed an organization called the National Interagency Council on Smoking and Health in July 1964. The council had 16 charter members and currently has 34 members.[13]

The chairman of the council during the labeling hearings was Emerson Foote, described by the Tobacco Institute as a "one-time advertising man, and 'reformed' smoker, who made a small fortune peddling cigarettes."[14] The characterization did not do justice to the career of this unusual man. Emerson Foote came to Madison Avenue in 1936 and began one of the advertising industry's most successful promotional schemes. He handled the Lucky Strike account and wrote most of the slogans that not only made his client prosperous but also popularized smoking throughout the nation. When he decided to join the health forces, he was chairman of the board of McCann-Erickson, one of the country's largest advertising firms. Foote explained that his decision to switch rather than fight for the cigarette manufacturers did not grow out of a dislike for cigarettes: "I am not against tobacco. I am against cancer, heart disease and emphysema."[15] Foote testified at the hearings and worked hard, but with no visible signs of success, to support the Federal Trade Commission's action.[16]

The council, on paper, looked like a powerful lobbying organization. *Barron's*, a national financial weekly, accused it of being a front for the bureaucracy, particularly the Public Health Service.[17] There is some substance to this charge. Two of the three officers of the organization during the labeling hearings were staff members of the Public Health Service, and for five years the headquarters of the council was maintained at Public Health Service offices in suburban Washington. Yet, this rather impressive coalition of health organizations was no match for the cigarette manufacturers. As the date for the congressional hearings approached, it seemed that the antismoking people were politically outclassed by the cigarette group. Cigarettes had high-priced talent, exceptional political experience, a tight organization, and powerful, entrenched support in Congress. Antismoking forces lacked large measures of these vital ingredients.

THE CONGRESSIONAL HEARINGS

The Senate Commerce Committee hearings attracted more attention than those of its counterpart committee in the House. The publicity that accompanied these hearings, coupled with the fact that some of the membership of the Senate committee were uncommitted on the smoking and health issue, underscored their importance. Those who supported the Federal Trade Commission rule were given favorable positions in the scheduling of their testimony, a sign that committee leadership was sympathetic to the commission's ruling. For example, the first slot of the second morning was given to a representative of the American Cancer Society. This early position helped to assure him of newspaper and television coverage. A spot later in the day would have drawn less public attention.

One of the difficulties that plagued the health groups throughout the congressional hearings was the absence of agreement on just what they wanted Congress to do. They agreed that cigarette smoking was harmful to health and that the government should do something about it. All of the health witnesses stressed these points. Members of Congress, bureaucrats, physicians, and the representatives of the public interest groups knew the medical arguments well and presented them with feeling. But this is where their agreement ended. Their failure to agree on a plan of action reflected their lack of political know-how and inability to organize a cohesive campaign. Senator Clements, on the other hand, had made certain the cigarette manufacturers avoided any disunity.

The disunity of the health groups became obvious early in the hearings. The Surgeon General suggested that the Federal Trade Commission was not the most appropriate agency to enforce the labeling and advertising requirement. He noted that the Department of Health,

Education and Welfare could provide the type of regulatory approach required for enforcement of the cigarette labeling regulations. Chairman Dixon did not take immediate exception to the Surgeon General's point of view. Nevertheless, he did stress in his testimony the necessity of Federal Trade Commission involvement because the absence of a health warning was an unfair or deceptive trade practice. Prevention of such practices was within the jurisdiction of the Federal Trade Commission, Dixon reminded the committee.

The health forces were further split on the wording of the warnings that they wanted to appear on packages and in advertising. Senator Neuberger favored "Caution—Habitual Smoking Is Injurious to Health"; Senator Bennett and Congressman Moss would have preferred this statement: "Warning: Continual Cigarette Smoking May Be Hazardous to Your Health." A third suggestion was proposed by the American Heart Association: "Caution: Habitual Cigarette Smoking Frequently Constitutes a Serious Hazard to Health."

These disputes were in sharp contrast to the ultrasmooth coordination and scenario employed by the cigarette interests. The case that the cigarette people made in support of their position was a good one. Their arguments were detailed, coherent, and generally persuasive.

THE CIGARETTE MEN TESTIFY

The cigarette lobbyists' presentations before Congress were much different from the presentations they made at the Federal Trade Commission hearing. Before the congressional committees they covered all aspects of the argument: the Surgeon General's report, other studies on the health consequences of smoking, the importance of unfettered competition to the economy and the American creed, tobacco's contribution to the nation, and the proper policy role of Congress vis-à-vis the states and administrative agencies. This full complement of arguments contrasted sharply with the limited legal argument presented at the Federal Trade Commission hearings.

Another significant difference in approach by the tobacco forces between the Federal Trade Commission and congressional hearings was the number of witnesses who appeared for cigarettes. At the Federal Trade Commission, one lawyer represented the manufacturers. In Congress, dozens of witnesses from a variety of professional fields appeared. The testimony of these witnesses was skillfully orchestrated by Earle Clements.

The heart of the industry case was given to each of the congressional committees by Bowman Gray, chairman of the board of the R. J. Reynolds Company, a competent and effective witness. His voice never rose above conversational tones. For two hours at the witness table of each committee, he chain-smoked his way through what proved to be a thoughtful synopsis of the industry arguments that were to follow. And although Mr. Gray disclaimed any medical expertise, he carefully laid the groundwork for the pro-smoking medical arguments. He touched base with the economists by noting that "unwise legislation in this field could produce repercussions which would be felt throughout the country's economy." He went on to warn that the balance of payments problem might even be exacerbated if exports of tobacco products fell.

Ideological and philosophical objections also appeared in Mr. Gray's testimony. Policy in a democracy should be made by Congress, not an administrative agency; and the will of the people embodied in their elected representatives should be supreme, he continued. On other philosophical questions, Gray argued that there was a right to advertise—a right that he labeled "an essential commercial" one. He acknowledged that he believed the Federal Trade Commission rule was "step one in the [government's] trying to get control of one industry." And he added, it was "a first step to get control of other industries."

After Mr. Gray came the parade of witnesses, the largest number of whom were medical doctors and professionals from allied fields. All of them cast doubt on the Surgeon General's report. The report, they claimed, was based on statistical rather than clinical evidence and was not sufficient proof that smoking caused diseases. A Virginia pathologist argued that the evidence "submitted . . . by proponents of the theory that lung cancer is caused by smoking . . . does not constitute scientific proof of this theory." Darrell Huff, author of *How to Lie with Statistics*, talked darkly about the Surgeon General's committee's work. He pointed to a number of statistical and methodological "warning signals" that perhaps indicated that some conclusions in the report were not warranted by the facts.

The majority of witnesses at the congressional hearings testified against the Surgeon General's report and the Federal Trade Commission's rule. Most of the professionals who testified identified their employers as independent research associations. However, nearly two years after the hearings, it was disclosed that a few of the witnesses had not properly or fully identified themselves. Senator Daniel Brewster (D.-Maryland) mailed questionnaires to those who testified on behalf of the cigarette industry. Sixteen of the 37 questionnaires he sent were returned. Some of those answering admitted that they had received large fees from the tobacco interests for their testimony. This came as a surprise to some members of the committee who thought they were hearing professional opinions untarnished by any possible financial connection with the industry. Senator Brewster suggested that there be a committee investigation of any possible conflict of interest that might have arisen at the labeling hearings, but the request died quietly and quickly.[18]

Cigarette manufacturers had a number of well-organized allies in Washington. While the Senate Commerce Committee was holding its hearings, the National Association of Broadcasters held its annual convention in town. There were over 500 radio and television executives in attendance. At a reception, more than 400 of the 535 members of Congress were entertained by these executives and treated to their views on the right to advertise. It has been estimated that more than one third of the members of Congress owned major stock holdings in radio and television stations. This could account for some of the sympathy in Congress for those who were threatened by government regulation of cigarette advertising.[19]

After the hearings, the Senate Commerce Committee quickly voted down Senator Neuberger's bill to accept the Federal Trade Commission's approach to regulation of cigarette labeling and advertising. The members of the committee, instead, reported out a bill very similar in form and content to the one eventually passed into law. Senator Neuberger attempted to amend the bill on the floor, but she was unsuccessful.

The bill went to President Johnson on July 13, and he maintained his silence on the legislation as he had done throughout the controversy. On July 27, within hours of the time the bill would have become law automatically without the President's signature, it was signed. Eight disenchanted members of Congress, in league with lobbyists for the Americans for Democratic Action, attempted to persuade the President to veto the bill. Their efforts were to no avail. The President signed the legislation in the privacy of his office. There were no guests, no glitter, and no souvenir pens, which ordinarily accompany the signing of a major piece of legislation. The bill was signed without ceremony, and the President's press secretary released the news without benefit of comment.

The passage of the Cigarette Labeling and Advertising Act marked the end of a well-organized campaign to move Congress to adopt an unusual oversight measure. The skills of the Tobacco Institute, enhanced by the sympathies of many members, helped to remove any doubts that might have existed in the Federal Trade Commission or elsewhere as to where ultimate policy-making authority resided. Congress is effective in disciplining errant agency policy makers, particularly when those agencies challenge the interests of powerful economic groups. Although the lengths to which Congress went to discipline the Federal Trade Commission were unusual, it is not unusual for members to prevent similar agency actions through less stringent, more informal methods.

THE FEDERAL TRADE COMMISSION RESCINDS ITS RULE

The day after the President signed the bill, the Federal Trade Commission issued an order vacating its trade regulation rule. In this order, the commissioners took note of the fact that the legislation did not change the findings or conclusions that were the basis of the labeling and advertising rule. Manufacturers were warned that any advertising that attempted to undermine the warning that was required on packages would be unfair and deceptive and could be stopped by the commission. Although the legislation prohibited the Federal Trade Commission from requiring a health warning, the July 28 commission order stated, "[The commission] will continue to monitor current practices and methods of cigarette advertising and promotion, and take all appropriate action consistent with the Act to prohibit cigarette advertising that violates the Federal Trade Commission Act."[20]

The legislation marked the end of a turbulent excursion into congressional politics for the Federal Trade Commission. In the summer of 1965, the commission settled down to its more normal routine and put to one side, at least temporarily, any plans for mounting a new rule-making proceeding in the cigarette and health field until the ban against its doing so expired in the summer of 1969. The commission set up its tar and nicotine laboratory and began gathering information for its yearly reports to Congress on cigarette smoking and advertising. Although things around the Federal Trade Commission grew quieter, the cigarette controversy continued. The nonsmoking genie was out of the bottle, and it began to appear and reappear in other, often unexpected, places. Congress had succeeded in silencing the Federal Trade Commission for a while, but it was about to hear from some of her sister agencies on the same subject in slightly different garb. The congressional action had won cigarette manufacturers some time, but the question of smoking, its relationship to health, and what the government might do about it was far from settled.

NOTES

1. See Walter J. Oleszek, *Congressional Procedures and the Policy Process,* 3rd ed. (Washington, D.C.: Congressional Quarterly Press, 1989), especially Chapter 10.

2. For one recent example of the haziness of the line between propriety and impropriety, the reader is referred to charges of undue influence leveled against members of Congress involved in the savings and loan debacle of the 1980s. Former Speaker of the House Jim Wright (D.-Texas) and Senators Alan Cranston (D.-California), Dennis DeConcini (D.-Arizona), John Glenn (D.-Ohio), John McCain (R.-Arizona), and Donald Riegle (D.-Michigan) all were implicated for intervening, unfairly, with the Federal Home Loan Bank Board (the agency responsible for regulating the savings and loan industry) on behalf of specific thrift institutions. The lawmakers claimed that their actions fell in the category of legitimate casework and were motivated by a desire to alleviate unnecessarily burdensome restrictions on constituents who operated struggling thrifts. As such, the members argued that their machinations fell well within the realm of ethical behavior. Many others, in both public and private spheres, disagreed. See Martin Mayer, *The Greatest-Ever Bank Robbery: The Collapse of the Savings and Loan Industry* (Toronto: Scribners & Sons, 1990).

3. PL 89-92 (1965), U.S.C., sect. 1331. The ban on FTC action in the area of advertising was extended for another two years in 1970. At that time, Congress also required that the FTC give six months' notice of, and supporting evidence for, any future plans to adopt trade regulation rules regarding cigarettes. See PL 91-222 (1970), 15 U.S.C., sect. 1331.

4. Four of the opposition votes were cast by liberal Democrats: Paul Douglas of Illinois, Robert Kennedy of New York, Gaylord Nelson of Wisconsin, and Joseph Clark of Pennsylvania. The fifth was from a Republican, Senator Wallace Bennett of Utah, a Mormon and longtime foe of cigarette smoking.

5. *Congressional Record,* H15962, July 13, 1965.

6. Organized in 1956, the Democratic Study Group (DSG) consists of House Democratic liberals who oppose the dominant conservative leadership in the House. The group first indicated its strength and principles when called upon to oppose the Southern Manifesto of 1956, a document sponsored by nearly all Southern Democrats, which opposed civil rights measures. The DSG proved effective in winning some liberal reforms in the early 1960s. For more on the DSG, see Richard Bolling, *House Out of Order* (New York: Dutton, 1965), pp. 54–58; and Mark F. Ferber, "The Formation of the Democratic Study Group," in *Congressional Behavior,* ed. Nelson W. Polsby (New York: Random House, 1971).

7. Elizabeth Brenner Drew, "The Quiet Victory of the Cigarette Lobby: How It Found the Best Filter Yet—Congress," *The Atlantic Monthly,* September, 1965, p. 76.

8. It is difficult to be certain about how much is spent on the institute's lobbying campaigns in any one year. Recent data peg advertising and promotional spending by the tobacco industry at about $4 billion a year (*USA Today,* June 9, 1994, p. 1) and a significant percentage of that amount is devoted to lobbying efforts.

9. Drew, "The Quiet Victory of the Cigarette Lobby," p. 79.

10. The American Medical Association (AMA) did not testify in Congress although it took the position publicly that Congress, not the Federal Trade Commission, should regulate the cigarette industry, if there had to be any regulation at all. This position drew criticism from the more liberal members of the organization who wanted the AMA to speak out on this health problem.

11. See Norton E. Long, "Power and Administration," *Public Administration Review,* vol. 9 (Autumn 1949), 257–264.

12. See Robert A. Katzmann, *Regulatory Bureaucracy: The Federal Trade Commission and Antitrust Policy* (Cambridge, Mass: MIT Press, 1980), and David M. Welborn, *Governance of Federal Regulatory Agencies* (Knoxville: University of Tennessee

Press, 1977) for good discussions of the law and politics governing the work of the federal independent regulatory agencies.

13. The following groups are members of the council: American Academy of Pediatrics, American Alliance for Health, Physical Education and Recreation, American Association for Respiratory Therapy, American Cancer Society, American College of Chest Physicians, American College Health Association, American College of Radiology, American College of Surgeons, American Dental Association, American Heart Association, American Hospital Association, American Lung Association, American Medical Student Association, American Pharmaceutical Association, American Public Health Association, American School Health Association, Association of State and Territorial Health Officers, Boys' Club of America, March of Dimes Birth Defects Foundation, National Association of School Nurses, National Board of Young Men's Christian Association, National Congress of Parents and Teachers, National Jogging Association, National League for Nursing, National Medical Association, National Student Nurses Association, Society of Surgical Oncology, U.S. Department of Defense, U.S. Department of Education, U.S. Department of Health and Human Services, Office on Smoking and Health, Public Health Service, and Veterans Administration.

14. From a speech by Franklin B. Dryden, assistant to the president, Tobacco Institute, Inc., before the 21st Tobacco Workers Conference, January 17–20, 1967, Williamsburg, Virginia, p. 12 (mimeo).

15. Roy Parker, Jr., "Ad Whiz Has New Target," *Raleigh News and Observer,* January 12, 1965.

16. Mr. Foote was succeeded as president of the National Interagency Council by former Surgeon General Luther L. Terry, who in turn was succeeded by his former assistant surgeon general, Dr. James L. Hundley. Dr. Hundley served as assistant chairman of Dr. Terry's Advisory Committee on Smoking and Health. The council devotes most of its efforts to holding conferences and promoting educational campaigns designed to discourage smokers from continuing their habit.

17. "Best Foote Forward?" *Barron's,* January 18, 1965.

18. Congress itself pays only the expenses of those witnesses it asks to testify; others pay their own expenses. The problem of witnesses paid by special interests is not serious so long as they disclose their connections. The problem of undisclosed connections is an ethical one; its implications remain unexplored by Congress.

19. Roy Parker, Jr., "Cigarettes Have Friends in Labeling Battle," *Raleigh News and Observer,* March 25, 1965.

20. "Vacation of Warning Requirements in Trade Regulation Rule Concerning Advertising and Labeling of Cigarettes," 30 *Federal Register,* p. 9484 (1965).

Congress
and the Bureaucracy:
A Balance of Power?

> This Indian Weed, now withered quite
>   Though green at noon, cut down at night,
>   Shows thy decay—
>   All flesh is hay:
> Thus think, and smoke tobacco.
>
>   From "Tobacco" by George Wither (1588–1667)

The struggle between Congress and the Federal Trade Commission was resolved only temporarily in favor of Congress by the moratorium imposed in the Cigarette Labeling and Advertising Act. The commission, joined by its newly acquired health constituency and other bureaucratic agencies, succeeded in keeping the cigarette controversy alive despite the congressional action designed to temporarily curtail the FTC's power. The agencies continued to work for acceptance of the idea of requiring a health warning in advertising even though the congressional ban against making such a requirement remained in effect until July 1, 1969.

In the years since Congress chose to exercise its oversight prerogative, the antismoking agencies have enlisted public support, found an ally in the Federal Communications Commission, and achieved more unity in pressuring for their goal of strengthening the health warning and extending it to advertising. Meanwhile, the political strength of the tobacco companies has eroded slightly as new health studies traced ever more serious medical consequences to cigarette smoking. The position of the manufacturers has deteriorated further in the eyes of many because the manufacturers have not voluntarily altered the direction of their advertising campaigns, which still portray smoking as good clean fun. The FTC claims that cigarette manufacturers are continuing to promote their products as harmless prerequisites to social acceptability.

The introduction of the 100-millimeter cigarettes in 1967 and 1968—giving the smoker more smoke, generally with higher tar and nicotine content, for the same price as regular or king-size cigarettes— was taken by some members of the commission as proof of the callous disregard by the manufacturers for government attempts to curtail smoking. More recently, "25 packs" have appeared on the market. Tobacco critics claim that these would permit smokers, who usually think of their smoking habit in terms of packs per day, to increase their consumption level over the standard 20-cigarette packs without being entirely conscious that they were smoking more.

BUREAUCRACY CONTINUES THE CONTROVERSY

The Public Health Service continued its efforts to reduce smoking through its National Clearinghouse for Smoking and Health and by the appointment of two advisory panels. The first group, composed of 14 experts, was asked by the Surgeon General to review recent medical research dealing with the effects of tar and nicotine on health. The panel reported that the scientific evidence suggested that lower tar and nicotine content in cigarette smoke reduced the harmful effects of smoking. This disclosure came shortly after Senator Magnuson had asked the Federal Trade Commission to reverse its ban on including tar and nicotine disclosures in advertising. He had also asked the commission to establish a laboratory to measure the quantities of these ingredients in every brand.[1] The commission quickly agreed to the senator's request and installed, in its headquarters' building, machines that smoke cigarettes and measure the amount of tar and nicotine in each one. The results of these tests are published regularly and distributed by the commission. Manufacturers have been encouraged to include the test results in their advertising, and since early 1971 all of them have done so. Since 1985, manufacturers have also been required to report information on tobacco additives to the FTC.

In the fall of 1967, the Surgeon General created a second panel—the Task Force on Smoking and Health—which included ex-advertising man and health interest convert Emerson Foote and retired baseball star Jackie Robinson. The task force captured considerable public attention when, in August 1968, it reported that some gains had been made in that the increasing rate of consumption had been slowed somewhat. Nonetheless, the task force condemned the industry for the content of its advertisements and asked the government for more stringent regulations, including the requirement of a health warning in advertising. The report was sufficiently critical of cigarette manufacturers to elicit this response from the Tobacco Institute: "[This report is] . . . a shockingly intemperate defamation of an industry which has led the way in medical research to seek answers in the cigarette controversy."[2]

The 1965 Cigarette Labeling and Advertising Act provided some opportunity for the bureaucracy to keep attention focused on the smoking and health issue through the requirement that both the Federal Trade Commission and the Public Health Service submit annual reports to Congress on smoking. According to the act, these reports were to contain current information concerning smoking and health together with recommendations for further legislative action. The reports provided an opportunity for both agencies to make very strong appeals for further action to curb smoking. Both the 1967 and 1968 reports of the Department of Health, Education and Welfare called for warnings to appear in advertising along with the disclosure of tar and nicotine content. Secretary of Health, Education and Welfare, Wilbur J. Cohen, appointed in the spring of 1968, concluded his letter to Congress with these words: "In my opinion, the remedial action taken until now has not been adequate." The letter was accompanied by a lengthy bibliography and analysis of the hundreds of medical articles and research studies published since the Surgeon General's 1964 report. The HEW acted much more aggressively in the cigarette health field under Secretary Cohen than it did in 1965 at the height of the controversy.

The Surgeon General's reports have grown increasingly strong on the adverse effects of smoking. The 1972 report hit a peak when it concluded for the first time that nonsmokers exposed to the cigarette smoke of others were being exposed to a health hazard. The report indicated that it was no longer enough to give up smoking; one had to stay out of rooms or other closed places where other people were smoking.

This disclosure led to moves to ban smoking in public places or at least restrict it to certain defined areas. A number of state and local jurisdictions have required that restaurants, for example, provide "no smoking" sections. In 1981, the Surgeon General's annual report called for study of the addictive nature of smoking. The report also concluded that no progress had been made in the search for a safe cigarette. Even the lower tar and nicotine cigarettes seemed to constitute a health risk because smokers, believing they were safer than with other cigarettes, smoked more often and inhaled more deeply—thereby increasing their health risks.

Subsequent Surgeon General's reports on smoking and health have continued to implicate tobacco in a growing range of health problems. In the 1982 report, Surgeon General Everett C. Koop attributed 30 percent of all cancer deaths to tobacco and called cancer from smoking "the chief preventable cause of death in our society." The 1984 report said that 80 to 90 percent of all chronic obstructive lung disease, and 50,000 of 62,000 deaths, were caused by smoking. In the 1985 report, Koop said that cigarettes were the main peril in the workplace, prompting the AFL-CIO to accuse him of undermining efforts to improve environmental and occupational health programs.[3] The 1986 Surgeon General's report focused on "passive" smoking and found that 2,400 lung cancer deaths per year resulted from the inhalation of "side stream" smoke at home or in the office.

The Federal Trade Commission also seems to have been encouraged rather than intimidated by the rebuke it suffered at the hands of Congress. In addition to its speedy action in setting up the tar and nicotine laboratory, the commission has submitted hardhitting reports to Congress. The first report, submitted in June 1967, contained five recommendations. These included a requirement that a warning statement appear in all advertising and that the statement itself be made stronger. The report suggested changing the warning to read: "Warning: Cigarette Smoking Is Dangerous to Health and May Cause Death from Cancer and Other Diseases." Furthermore, the commission called for more appropriations for itself and for the HEW to increase its campaigns to bring the antismoking message to the public with greater effectiveness.

The commission's second report was even bolder than its first. It contained some analysis of advertising content and an exposé of what the Federal Trade Commission felt was a blatant attempt to mislead the public. An article by Stanley Frank appeared in the January 15, 1968, issue of *True Magazine* dismissing the evidence against smoking as inconclusive and inaccurate. Less than two months later an article with similar conclusions appeared in the *National Enquirer* titled, "Cigarette Cancer Link Is Bunk." It was written by Charles Golden. Within a few days *The Wall Street Journal* disclosed that the articles were placed in these two national publications by the tobacco interests. Stanley Frank and Charles Golden were the same person—who later became a staff member of the public relations firm retained by the Tobacco Institute. The institute ordered more than one million reprints of the *True* article, which were mailed to doctors, medical researchers, educators, and nearly every member of Congress. The FTC estimated that this campaign cost the institute at least $175,000. This journalistic–public relations episode led the commission to conclude that these actions were " . . . not the acts of an industry either confident of its facts nor solicitous of its reputation."[4]

Perhaps it was this obvious attempt by the tobacco manufacturers to discredit the government's work in the smoking field that stiffened the Federal Trade Commission's position in its 1968 *Report to Congress.* The 1968 report contained a recommendation that was not included the previous year. The commission recommended that cigarette advertising on television and radio be banned entirely. If the advertising could not be banned, the commission suggested that the hours at which such advertisements appear be limited and that the total amount of advertising also be regulated. The report was adopted by the FTC with only one dissenting vote. Commissioner Nicholson and Chairman Dixon noted in concurring opinions that they hoped the government would not have to go so far as to impose a ban on radio and television advertising. Yet even they were adamant in their expressions of need for more stringent requirements, particularly the requirement that a health warning appear in all advertising. In later years the FTC reports continued to argue for radio and television ad bans as well as the requirement that a strengthened health warning be included in printed advertising.

Probably the most important event to occur during the four-year moratorium on the Federal Trade Commission was the dramatic entrance of the Federal Communications Commission (FCC) into the smoking and health controversy. This commission, like the other independent regulatory bodies, has generally shown very little interest in moving against the wishes of those it regulates. Yet, with relatively little prodding, the FCC was persuaded to require that broadcasters air antismoking publicity more frequently. The FCC's action favoring the antismoking people, against the wishes of the broadcasting industry, is interesting politically because of the very limited support it had in any quarter, including the health groups themselves.

The requirement for more antismoking publicity was adopted when the Federal Communications Commission was persuaded to apply its fairness doctrine to cigarette commercials. Application of the fairness doctrine in this case meant that any station that carried cigarette ads was obliged to give the public the other side of the issue, that is, inform them of the health hazards in smoking. The FCC was prompted to act when it received a letter from a young New York lawyer, John F. Banzhaf, III. Mr. Banzhaf requested that the commission require WCBS-TV in New York City to give free, to responsible health groups, the same amount of time as that sold to tobacco companies for the purpose of promoting the virtues and values of smoking. The FCC did not require that precise amounts or exactly equal time be given, but it did require stations to provide "a significant amount of time for the other viewpoint."[5]

The commission's decision came as a surprise to nearly everyone. The president of the National Association of Broadcasters called the action an "unwarranted and dangerous intrusion into American business. . . . "[6] Members of Congress were caught off guard by the FCC's announcement. One tobacco-state congressman, Walter Jones (D.-North Carolina), attempted to rally support for the cigarette manufacturers among other industries, the advertising of whose products he claimed might in the future meet a fate at the hands of the FCC similar to that of cigarette advertising. He warned that other groups, for example, those opposing the consumption of alcoholic beverages, might soon request that the fairness doctrine be applied to them. Senator Magnuson, on the other hand, announced his support for the FCC action, terming it a major victory for health forces.

There was some surprising opposition, or at least nonsupport, for the FCC action from some of the health groups. While the initial reaction of these groups was favorable, they later started having misgivings, which surfaced when appeals were filed in the U.S. Court of Appeals for the District of Columbia by two Washington law firms— Covington and Burling and Arnold and Porter—on behalf of the cigarette manufacturers. The misgivings of groups like the American Cancer Society were based on the fear that the courts might agree with the complaint and dismiss the FCC opinion. They would then be in the position of having been antagonistic to radio and television stations and the networks. The Cancer Society and its allies knew that they were dependent upon the owners of the stations and the networks for the free announcements that promoted their own fund-raising drives. They chose a prudent course in this legal struggle, hoping to avoid putting their good will and free time with station owners in jeopardy. Consequently, health group support for the FCC was so quiet and nonaggressive as to be, essentially, nonexistent. The fears of the health groups were unjustified, for on November 21, 1968, the U.S. Court of Appeals decided that the FCC could use its fairness doctrine to require free time for antismoking commercials.[7]

An amusing variety of antismoking ads began to appear on radio and television. Informative and dramatic, it seems certain that they contributed to the reduction in cigarette consumption noted first in 1968. The Federal Communications Commission's ruling helped the health groups get their message aired. The American Cancer Society reported that in the three and one-half years before the FCC applied its fairness doctrine to cigarette ads, it distributed a total of 982 pre-recorded antismoking commercials for radio and television. In the eight months after the FCC's decision, the Cancer Society distributed 4,723 such commercials.[8]

The work of Banzhaf in persuading the FCC to apply the fairness doctrine to cigarette commercials was one of the most significant events in the whole labeling controversy.[9] The total ban enacted by Congress on airwave advertising that became effective in 1971 won the support of the cigarette manufacturers largely because they wanted to avoid the "anti" commercials. As the ad ban began, the FCC ruled that television and radio stations could carry antismoking commercials as a "public service" after the ban became operative but would not be required to carry the opposite views of the cigarette companies. This seemed unfair to the manufacturers, who decided to appeal the FCC's rule to the courts, where they were rebuffed.

John Banzhaf, Ralph Nader, and the numerous organizations they have created and inspired are frequent users of the policy-making powers of administrative agencies to bring about changes in policy favorable to consumers. Crusades to eliminate dangerous products from the marketplace and deceptive practices in advertising rely on agency action for their support. The consumer movement that began in the 1960s has given greater force to administrative law as a tool of social change. The procedures and the laws that agencies use for policy making are not new for the most part. What is new is their use by organized, professionally staffed consumer groups. Agency power marshaled for the consumer is often less than enthusiastically received by Congress, as in the cigarette controversy. One study notes, " . . . the administrative process has proved to be the key element in consumer protection policy and the implementation of that policy invariably has taken a different path than that envisioned by the original proponents of the legislation."[10] The agencies and Congress define their agendas differently in the field of consumer protection.

FEDERAL COMMUNICATIONS COMMISSION INTENSIFIES THE CONTROVERSY

As the July 1, 1969, expiration date of the Cigarette Labeling Act of 1965 approached, the cigarette controversy began appearing on the agendas of government agencies again. In one bold move that raised concerns among the members of the old tobacco subsystem, the Federal Communications Commission unexpectedly announced in February 1969 a proposed rule that would prohibit cigarette advertising on radio and television.

The FCC announcement at a news conference and in the *Federal Register* put Congress on notice that it would have to take some action before the July 1 expiration date. There were several paths this action could have taken. Congress could have chosen not to act at all, allowing the 1965 legislation to expire. This would have permitted the FCC to adopt the rule it had proposed in February and would also have allowed the Federal Trade Commission to act if it so desired. On the other hand, Congress could have extended the ban on agency action incorporated in the 1965 legislation, or it could have passed almost any bill strengthening or weakening the health warning label, including a requirement that it appear in all advertising.

The antismoking interests found themselves in an unusually good position, because for once they could advance their cause by seeing that Congress failed to act. If Congress could be persuaded to remain silent, the health interests thought their desires would be implemented by agencies released from the congressional ban on rule making. Senator Moss, a long-time advocate of strenuous action against the health hazards of cigarette smoking, put the Senate on notice as to what his strategy would be, in a speech on January 31, 1969:

> For the first time, the legislative advantage lies with the public. It is the cigarette industry which has the burden of getting Congress to act. If there is no new legislation extending the ban on agency regulation, then the agencies will again be free to act on July 1.
>
> . . . I want to serve notice here and now that I shall do all within my power to see that no such law to continue the ban passes.
>
> Although, as my colleagues know, I have long and steadfastly opposed rules which make it possible for a small group of Senators to prevent the passage of legislation through a filibuster, when it comes to a matter involving the lives and health of millions of Americans, I shall not hesitate to take full advantage of the existing rules, and to enlist the support of my many colleagues of like mind in the Senate—and there are many—to stop the passage of "disabling" legislation.[11]

Despite this strong statement from Senator Moss, the tobacco lobby was fully prepared for the expiration date and committed to seeing that Congress act to protect manufacturers from agency machinations. The House Interstate and Foreign Commerce Committee held 13 days of hearings in April and May, two months before the ban was due to expire. The 1969 hearings were a repeat of their 1965 predecessors. The tobacco industry position was again carefully and skillfully orchestrated before the committee. Most of the arguments and many of the witnesses were the same as those used in 1965. Michael Pertschuk, chief counsel for the Senate Commerce Committee and intimately involved in the cigarette controversy from the earliest days when he was on Senator Maurine Neuberger's staff, sensed history repeating itself:

> There is a new president and a new party in the White House and there is a new Congress. But, there is nothing in this new Congress to suggest a weakening of the proportionate strength of the tobacco-state congressmen. Ten congressmen out of the thirty-six on the House Interstate and Foreign Commerce Committee came either from tobacco-growing districts or districts closely allied politically and economically with those tobacco-growing districts.[12]

The bill reported out of the committee and passed by the House on June 18 was a nightmare for the health interests. It prohibited the states permanently, and federal agencies for six more years, until July 1, 1975, from acting on cigarette advertising, in exchange for a slightly strengthened warning, which would replace the existing warning on packages.

The reaction in the Senate and elsewhere in government was severe. The tobacco interests were regarded as having overplayed their hand. What followed was a good example of politics extended beyond the usual subsystem. Numerous agencies, public and private, state and national, began to propose policies favorable to the health interests. In June, the California Senate voted to ban all cigarette advertising in California, *The New York Times* announced it would no longer carry cigarette ads without health warnings, and the FTC started its hearings on a revival of its trade regulation rule on July 1, the day the original congressional ban expired.

By the time the Senate hearing was held on July 22, 1969, the tobacco interests sensed that their victory in the House was too unpopular to stand. They retreated strategically in the face of certain Senate opposition led by their powerful critics, Senators Moss and Magnuson.

The Senate Commerce Committee's Consumer Subcommittee, chaired by Senator Moss, held the hearing. In the Senate there were few parallels with 1965. This time it was a short, one-day hearing. Only five tobacco witnesses appeared. Joseph Cullman III, chairman of the Tobacco Institute's executive committee, announced that the cigarette manufacturers were willing to withdraw all radio and television advertising beginning January 1, 1970, provided Congress would extend antitrust immunity to cover an intercompany agreement to do so. From that point on, the tobacco interests adopted a statesmanlike posture. Voluntary action and lack of opposition to congressional action characterized their public positions. The bill that emerged from Congress the following March banned cigarette ads from radio and television beginning January 2, 1971, and strengthened the warning on packages. One concession to the tobacco interests was the provision that the Federal Trade Commission had to give Congress six months' notice of any rule-making activity affecting cigarettes. Another provision of the act gave the FTC the authority to consider the warning requirement for all printed advertising after July 1, 1971. Preemption of state action was continued.

Six radio station owners appealed the broadcast prohibition to the courts. In March 1972, the Supreme Court upheld the congressional action. The cigarette manufacturers did not join in the appeal, largely because once again, just as in 1965, congressional action in the cigarette controversy provided manufacturers with some distinctive advantages. Most importantly, the ban on cigarette ads reduced the impetus for airing antismoking ads. Although the FCC encouraged broadcasters to continue airing antismoking PSAs, the agency could no longer *require* airing of these very effective announcements about the hazards of smoking,[13] and their frequency of airing dropped off precipitously after the ad ban went into effect. In addition, the ad ban eliminated the need for costly television and radio commercials.

The numbers speak for themselves: Marketing budgets of the big manufacturers were down an estimated 30 percent in 1971, while gross sales jumped 3 percent. At the same time, however, another provision of Congress's Public Health Cigarette Smoking Act (PHCSA) strengthened the package warning by changing the wording from "*Caution:* Cigarette Smoking *May Be Hazardous* to Your Health" to read: "*Warning:* Cigarette Smoking *Is Dangerous* to Your Health." (Changed words in the warnings are in italics.) This provision was less well received by the tobacco interests; its inclusion in the bill was evidence of their declining influence, generally, in regulatory matters.[14]

Also indicative of tobacco's waning influence are two important voluntary agreements—the result of trade practice conference negotiations—reached between the FTC and the cigarette manufacturers after final passage of the PHCSA. First, in the summer of 1970, the commission proposed to issue a trade regulation rule requiring that tar and nicotine information appear in all cigarette advertising. By the end of the year, the cigarette manufacturers agreed among themselves to do this, and the commission approved the informal agreement and dropped its rule-making proposal. The agreement, although voluntary, had more bite than the advertising guidelines agreed to in the 1950s, precisely because the FTC had adopted trade regulation rule procedures in the intervening years and claimed the power to enforce such rules if necessary.

Three months after the congressional ban on advertisements went into effect in January 1971, the FTC had the cigarette companies back at the bargaining table and consenting, in a second voluntary agreement, to include a health warning in all their printed advertising. By mid-year, the FTC was hammering away at the manufacturers again, threatening to initiate adjudicatory procedures for false and deceptive advertising if the cigarette companies did not agree to make their ad warnings more prominent.[15] Within six months the FTC had succeeded in forcing six major cigarette companies to agree to a consent order that required ad warnings to be "clear and conspicuous" in all printed advertisements. Finally, eight years after the Surgeon General issued his seminal 1964 report and eight years after the FTC announced its rule-making intentions, the regulatory policies that the FTC had proposed were adopted in their entirety.

REGULATORY UPDATE

Clearly, passage of the Cigarette Labeling Act of 1965 and the Public Health Cigarette Smoking Act of 1969 were only partial victories for the FTC and other like-minded agencies in the federal bureaucracy interested in putting more teeth into regulation of the tobacco industry. They were important victories, nonetheless, especially given the strength of the interests these agencies were up against. The passage of these two acts by Congress stands as a testament to the power, not of the legislative branch, but of the executive agencies and the bureaucrats who work in them. Commissioners at the FTC and the FCC, the Surgeon General and others in the Public Health Service, and countless other technocrats who worked within the federal agency structure played key roles in reviewing scientific evidence, developing testimony for Congress, and pushing for the development of agency-making powers when many—most vociferously those in the tobacco subsystem—argued that no such powers existed under the U.S. Constitution.

Since the early 1970s, federal agencies have broadened their reach and strengthened their hand in the regulation of smoking in the same manner as they had in the 1960s; characteristically, in two-steps-forward, one-step-back fashion. But while no decisive blows to the tobacco industry have been leveled to date, the accumulating total of bureaucratic efforts had left the tobacco industry reeling by 1994, when cover stories in weekly magazines appeared with apocalyptic titles such as "Should Cigarettes Be Outlawed?"[16] and "Tobacco: Does It Have a Future?"[17] and "How Do Tobacco Executives Live with Themselves?"[18]

The FTC, either advancing the cause of regulation or retreating in the face of opposition, has been central to the debate all along. One of the FTC's steps backward occurred in April 1972 when a U.S. district court cast a shadow of doubt on the FTC's policy-making capabilities, ruling that the commission could not require the posting of octane ratings on gasoline pumps. The decision was later reversed by the U.S. Court of Appeals, however, and the Supreme Court denied certiorari, allowing the appeals court ruling in support of the FTC to stand. The FTC, bolstered by this decision legitimating its rule-making power, was successful in urging Congress to ban ads for "little cigars" shortly thereafter in the fall of 1973.[19]

In 1975, the FTC gained even more power when President Ford signed the FTC Improvements Act, a law providing the commission with a statutory basis for rule making and providing easier access to FTC proceedings for consumers. The good will and congressional trust apparent in this legislation did not last for long, however, for by the late 1970s, the FTC was back on the defensive for taking too much of an activist, consumer-oriented approach to its responsibilities. Several attempts were made by Congress in this time frame to restrict the FTC's jurisdiction and cut back its appropriations. (On two occasions in 1980, Congress actually allowed funding for the commission to expire.) Congressional (and industrial) opposition grew to such intensity in this period that the FTC was frequently singled out as the prime reason to push for the reform of government regulatory processes in general. Congressional discontent with the FTC peaked when the commission began to take on some of the most politically well-connected groups in the country, including segments of the insurance, drug, funeral, and advertising industries. Finally, on May 28, 1980, Congress passed a second FTC Improvements Act to reign in the agency. Among other things, the act called for a two-house legislative veto of commission rules, and specifically excluded children's advertising from commission jurisdiction.

This legislative slap in the face proved to be only a temporary setback for the FTC, for the commission was back in front of Congress in May 1981 with calls for a new, more effective health warning system for cigarette packaging that would include sterner language and larger type. The commission's 1981 staff report on cigarette advertising that highlighted the fact that large portions of the population were not fully aware of the dangers of smoking also drew a fair amount of attention and support for stricter regulation.[20] The FTC's advocacy on these issues did not produce immediate results, but the commission's machinations did ultimately bear fruit when on October 13, 1984, President Reagan signed the Comprehensive Smoking Education Act into law (P.L. 98-47). Among other things, the new law replaced the 1970 version of the package warning with a series of four stronger, more specific warnings. The FTC may have been restricted or dissuaded from acting on its own by the FTC Improvements Act of 1980, but the commission proved to be an effective advocate for change, nonetheless.[21]

The FTC took another small step backward in August 1986 when an administrative law judge dismissed an FTC complaint filed against R. J. Reynolds for misrepresenting results of the Multiple Risk Factor Intervention Trial (known as the "MR FIT" study). MR FIT was a long-term scientific analysis of the health hazards of smoking funded by several not-for-profit health groups. The FTC claimed that a Reynolds advertisement falsely represented this report as tending to refute the link between smoking and heart disease. The administrative law judge hearing the case ruled that the Reynolds advertisement was an editorial statement fully protected by the free speech guarantees of the First Amendment. The FTC appealed for another hearing but later backed off when in October 1989 it convinced R. J. Reynolds to sign a consent order that forbade further references to MR FIT in its advertising. Once again—ultimately, if indirectly—the FTC got its way.

Clearly, the FTC's effect on the regulatory debate has been roundabout, but telling, over the course of the last 30 years. This advocacy has been mirrored in other parts of the federal bureaucracy as well, to similar effect. One place where this sort of entrepreneurial politics[22] has been most evident over the years is in the Surgeon General's office. It is hard to imagine the debate over tobacco regulation getting started at all if it had not been for Surgeon General Luther Terry and his well-orchestrated release of the Advisory Committee report on *Smoking and Health* in 1964. Since that time, the Surgeons General have been at the front of the pack in leading the regulatory charge against the tobacco subsystem. The Surgeon General's office may not have had the regulatory tools of the FTC to work with, but the country's chief public health officer does have credibility and legitimacy in the eyes of the public, and his or her pronouncements are inevitably perceived as newsworthy by the media. This combination of legitimacy and exposure make it possible for the head of the Public Health Service to make claims about smoking that help shape public opinion and construct a social reality that enables regulators in all three branches of government to contemplate formulating restrictive policies they would never consider otherwise.[23]

Among the more prophetic of these reality-shaping pronouncements came on January 11, 1971. The congressional ban on cigarette advertisements had only been in effect ten days when the Surgeon General proposed a government initiative to ban smoking in public places, claiming that nonsmokers in smoke-filled rooms experienced a significant health hazard. Important grass-roots movements to ban or limit smoking in designated public spaces in the 1980s and 1990s can trace their beginnings to the early 1970s when the Surgeon General began making these sorts of claims about the health hazards of second-hand smoke.[24] This authoritative statement on the detrimental effects of second-hand smoke also gave federal bureaucrats cause for action. In May 1973, two years after the Surgeon General's announcement, the Federal Aviation Administration began requiring that smokers and nonsmokers be segregated by section on commercial airlines. The Interstate Commerce Commission (ICC) restricted smoking to the rear 20 percent of all commercial interstate buses in May of the following year. In 1976 the Interstate Commerce Commission (ICC) extended its ruling to trains, and executives in the General Services Administration (GSA) began issuing smoking guidelines for buildings in which nearly one million government employees worked.

Another round of regulation along these lines was inspired by release of the Surgeon General's annual report in 1986. Many of these reports over the years have focused on a specific theme, and this one renewed and updated charges relating to the problem of second-hand smoke first raised a decade and a half earlier.[25] Later that same year, the GSA, the Department of Defense, and the Veterans' Administration all took steps to establish smoke-free rules for common areas under their jurisdiction, while the Environmental Protection Agency (EPA) issued its own draft report citing second-hand smoke as carcinogenic.[26] Each of these actions was made possible, at least in part, by the path-making claims issued by the nation's leading government authority on health, the Surgeon General.

Today, smoking is prohibited on all regularly scheduled interstate buses because of more recent rules promulgated by the ICC. Congress has banned smoking on all domestic flights, regardless of length (excepting flights to Alaska and Hawaii). And the DoD has banned smoking in all indoor spaces on military bases, worldwide (except in restaurants, recreational areas, and domiciles). Even more inclusive rules are in the offing according to the Labor Department's Office of Safety and Health Administration (OSHA), which recently announced its intention to prohibit smoking in the roughly 6 million enclosed business sites under its jurisdiction nationwide (*including* restaurants and bars where food is served). Each of these initiatives gained significant impetus, it can be argued, from the Surgeon General's pronouncements on the dangers of second-hand smoke—and smoking in general—over the years. And each action, with the exception of the congressional ban on airline smoking, was promulgated by a government agency, acting outside what is traditionally thought (and taught) to be the normal, legislative-centered law-making process.

It appears now that these sweeping administrative actions may be joined by legislation designed to establish all public spaces, nationwide, as smoke-free zones. Throughout 1994, the House Energy and Commerce Subcommittee on Health and the Environment, chaired by Henry Waxman, (D.-California) held hearings on the Smoke-Free Environment Act. This act, if passed as constructed, would ban smoking in every building in the nation that is regularly entered by ten or more people at least one day a week. (Smoking would be allowed only in sealed rooms if those rooms were equipped with separate exhaust systems.) It should surprise no one who appreciates the important role played by the Surgeons General in setting the stage for smoking regulations over the years to learn that six former Surgeons General (from four Republican administrations and two Democratic administrations) were called to testify in favor of the act before Waxman's committee February 7, 1994. Clearly, those who did the scheduling of this event were hoping to enlist the Surgeons General in a bid to construct a social reality amenable to the next round of regulation.

Cabinet-level secretaries are also in the business of constructing social realities. Like Surgeons General, they can compensate for their lack of explicit regulatory power by helping to shape and guide the public agenda. Health, Education and Welfare Secretary Joseph Califano was, no doubt, one of the most vociferous critics of the tobacco industry, even if his short-term successes were marginal. Califano launched a vigorous antismoking campaign in 1978 on the fourteenth anniversary of the Surgeon General's 1964 report, declaring smoking to be "Public Enemy Number One." Most of Califano's specific policy initiatives were not well-received initially. The broadcast media were cool to his idea of airing more antismoking announcements, the FAA declined to ban smoking on all airline flights, the business community largely ignored Califano's requests that they volunteer to set up smoking guidelines, and Congress balked at the idea of raising excise taxes on cigarettes. Even Califano's boss, President Carter, was less than enthusiastic about Califano's agenda. Carter wrote in the margin of one staff memo that encouraged him to take a stand against tobacco subsidies, "I refuse to be drawn into this fruitless issue."

About the only place Califano's call to arms had immediate impact was at the FDA, where it was agreed that warnings about the adverse health effects of smoking should be required on all packages of birth-control paraphernalia. Still, even though negative reaction to Califano's antismoking initiatives by members of Congress from tobacco-producing states helped precipitate his unceremonious dismissal as HEW Secretary in 1979, much of Califano's larger agenda was realized in the long term. The vast majority of businesses now have smoking policies in place. Indeed, many companies now ban smoking entirely and some have gone on record as refusing to hire smokers in the future.[27] Congress doubled the per pack excise tax on cigarettes in 1982, and has recently considered a tax of a dollar or more per pack to defray the cost of health care reform. And smoking on domestic airline flights has been illegal since 1989 thanks to legislative action.

While Joseph Califano certainly helped to create an atmosphere in which antismoking rules and regulations would be acceptable in the long run, some of the credit for more recent developments must surely be attributed to one of Califano's successors: Dr. Louis Sullivan, Secretary of Health and Human Services in the Bush administration and outspoken advocate of the anti-tobacco cause. On February 20, 1990, Sullivan testified before the Senate Labor and Human Resources Committee that cigarette smoking costs the nation $52 billion in health expenses and time lost from work every year, and pointed out that "cigarettes are the only legal product that when used as intended, cause death." On April 10 of the same year the Secretary asked sports fans and promoters to boycott sports events sponsored by tobacco companies in a speech to the First International Conference on Smokeless Tobacco. Within two years, chewing tobacco was banned at minor league baseball parks for fans and players alike, and a number of major league baseball parks began banning smoking: Camden Yard, the new and celebrated home of the Baltimore Orioles, was one of the first. Through health care pronouncements such as those made by Sullivan and Califano, together with education programs initiated by HHS, bureaucrats have proven able to create a climate conducive to policy change.[28]

Recently, a number of developments have taken place which suggest that the tobacco subsystem is approaching a nadir in its ability to control the policy agenda. On February 25, 1994, Dr. David Kessler, commissioner of the FDA, threatened to regulate cigarettes as drugs if it could be determined that cigarette manufacturers manipulated nicotine levels in their products over the years in an effort to better "hook" consumers. In April, top executives of the leading tobacco companies appeared before the Waxman subcommittee for what was described as a "grilling" about their promotional and manufacturing practices. In May, internal papers from the Brown and Williamson tobacco company were leaked to key members of Congress and the press. The documents tended to support the claim that the industry knew as early as the 1940s that cigarettes were addictive. The documents also pointed to a patent, applied for by Brown and Williamson, for a tobacco plant cryptically called "Y-1" that was genetically engineered to increase nicotine content. Apparently, Brown and Williamson had used Y-1 in at least one of its brands to increase the nicotine yield to smokers. Tobacco executives claimed that nicotine levels of cigarettes are often altered to enhance the taste and flavor of these products, but policy makers, hot on the trail blazed by Kessler, were clearly skeptical.

Meanwhile, bureaucrats in the state of Mississippi sued the tobacco industry to recover smoking-related health care costs paid by the state (*Mississippi* v. *American Tobacco et al.*). In a similar, but even more important legal development, Florida passed a bill in May 1994 that would allow the state to sue tobacco companies for the state's share of Medicaid costs associated with smoking-related illness (estimated at $200 million to $300 million per year in Florida). The new law allows the state to use statistics that indicate the general relationship between smokers—as a class—and illness, rather than forcing the state to establish a clear causal link in each case where it attempts to recover costs. The measure also authorizes the state to use "market share" theory to attribute percentages of liability to tobacco companies according to the company's market share (rather than requiring the state to demonstrate that a particular company's brand was at fault in a particular case). Finally, the new law prohibits tobacco companies from claiming immunity from liability since smokers are fairly informed about the health hazards of smoking by package and ad warnings. The new Florida law argues that the state is essentially an innocent third party and is forced to cover smokers' Medicaid costs, regardless of whether the smokers are fairly warned or not.

The month of June 1994 was no better for the tobacco interests. Like the phoenix, Joseph Califano was back on Capitol Hill, this time as the executive director of a nonprofit organization committed to addressing health and substance-abuse concerns. He gave important testimony to the Waxman subcommittee about the extent of the health care costs incurred because of smoking-related disease at a crucial time in the congressional debate about national health care reform. FDA Commissioner David Kessler also made a repeat appearance, this time charging that some ammonia compounds cigarette manufacturers regularly add to their products are included strictly for the purpose of increasing the delivery of nicotine to the smoker. Shortly thereafter, another high-level bureaucrat—Attorney General Janet Reno—announced that the Justice Department would undertake a preliminary review of complaints brought by members of Congress that tobacco company executives misled them in the congressional testimony taken earlier in the year about the industry's knowledge of health hazards and its alleged manipulation of nicotine levels.

All this activity illustrates well how much the tobacco subsystem has changed over the years. Beginning in 1964, with the release of the Surgeon General's landmark report on *Smoking and Health,* the small group of people that had constituted the tobacco subsystem in Congress, in the agencies, and in the tobacco companies, slowly but inexorably lost what had been a fairly steady and unchallenged grip on the reins of the policy-making process. Indeed, the number of individuals, groups, agencies, institutions, and levels of government that are involved in policy making today is so great that, according to political scientist Hugh Heclo, it no longer even makes sense to talk in terms of policy subsystems, iron triangles, or subgovernments where a narrowly defined set of interested parties privately broker policy for their own selfish ends. Rather, Heclo suggests, we should think in terms of *issue networks.*[29]

Heclo writes that today "the iron triangle concept is not so much wrong as it is disastrously incomplete. . . . The notion of iron triangles and subgovernments presumes small circles of participants who have succeeded in becoming largely autonomous. Issue networks, on the other hand, comprise large numbers of participants . . . and include individuals and organizations with intellectual, professional, and emotional interests that serve to broaden the basis for conflict with the more narrowly focused economic and electoral interests held by members of the more traditional issue subsystem."[30] The case of cigarette regulation appears to provide some verification of Heclo's theory: *Issue network* clearly seems more descriptive than *policy subsystem* when it comes to the regulatory realities of tobacco politics and policy making in the 1990s. This is especially the case when one includes the myriad policy-making actors at the state and local levels where a great deal of the regulatory action has taken place in recent years. The dissident individuals, groups, and institutions that have opposed the position of the traditional tobacco subsystem have effectively altered the policy-making process by penetrating the subsystem, expanding it, and creating something very different in its place: *The Tobacco Network* (see Figure 8-1).

Regardless of the terminology used, however, one thing is certain: As long as the number of actors and policy interests advanced con-

Figure 8–1 Tobacco Dissidents + the Tobacco Subsystem Combine to Become the Tobacco Network

Executive Agencies of State and Local Government

FTC (especially P. Elman, P. Dixon, M. Pertshuk); FCC; Public Health Service; Surgeon General (especially L. Terry, C.E. Koop, J. Elders); HHS (especially W. Cohen, J. Califano); ICC; FAA; National Interagency Council on Smoking & Health (especially Emerson Foote); Department of Labor; OSHA; EPA (especially W. Reilly); FDA (especially D. Kessler); CPSC; and members of advisory committees (most notably at the FTC and the EPA)

Federal Agency Dissidents

Congressional Dissidents

Tobacco Subsystem

National Interest Group Dissidents (See Note 1 below.)

Advocates of Public Health Issues & Supporters of the FTC in Congress
M. Neuberger (D-OR);
W. Magneson (D-WA);
F. Moss (D-UT);
J. Moss (D-CA);
H. Waxman (D-CA);
M. Synar (D-OK)

Policy Entrepreneurs

Public Health Groups

Other Interested Groups

State and Local Legislatures

Grass-Roots Organizations

Note 1: **Policy Entrepreneurs** J. Banzhaf (ASH); J. Califano (Center on Addiction and Substance Abuse, Columbia U.); R. Dynard (Tobacco Products Liability Project); M.Edell (Cipollone family lawyer); M. Pertschuck (Advocacy Institute); P. Reynalds (Citizens for a Smokefree America)

Public Health Groups American Medical Association (AMA); Cancer, Heart, Lung, & TB associations and allied health groups

Other Interested Groups Americans for Dem. Action (ADA); National YMCA; National PTA

Note 2: Dashed lines are used to indicate the fluidity and permeability of a Tobacco Network in which dissident forces emerge and, at times, combine with each other to encroach on a policy area that had traditionally been the exclusive domain of members of the old Tobacco Subsystem.

tinues to grow, the policy process will continue to become more volatile and unpredictable. With health groups becoming increasingly powerful, and with agency heads becoming bolder and more effective in challenging vested interests, it seems highly unlikely that a smaller, insular subsystem—one in form similar to the tobacco subsystem of the 1960s—will reemerge anytime soon.

NOTES

1. William G. Meserve, staff counsel to the Senate Commerce Committee, discussed some of these developments in a speech titled, "Cigarettes and Congress," before the California Conference on Cigarette Smoking and Health, October 29, 1967.

2. Victor Cohn, "Smoking Crisis: U.S. Task Force Asks Funds for Fight on Cigarette Ads," *The Washington Post*, August 17, 1968.

3. *The Washington Post*, December 20, 1985, p. A9.

4. Federal Trade Commission, *Report to Congress*, June 30, 1968, p. 30 (mimeo).

5. Federal Communications Commission, Public Notice, 1188-3, June 5, 1967 (mimeo).

6. "Wasilewski Opposes Fairness Doctrine Being Applied to Cigarette Spots," *TV Code News*, 6, no. 6 (June 1967), 3.

7. *John F. Banzhaf, III v. Federal Communications Commission*, 405 F. 2d 1082 (1968).

8. Robert E. Dallos, "Perry Mason's TV Foe, Dead of Cancer, Left Anti-Smoking Film," *The New York Times*, September 13, 1968, p. 55.

9. After bringing his complaint to the FCC, Banzhaf went on to become the founder and executive director of an organization called ASH (Action on Smoking and Health) that endeavored to raise a legal defense fund of $100,000 to help protect and defend the FCC's decision. Among the sponsors of ASH were many of those individuals associated with the antismoking forces, including Maurine Neuberger.

10. Mark V. Nadel, *The Politics of Consumer Protection* (Indianapolis: Bobbs-Merrill, 1971), p. 29.

11. *Congressional Record*, January 31, 1969, p. S1124.

12. Michael Pertschuk, "A Look Backward and a Glance Forward," *A Summary of Proceedings*, National Interagency Council on Smoking and Health, September 1970, p. 22.

13. Impact of public service announcements is difficult to sort out. But in 1966, after the Surgeon General's report and the beginning of health warning labels, only 47 percent of smokers expressed health concerns about their habit. In 1970, after the PSAs had run for about two years, 69 percent of smokers reported having health concerns about smoking. Meanwhile, per capita consumption of cigarettes dropped 6.9 percent in this four-year period (consumption had dropped only about 2 percent between 1962 and 1966). By the end of 1971, with public service announcements off the air for a year, per capita consumption began rising again, a rise that continued for the next several years. See Robert A. Kagan and David Vogel, "The Politics of Smoking Regulation: Canada, France, the United States," in *Smoking Policy: Law, Politics, and Culture*, eds. Robert L. Rabin, and Stephen D. Sugarman (New York: Oxford University Press, 1993), p. 35.

14. See Bernard Rosen, *Holding Government Bureaucracies Accountable* (New York: Praeger, 1982), p. 117; *Tobacco Situation*, Washington, D.C.: Economic Research Service, U.S. Department of Agriculture, March 1972.

15. The threat of case-by-case action allowed the FTC to bring pressure to bear on cigarette manufacturers while at the same time avoiding congressional sensitivity regarding the more general rule-making procedures invoked by the FTC in the past.

16. *The New York Times Magazine*, March 20, 1994, p. 34.

17. *U.S. News and World Report*, April 18, 1994, p. 32.

18. *Business Week*, July 4, 1994, p. 24.

19. "Little cigars" were cigars made the same size and shape of cigarettes by the tobacco companies to avoid regulation. They were not covered under laws passed by Congress, which applied, according to the letter of the law, only to traditional cigarettes.

20. In a survey done for the report, 50 percent of women did not know that smoking could cause miscarriage or stillbirth, and 40 percent of the high school seniors believed smoking was "no great health risk."

21. Despite passage of the law requiring more stringent warnings, the influence of the tobacco lobby remained strong. Earlier formulations of one of the four warnings specified that smoking could cause death as well as miscarriage in pregnant women. Mention of this possibility was deleted in committee mark-up sessions.

22. James Q. Wilson uses the term *entrepreneurial politics* to refer to situations where a government official (or agency) advocates for the community interest over the interests of a smaller, self-interested group (in this case, the tobacco industry). James Q. Wilson, *Bureaucracy: What Government Agencies Do and Why They Do It* (New York: Basic Books, 1989), p. 77.

23. See Ronald J. Troyer and Gerald E. Markle, *Cigarettes: The Battle over Smoking* (New Brunswick, N.J.: Rutgers University Press, 1983), pp. 26, 77, 144, for a discussion of how authoritative claims made by scientists and government leaders can help to construct a mass social reality that is conducive to change. According to Troyer and Markle, claims made by federal officials have a stigmatizing sociological effect that eggs along changes in public attitudes that, in turn, make further regulation by government possible.

24. In 1986, approximately 100 municipalities nationwide reported having ordinances related to restricting smoking in public places. By 1991, the number of municipalities with smoking ordinances in place had swelled to over 450. Kagan and Vogel, "The Politics of Smoking Regulation: Canada, France, the United States," p. 37.

25. *The Health Consequences of Involuntary Smoking* (U.S.DHHS, Surgeon General, 1986) brought to light the importance of "side stream" smoke (also referred to as Environmental Tobacco Smoke: ETS), noting that ETS was at least as rich in carcinogens as inhaled tobacco smoke. The report also noted that "passive smokers" have significantly higher rates of lung cancer and various other respiratory conditions. Rabin and Sugarman, *Smoking Policy*, pp. 3–4.

26. The EPA's final report was issued in 1992 after being endorsed by an independent panel of experts; some, including the panel's chairman, with close ties to research supported by the tobacco industry ("Environmental Tobacco Smoke," U.S. EPA 1992). The report confirmed the links between ETS and elevated rates of lung cancer and other respiratory conditions and estimated that ETS was responsible for approximately 3,000 lung cancer deaths and about 37,000 cardiovascular-disease-related deaths per year (about the same number of deaths attributable to automobile accidents). ETS was also identified as responsible for between 150,000 and 300,000 lower respiratory ailments in children.

27. In 1986, 36 percent of companies responding to a survey on smoking regulations indicated that smoking policies were in place and 2 percent of companies responding reported that smoking was prohibited in all of their buildings. By 1991, 85 percent of companies responding indicated the presence of smoking policies and the percentage of companies banning smoking had jumped to 34 percent. Rabin and Sugarman, *Smoking Policy*, p. 19.

28. The Reagan administration waged a continuing battle with Congress about

the size of the budgets of the Public Health Service (PHS), including the Office of Smoking and Health. While the administration was successful in at least slowing the growth rate of the PHS budget, the bureaucracy found ways to circumvent some of the administration's efforts. For example, in 1984, when the administration tried to deemphasize activities of the Office of Smoking and Health, bureaucrats repackaged its antismoking program into an anti-cancer program and nested it in the National Cancer Institute (also a part of the PHS) where it was easier to hide from the knife of the administration's budget cutters.

29. The term *issue network* comes from Heclo's "Issue Networks and the Executive Establishment," reprinted in Richard J. Stillman II, *Public Administration: Concepts and Cases,* 4th ed. (Boston: Houghton Mifflin, 1988), pp. 408–417.

30. Ibid., pp. 408–409.

Chapter

9

The Bureaucracy
and Democratic Policy Making

A cigarette is the perfect type of a perfect pleasure. It is exquisite, and it leaves one unsatisfied. What more can one want?

Oscar Wilde (1854–1900)

The ebb and flow of power experienced by the FTC over the years reflects well the ongoing tensions between agency activism and restraint that exist in the American policy-making process. At times, it seems as though the FTC and other bureaucracies on the antismoking side of the debate enjoyed a great deal of leverage in shaping the cigarette regulation controversy. The political power and delegated authority possessed by bureaucratic agencies made both the initiation and continuation of this controversy possible. Had the decision on cigarettes and health been left to Congress alone, it is safe to assume that the manufacturers would have triumphed and no regulations of any significance would have been promulgated. In the long term, the cigarette labeling controversy is a clear example of an agency's power to influence and even formulate public policy.

At the same time, agencies interested in regulating the tobacco industry found themselves rebuked and rebuffed in the policy-making process on more than one occasion. Congress watered down the labeling restriction proposed by the FTC in its Cigarette Labeling Act of 1965 and imposed a four-year ban on FTC regulation of the industry. Congress extended the ban on FTC rule making for another year in 1970 with passage of the Public Health Cigarette Smoking Act, a law that also required the FTC to give six months' notice of any agency intentions to initiate rule-making procedures that would affect the tobacco industry. The FTC and its allied agencies forced the issue onto the government agenda, and that fact suggests that agencies enjoy a measure of policy-making power. But at the same time, it is true that Congress successfully blunted the most significant thrusts of anti-smoking bureaucracies by passing laws in 1965 and 1970 that were sympathetic to tobacco industry interests (the industry opposed neither of these laws). This suggests that agency power is limited.[1] In the final analysis, neither critics nor champions of agency discretion would find anything absolute to write about in this history of events.

BUREAUCRATS HAVE TOO MUCH POWER

For those who argue that government agencies have too much power, the case is clear and relatively straightforward. Criticisms of bureaucratic policy-making powers are made on the grounds that bureaucrats have the ability to act capriciously, unchecked by public opinion or other governmental institutions and undisciplined by the rigors of standing for election. As the tobacco industry argued in the congressional hearings of 1965, there is divergence between the way policy is made when bureaucrats are allowed to play an important role and the manner in which traditional theories of representation suggest policy should be made. The cigarette manufacturers emphasized that the FTC did not have, or at least should not have, the power to make policy—a power that was rightly the prerogative of Congress alone.

This position has attracted support from many quarters over the years. Individuals and groups who think their interests are threatened by agency action frequently adopt the narrow view that agencies, under the Constitution, are prohibited from making policy. Some argue that agencies are only the servants of Congress and that the lack of full congressional control over the bureaucracy is a serious obstacle to democratic governance.[2]

There is no question that the bureaucracy enjoys a measure of political power that is not anticipated or acknowledged by those who have written over the years about the supposedly clear dichotomy between politics and administration,[3] and information is an important key to that power. Bureaucrats control the flow of information to other policy makers and the general public, and their expertise in collecting and interpreting this information provides these individuals with an important base of political power. Over the years, Americans have come to depend on these educated government elites to help construct a shared social reality regarding a range of important questions associated with health and safety. The data that is relevant to these issues of social concern is often technical, arcane, and hard to find and interpret, and this fact gives government bureaucrats their entrée. The process of using information to construct a social reality about the hazards of smoking in the psyche of the collective public has made it easier for bureaucrats to assume a policy-making role and has, in turn, made it easier for antismoking members of Congress to advance their cause with their colleagues. Control over information about the hazards of smoking has given the bureaucracy political power—some would argue too much political power—when it comes to regulating private industry in the name of the public interest.

In recent decades, the role of the media in the policy-making equation has only enhanced the bureaucrat's ability to steer policy in one direction or another. Surgeon General Luther Terry's strategically orchestrated release of the report of the Advisory Committee on Smoking and Health in 1964 magnified the impact of that report well beyond what may have been expected had the report been quietly released on a typical, otherwise-busy weekday. An interest-piquing news blackout followed by a high-profile press conference led to splashy headlines in the Sunday papers and helped propel the smoking and health issue up on to the government agenda. The FTC began holding rule-making hearings within weeks of the report's release, and President Johnson was signing the Cigarette Labeling and Advertising Act of 1965 only eighteen months later. The final policy product might not have been everything the Surgeon General had hoped for, but strategic use of the media as a conduit of information, interpretation, and evaluation made the passage of some policy almost inevitable.

The provision in that legislation requiring the Surgeon General to issue regular reports on the smoking and health controversy provided the bureaucracy with a regular timetable for issuing what has turned out to be "a steady output of progressively grimmer official reports on the consequences of smoking."[4] These reports have made it possible for bureaucrats to keep the policy issue alive and coax the regulatory process along. Bureaucrats who release newsworthy reports and make controversial claims about the health hazards of second-hand smoke (e.g., Surgeons General Koop and Sullivan and EPA Commissioner William Reilly), manipulation of nicotine levels (e.g.,

FDA Commissioner David Kessler), and the impact of the tobacco industry's promotional activities in encouraging young Americans to take up the smoking habit (e.g., Surgeon General Joycelyn Elders) have reinforced efforts of the antismoking segments of the American government and paved the way to increased regulation of the tobacco industry.[5]

Critics who worry about bureaucratic accountability might describe activist, free-wheeling agency heads such as Sullivan, Koop, Elders, Reilly and Kessler as minions run amuck. Yet it can reasonably be argued that the master–servant view of the relationship between legislators and bureaucrats advanced by Wilson, Goodnow, and others is no longer tenable from either a practical or a legal perspective. In practice, the demands of a complex society require the specialized skills of bureaucrats in policy making. It is in large part this conflict between traditional democratic theories and the demands of the modern state that is at the heart of the debate over the policy-making powers of bureaucratic agencies. Professor Peter Woll has summarized the situation neatly:

> It is difficult to grasp the concept that the bureaucracy is not subordinate to one or more of the three initial branches of American government. But the fact is the three primary branches have necessarily supported the creation of a semiautonomous bureaucracy as an instrument to enable our government to meet the challenges it has faced. Given the needs of modern government for economic regulation, specialization, continuity, and speed in the dispatch of business, to mention only a few, it is the bureaucracy that has stepped in to fill the gap created by the inability of the other branches to fulfill all of these requirements. The other branches, particularly the Presidency and the Supreme Court, have also greatly expanded their ability and willingness to meet the challenges of the twentieth century, but they could not possibly solve by themselves the extraordinary problems that have confronted our government.[6]

At the same time, before we go too far down the path in believing that bureaucrats enjoy wide, nearly unchallenged discretion in steering the policy process and shaping the results, we must return to the political reality of the regulatory process where multiple checks are imposed on bureaucrats. The constitutional system of separated powers, statutory law that prescribes certain administrative procedures and proscribes others, accessibility of the regulatory process to private individuals, and "reflective representation" are among the forces in American government ensuring that bureaucrats hardly have the clear course in policy making.

EXTERNAL CHECKS ON BUREAUCRATIC AUTONOMY

Criticisms of agency power often gloss over two important points. First, much of an agency's discretion in policy-making matters is specifically delegated to it by enabling legislation passed by Congress, as discussed in Chapter 4. Second, there are very real checks on administrative policy-making discretion that exist in our system of separated powers. Indeed, it may be easier to make the opposite case; that there are too many restrictions on the ability of agencies and commissions to advance policy in the public interest. Certainly, bureaucrats in other Western democracies—Canada, Great Britain, and France, for example—have more policy-making leverage than their brethren in the United States. And in the case presented here, it is clear that while commissioners at the FTC helped to move the regulatory process along, they were restricted at each step of the way by a Congress that was more sensitive to the interests of the tobacco manufacturers than to bureaucrats who were aligned with the health lobby.

In fact, there are numerous examples of agency power being checked at the national level when the agency moves beyond the boundaries of what Congress had intended. The surgically precise limits placed on FTC authority in the congressional acts of 1965 and 1970 are good examples of just what Congress is capable of. Passage of the FTC Improvements Act in 1980 provides another example of effective congressional oversight. As one correspondent described the situation at the time, "With a fervor worthy of St. George, Congress has galloped off to tame the regulatory dragon"[7] by limiting the FTC's jurisdiction and establishing a legislative veto system for rules promulgated by the commission.[8] The various statutes under which the FTC operates are, like the laws governing most government agencies, general in nature. They express broadly defined goals while the details are left to the bureaucracy to write. When the bureaucracy moves outside the boundaries of congressional intent, as the FTC did late in the 1970s, the Congress has only to pass new laws that effectively rein in the offending agency.

In addition, it should be noted that an FTC run amuck, the prevailing view held by Congress in the late 1970s, is hardly representative of perceptions held by members of Congress and other FTC watchers over time. Rather, the years leading up to passage of the FTC Improvements Act of 1980 were marked by criticisms that the agency was too timid rather than too powerful. A 1957 report submitted by a subcommittee of the House Committee on Government Operations concluded that "the Federal Trade Commission has failed in its statutory duty to 'prevent deceptive acts or practices' in filter-cigarette advertising. The activities of the commission to prevent this deception were weak and tardy. . . . The Federal Trade Commission has failed to approach the problem of false and misleading advertising with vigor and diligence."[9] In 1969, Philip Elman, one-time commissioner at the FTC, argued before a Senate committee that FTC actions regarding cigarette advertising were an exception in an otherwise lethargic picture in which the commission fails to perform "effectually any of the roles given it by Congress."[10] In the few instances in which the FTC has acted forcefully, "the Congress has acted to reverse or limit the Commission's decisions."[11] Likewise, a 1969 study by a group of law students working for Ralph Nader concluded that "the singularly unusual case of the FTC's action on deceptive cigarette advertising is indicative of what the FTC would be capable of if properly directed and motivated."[12] These sentiments helped build support for the FTC Improvements Act of 1975 in which Congress added substantially to the agency's regulatory powers. The FTC may have become—in the eyes of some members of Congress—too brazen late in the 1970s, but this sentiment was relatively localized in time and did not last for long.

Ultimately, Congress exerts considerable influence over the regulatory commissions. Often the aggressiveness of the commissions, or lack thereof, is a reflection of congressional attitudes toward the agency's agenda. For example, the FTC became more active in the years preceding 1980 partly in response to criticisms, from Congress and elsewhere, that the agency was too weak, and partly as a reflection of a Congress increasingly interested in consumer affairs, generally. When the commission lost that congressional backing in a more conservative Congress later in the 1970s and on into the 1980s, it became the focus of a major assault on regulatory processes and regulation itself. As such, Congress should be understood to exert considerable influence over the FTC and other bureaucracies, in accordance with the separation of powers.

The President also exerts considerable influence over the activities of agencies in the executive branch. Political principles monitor bureaucratic agents and use both rewards and sanctions to bring agency behavior into line with presidential priorities when bureaucrats stray from the desired course. In the case of the FTC, presidential appointments have been instrumental in changing the agency's course at different times in history. Although Congress had been nudging the FTC in the direction of taking a more consumerist orientation through the early- and mid-1970s, the agency was not as responsive as some would have hoped until President Carter appointed

Michael Pertshuk to head up the commission in 1977. The FTC assumed a much more consumer-friendly orientation shortly after Pertshuk's arrival. Then, in 1981, with relatively conservative views about the role of government sweeping across the country, President Reagan appointed James Miller III to chair the commission. Miller ushered in an era during which the FTC took a much more sympathetic stance toward business.[13] Political appointment, a shared tool of the President and Congress, is among the most effective and frequently used tools employed by political leaders to control the activities of bureaucrats.[14]

The judiciary provides another important check on bureaucratic discretion in America's system of separated powers. Recourse to the courts is one of the protections provided an individual who believes that an agency action has interfered with one's fundamental rights and liberties, or simply that the agency has injured someone by mistakenly applying the law. The right to appeal an administrative decision to the courts is well established, although the extent to which a court will consent to fully substitute its judgment for that of an administrative agency is one of the most tangled areas in American jurisprudence.

One of the reasons for this lack of clarity is that legal experience in administrative law is not as great as in other areas, which benefit from centuries of common law experience. In some respects, the functions of administrative agencies fall outside the traditions of and are incompatible with the common law, making it unclear precisely on what grounds agency actions can be overruled by the courts, and which actions, if any, are excluded from review.[15] Generally, the courts are most interested in seeing that agency procedures do not infringe upon an individual's fundamental rights and that agency decisions are based upon a proper understanding of relevant statutes and judicial precedents. Here, the courts seek to determine if the agency has acted fairly, without caprice, and in a manner that is not arbitrary.[16] Guidelines for these procedures are found in the constitutional guarantees of due process, as well as in the statutory law that speaks directly to questions of administrative process.[17]

The federal courts have been especially active in overseeing state and local bureaucracies. Decisions in landmark cases such as *Miranda* v. *State of Arizona* and *Brown* v. *Board of Education* are just two of many instances where the courts have impinged directly and dramatically on the operations of subnational bureaucracies.[18] Federal court rulings have effected federal agency activities of all kinds at the federal level, as well, including the regulatory activities of the FTC. The 1972 decision of a U.S. district court prohibiting the FTC from requiring the display of octane ratings on gasoline pumps and stripping the commission of the rule-making power it had carefully nurtured into existence provides one good example of judicial oversight.[19] The U.S. court of appeals eventually reversed the lower court decision, but critics of bureaucratic overreaching were allowed their day in court. Although they lost in the end, the FTC's detractors were able to call on the federal judiciary in their attempt to postpone the development of rule-making procedures at the commission.

Ultimately, whether the judiciary is called upon to decide matters of substance or procedure, there should be no question about the important check on administrative power supplied by the federal court system. As Bernard Rosen has suggested:

> Knowing that the courts are there, knowing that an increasingly litigious citizenry—individuals and organizations—is prepared to go to court . . . strongly encourages administrators to be mindful of the intent of the law and the rights of individuals as they make policy and manage programs.[20]

Clearly, the separation of powers provides a set of powerful external checks on the policy-making discretion of administrative agencies. But if the norms of democratic decision making are to be adhered to, it also is important that the internal operations of administrative agencies adhere to democratic principles. Citizens must be provided with the opportunity to participate in the formulation of policies that are every bit as binding on their lives as acts of legislatures. Elections expose legislators and Presidents to public pressures while administrative agencies are insulated from the electoral process and perhaps from responding to the public. Somehow citizen participation and a responsiveness to the public interest must be built into the regulatory process to enhance the system's conformity with theories of representative government.

Techniques have been developed over the years to achieve fairness in administrative proceedings. The Administrative Procedure Act of 1946 provides some democratic guidelines for agency decision making. The *Federal Register* is another tool that adds a measure of democracy to the process by keeping interested parties informed of actions (both taken and proposed) by administrative agencies. The use of independent administrative law judges and independent advisory committees both add democratic dimensions to agency policy-making routines, as well. Making the administrative agencies accessible to private individuals and groups also enhances the process. Finally, "reflective representation" helps to round out the forces that conspire, collectively, to bring the process and outcomes of agency policy making into line with the tenets of representative, democratic governance.

ADMINISTRATIVE PROCEDURES ACT

Demands to adopt court-like procedures for administrative agencies came from such quarters as the American Bar Association as early as the 1930s. The expansion of government activity during the New Deal sounded the alarm for many who were genuinely concerned about the infringement of fundamental rights that individuals might suffer at the hands of irresponsible bureaucrats. Others sought simply to curb the regulatory powers of government over business and industry.

Pressures for the adoption of stricter, more uniform administrative procedures were delayed by World War II but were revived shortly after the end of the war. In 1946, Congress passed the Administrative Procedure Act (APA),[21] which sets out procedures to be followed by agencies when they engage in rule-making and adjudicatory proceedings. The procedures have some relationship to those used by courts, although they are not quite as formal or as carefully stated. Certain elements of congressional hearing procedures are also incorporated in the act. There are several exemptions from the requirements of the act, in recognition of the fact that there are large numbers of issues before agencies that could not be effectively handled under these formal procedures.

If every policy-making action of an agency were to be treated as a judicial proceeding or a legislative hearing, the decision-making process would grind to a halt. So the first difficulty faced by those who wrote the APA was to decide which agency actions the act covered and which it did not. All military and foreign affairs functions were exempted from its requirements. Also exempted were "any matters relating to agency management or personnel or public property, loans, grants, benefits, or contracts." Framers of the act then went on to differentiate between rule making, or quasi-legislative functions, and the adjudicatory functions of agencies. The most formal procedures in the act apply to all adjudicatory functions, but to only some agency rule-making functions. There also is a distinction made in the act between *formal* and *informal* rule making.

In informal rule making, only some of the required adjudicatory procedures are employed; for example, hearings are conducted, a public record is kept, and certain rules of evidence are followed. However, the most important difference between formal and informal processes is that in the former a public hearing is required and in the latter, the decision as to whether or not to hold a hearing is left up to the agency. How does an agency know when it must hold a public hearing? A hearing is required only when the legislation under which the agency operates requires it. There are only a few statutes that require formal hearings for all rule making; in fact, none of the 11 major acts that the Federal Trade Commission administers require hearings in rule making. When agencies are not required by legislation to hold a hearing, the rule-making section of the Administrative Procedure Act is followed only if the agency decides it should be followed.[22]

In formal rule making, or when an agency elects to do so, the Administrative Procedure Act requires that a public notice of rule making be given, including: (1) a statement of time, place, and nature of the proceedings (also giving details of plans for a hearing if one is to be held); (2) reference to the authority under which the rule is proposed; and (3) the terms and substance of the proposed rule. The APA goes on to say that those affected by a proposed rule must be given time to respond in writing. Thirty days' notice has to be given before a rule becomes effective, and interested persons have the right to petition for amendment or repeal.

Frequently, agencies elect to use formal rule-making procedures even when they are not required to, particularly when the proposed rule will affect large numbers of groups or individuals. There are several reasons for favoring the formal process, not the least of which is the practical matter of enlisting support for the rule. If those affected by a rule participate in its formulation, chances are they will better understand its provisions and the rationale behind it. This is no guarantee of support for the measure, but the rule that emerges from the more formal process should be easier to enforce than one made behind the closed doors of a bureau chief's office.

The Federal Trade Commission followed formal procedures in all of its rule making regarding the tobacco industry. The commissioners never seriously considered adopting cigarette labeling and advertising regulations without holding formal hearings because they sensed how controversial the issue would be. They knew that if they adopted the rule without hearings, the cigarette manufacturers could seize upon the secretiveness of their action to argue that the FTC was undemocratic, arbitrary, and dangerous. To protect itself from such accusations, and with genuine interest in determining if anyone had sound arguments for rejecting their proposed rule, the commission set in motion the procedural machinery described in the Administrative Procedure Act for formal rule making, thereby making both the regulatory process and the end result of those deliberations more tenable from a democratic principles standpoint.

WRITTEN RECORDS

President Lyndon Johnson signed the Freedom of Information Act (FOIA) on Independence Day, July 4, 1966. In 1974, the FOIA was amended and incorporated into the legal code as part of the Administrative Procedures Act. The FOIA gives any person the right to ask for and receive government documents that he or she describes in writing, unless there is a specific exemption that permits the agency to refuse (e.g., for reasons of individual privacy or national security). In announcing its guidelines for enforcing the act, the attorney general said, "If government is to be truly of, by, and for the people, the people must know in detail the activities of government. Nothing so diminishes democracy as secrecy."[23]

The idea that democratic principles could be advanced by openness in government was not a new one in the 1960s, however. Rather, the creation of written, publicly accessible records of agency activities has been a central democratic component of agency decision making in the United States at least since 1936, when the *Federal Register* came into existence.

The *Federal Register* brought some order to administrative chaos that existed before its publication. Prior to that, there was no single published document containing the official actions of agencies and no effective way for the government to communicate with its constituents about the actions taken by administrators. Nor was there any way for various segments of the public and private sectors to know what decisions agencies were making or how those decisions changed the law. As the quantity of administrative decisions grew, it became literally impossible for the left hand of the bureaucracy to know what the right hand was doing. The resultant disorder was bad, not only for administrative effectiveness but also for citizens, who had little access to information about what their government was up to.

The need for an official publication containing administrative actions came forcefully to the attention of the public in 1935 in an important and critical Supreme Court decision.[24] The Court, in striking down the National Recovery Act, noted that enforcement officials of the administration, industrialists, and the lower courts had not been informed that certain administrative regulations promulgated under the act had been revoked. Some of the worst fears of the legal community were confirmed in this case of ill use of administrative policy-making powers. This failure of administration prompted Congress to pass the Federal Register Act in 1935, the same year the Court handed down its decision.

The Federal Register Act requires that all documents having general applicability and legal effect must be published in the *Register*.[25] This includes such items as general statements of agency powers and procedures and copies of the forms it uses for applications and other purposes. The Administrative Procedure Act spells out in detail those actions of agencies that must be published. It states, for example, that notice of proposed rule making shall be published in the *Federal Register*. Accordingly, the FTC published in the *Register* a notice of rule-making proceedings in 1964 indicating its intention to establish trade regulation rules for the advertising and labeling of cigarettes. The notice contained a draft of the proposed rule, an explanation of the legal authority upon which the action was to be taken, and the dates for hearings before the commission. The public was also informed in the notice that they could file written data, views, or arguments concerning the rule or the subject of the proceeding in general.

The Federal Trade Commission makes it a practice not to rely exclusively on the *Register* for dissemination of information concerning its rule-making proposals. For example, copies of the cigarette notice were mailed to a large number of companies, associations, and individuals who might conceivably have had some interest in the proceedings. Then, shortly after the notice was placed in the *Register*, the FTC directly solicited statements from state and local health officers and associations, physicians, medical scientists, behavioral scientists, chemists, cigarette manufacturers, and many others.

The response to the notice of proposed rule making was substantial. Several individuals and groups asked that they be scheduled for oral testimony at the hearings; others submitted lengthy statements. Still others presented petitions or wrote brief letters stating their position. Much of the correspondence was not directly solicited. Some appeals came from high school students who had been recently exposed to antismoking movies, and others came from gratified parents looking for official support in their private campaigns to keep cigarettes from their children. All of the communications were placed in the public record of the hearing. They were available to anyone who wanted to read them before, during, or after the commission hearings. By the time the hearings began, the draft of the rule had been more widely circulated and commented on than if Congress itself was proposing legislation.

Clearly, the two-way flow of information generated by the FTC in this case opened up the political process and helped to allay what some have described as the "deep-seated suspicions that now surrounds non-elective bureaucracies in a representative U.S. system."[26] The wide circulation of draft rules and gathering of information added a democratic flavor to the FTC's decision-making process that, otherwise, could easily be viewed as elitist, and maybe even autocratic.[27]

ADMINISTRATIVE LAW JUDGES

The use of quasi-judicial agents—administrative law judges—is another internal dimension of the bureaucratic policy process that has the potential for enhancing the democratic character of that process.[28] All of the regulatory commissions and several other agencies have assigned to them contingents of highly specialized individuals to serve in this capacity. Today there are over 1,000 administrative judges serving in 30 different Cabinet-level departments and independent regulatory agencies in the Federal government.[29] The largest number of judges, by far (858), are assigned to the Social Security Administration in the Department of Health and Human Services. In contrast, most agencies have only a couple of judges dedicated to hearing cases. The FTC, with its contingent of two administrative law judges, is more typical.[30]

The need for a cadre of judges or examiners arose shortly after creation of the Interstate Commerce Commission (ICC) in 1887. For nearly 20 years the commissioners of the ICC presided over all hearings. It became apparent during this period, however, that the work load was too great and, further, that greater specialization and expertise were required for hearing and understanding the complexities of the cases before the commission. Congress came to the aid of the Interstate Commerce Commission in 1906, authorizing it to employ "separate agents or examiners." These individuals were hired to hear cases and write opinions which were then passed on to the commission, where final decisions would be made.

The appointment of hearing examiners in 1906 did help to relieve the burden on the ICC commissioners but also led to severe criticism of agency adjudication. As the number of hearing examiners grew, they became closely attached to their agencies and dependent upon them for salary increases and the like. As a result, they became less independent, making it difficult for them to maintain impartiality. Consequently, examiners bore the brunt of criticism from those who saw the concept of an independent judiciary being eroded by agency adjudication presided over by individuals who had become overly dependent upon and beholden to their respective agencies.

In 1941, the U.S. attorney general issued a report requiring that agencies give more independence to hearing examiners. This report was also influential in persuading Congress to legislate on the question of hearing examiners' separation from their agencies. The Administrative Procedure Act of 1946 empowered the Office of Personnel Management (OPM, formerly the U.S. Civil Service Commission) to supervise the corps of examiners. The OPM, not the employing agency, was henceforth responsible for the hiring, setting rates of pay, removal, and discipline of the growing cadre of examiners who would, over time, become known as Administrative Law Judges (ALJs).

To further insure the more detached, judicial demeanor of these examiners/judges, the APA requires that they behave according to the canons of judicial behavior. They cannot, for example, consult any party to the case outside of the hearings over which they preside (ex parte communication), unless all parties participate in the consultation. And like their counterparts in the courts, administrative law judges are expected to refrain from discussing their cases with anyone outside the hearing room. The APA also requires that all communications with the judge during a hearing be made part of the public record. Furthermore, the judge is prohibited from participating in any of the agency's investigatory activities related to the development of a case he or she might hear. A judge first learns of a case and its details when the public hearing is scheduled.

Most of an administrative judge's time is devoted to adjudicatory proceedings, not rule making. In fact, the special, formal demands of adjudication were the chief reason for the creation of these interesting and unusual government positions. Nevertheless, one occasionally finds a judge presiding at rule-making hearings. The administrative judges in the Department of Labor, for example, preside at hearings devoted to interpreting sections of the Fair Labor Standards Act. In another example, commissioners at the FTC assigned a rule-making case involving regulation of children's television advertising to the docket of a judge. The FTC usually is reluctant to ask judges to preside at these kinds of hearings, however, because of the independence that ALJs bring to the job. This independence, both necessary and desirable in adjudication, is neither necessary nor desirable in rule making. Agencies like to have more control over policy development through rule making than the use of administrative law judges allows, especially when rules as controversial as cigarette labeling and advertising are being considered.

Even in their more limited role of hearing adjudicatory cases, ALJs play an important, counterbalancing role in checking agency power. The 1986 decision of an administrative law judge in the MR FIT (Multiple Risk Factor Intervention Trial) case brought by the FTC against R. J. Reynolds is a good example. The FTC argued that R. J. Reynolds had twisted and exaggerated the results of the MR FIT study in an advertising campaign designed to cast doubt on the scientific evidence about the hazards of smoking. But the administrative law judge hearing the case ruled that the advertisement was an editorial statement fully protected by the free speech guarantees of the First Amendment. The FTC appealed for another hearing (to no immediate avail) but later backed off when, in October of 1989, it convinced R. J. Reynolds to sign a consent order that forbade further references to MR FIT in its advertising. In the end, the FTC got its way, but not for two years and only after negotiating a settlement with R. J. Reynolds. The FTC was prohibited, on first amendment grounds, from acting capriciously, by one of many administrative law judges who play an important role in a system of internal checks and balances on agency power.[31]

ADVISORY COMMITTEES

With the increasing participation of the bureaucracy in policy making, advisory committees (or advisory councils, as they are sometimes called) provide one way of keeping bureaucrats in tune with public opinion. This, in turn, makes the regulatory process more democratic than it might be, otherwise. In theory, the thousand or so advisory committees made up of private citizens now active in federal government make it possible for individuals outside the bureaucracy to have an impact on the direction and substance of agency policy making.

In reality, the quality and usefulness of advisory committees has varied greatly over the years. Due to the particularized activities of agencies, membership on advisory committees tends to be limited to those who have some specialized knowledge, experience, or expertise. Often, those who find their way to an advisory committee owe allegiance to—or are somehow beholden to—the very groups the host agency is supposed to be regulating in the public interest. The rush to select individuals who have special knowledge or an industry bias makes it difficult for true outsiders (e.g., those who might represent a nonspecialized, broader perspective) to gain an appointment to an advisory committee so that they may be in a position to have an influence on policy making. This leaves many observers of the administrative process skeptical of the value of advisory committees as vehicles for public interest representation.[32]

The old Business Advisory Council (BAC) of the Department of Commerce was an important force in United States commercial policy making for nearly 30 years and was one body that fueled skepticism about the ability of such committees to serve as a check on bureaucratic power in the public interest.[33] The BAC provided a powerful and direct link between government and business before it was eventually eliminated as a public body and reconstituted as a private organization. The rewards for service on it included the opportunity to ensure the right of self-regulation for the business community. While it was still in operation, the prestigious and powerful members of the BAC were privy to decision making in the Department of Commerce and other agencies. Corporate leaders who made up the 60-member council also had close ties with the White House, particularly during the Eisenhower years. Cabinet members tripped over each other for invitations to speak before the council, which met secretly at swank resorts around the country about six times each year.

No one really knows just how powerful the Business Advisory Council was, but many outsiders suspected that it wielded more power than it should have. A committee of the House of Representatives decided to investigate the BAC in 1955, but the council denied the committee access to its files. Ultimately, the House committee reprimanded the ICC and other agencies for allowing groups like the BAC to make decisions for them. In one particularly sharp rebuke, the House committee reviewing the situation said that current practices had led to:

> a virtual abdication of administrative responsibility on the part of Government officials in charge of the Department of Commerce in that their actions in many instances are but the automatic approval of decisions already made outside the Government in business and industry.[34]

The Advisory Committee on Smoking and Health, appointed by Surgeon General Luther Terry in 1962 to report on the health effects of cigarette smoking, is an example of an advisory committee being used more constructively: to check the power of economic and bureaucratic elites in the tobacco subsystem who conspired to rig or derail the regulatory process for their own private interest. As such, this advisory committee played a significant, if not a lasting, role in the policy process (the committee had a life span of little more than a year). This group had a significant impact largely because its members, all of whom had impressive academic and scientific credentials, were highly regarded and also because its final report was neatly packaged and presented. Clearly, dissemination of this report proved to be a turning point in the debate about whether or not the sale and advertising of tobacco products should be regulated.

A similarly constructed and respected advisory committee, operating under the aegis of the Environmental Protection Agency, was created in the late 1980s to assess the data on the health hazards of environmental (second-hand) tobacco smoke (ETS). The credibility and ultimately the impact of the final report issued by this group was bolstered by the perceived neutrality of the group's members. (Some even criticized EPA Director William Reilly for selecting members who were too closely aligned with the tobacco industry.) The findings of this committee in 1986 provided ammunition to the seven flight attendants who shortly thereafter filed a class action suit against six major tobacco companies for the increased risk of disease the attendants claimed to have suffered from years of exposure to second-hand smoke. The report also helped set the stage for the Occupational Safety and Health Administration (OSHA) to begin considering second-hand smoke as a workplace safety hazard. The report of the EPA's advisory committee also added impetus in the Congress to consider regulations in 1994 that would effectively ban smoking in nearly every building in the country that is regularly entered by the public.

As early as the 1940s, the government had tried to eliminate, or at least limit, the excesses of some advisory committees so that they would operate more like Luther Terry's and William Reilly's committees and less like the BAC. The Justice Department has issued regulations governing agendas and the selection of committee chairmen, and various Presidents have issued executive orders intended to reform the selection and conduct of committee members (most notably Kennedy in 1962, Nixon in 1972, and Carter later in the 1970s). The U.S. Congress has also been involved in the process. Members held hearings on advisory committees on and off throughout the 1950s and 1960s, all of which led up to passage of the Federal Advisory Committee Act (P.L. 92-463) in 1972, a law which speaks to the conduct and membership issues that have been raised over the years.[35] In 1987, the General Services Administration (GSA; the agency charged with responsibility for implementing the provisions of the 1972 act) published new proposed regulations to tighten even further committee management at the agency level.

Nevertheless, the power and propriety of advisory groups still depends on the degree of enthusiasm bureaucrats have for creating balanced, impartial groups (to the degree that is possible) and following their advice. Meanwhile, where the departmental ethos is one of close cooperation with the groups that the department supposedly regulates, abuses will continue. Ultimately, advisory committees will succeed in checking the power of economic and bureaucratic elites in favor of the public interest, generally defined, only when agencies make a determined effort to include within their structure individuals who have had, currently have, or will have, no personal stake in the outcome of the regulatory process.

ACCESSIBILITY

Responsiveness to complaints of individual citizens is another measure of democratic governance on which the bureaucracy has the potential (and in some cases, the track record) for scoring well.[36] To be sure, members of Congress have become increasingly attentive to the pleas of individual citizens, and have worked hard to respond to the personal complaints of their constituents (e.g., by setting up district offices and hiring staff members). Case work responsiveness is not the same as policy responsiveness, however. When it comes to policy making, Congress is notoriously sensitive to the will of groups who are well-organized, well-connected, and well-financed even when the interests of those groups run counter to the opinions of a wide, enduring majority of the general public. The fact that the United States is the only Western democracy in the world without a national health care plan (despite strong and enduring support for the rudiments of such a plan) is often attributed to the strength of the small business lobby, the insurance lobby, and various provider interests groups (especially physicians' groups), all who oppose national health care reform because members of these specialized interests would stand to suffer financially under such reforms. Members of Congress may be elected by majorities of voters, but time and again, members have demonstrated sympathy for minority policy positions advanced by relatively small groups who have the financial resources to make their voices count in the legislative policy-making process.

Likewise, while many individual nonsmokers (and smokers) might prefer tough controls on tobacco, they are not organized enough to counterbalance the influence of tobacco interests in the halls of Congress. For those private individuals and groups who are interested in having an impact on the policy-making process here and on other issues, the bureaucracy provides an alternative route to influence. John Banzhaf, a policy entrepreneur of the first order, is one individual whose experience serves as testament to the responsiveness of bureaucracies. Banzhaf, a New York City lawyer in private practice, filed a petition with the Federal Communications Commission, a move analogous to filing a complaint in the court system, in that in both cases, the adjudicating body is relatively insulated from interest-group pressures. Ultimately, Banzhaf's complaint led to the FCC ruling in 1967 that applied the fairness doctrine to cigarette advertising.[37] The cigarette manufacturers appealed the decision of the FCC to the U.S. Court of Appeals for the District of Columbia, but despite the political and economic advantages enjoyed by the industry, Banzhaf prevailed and the political throw-weight of economically powerful groups was neutralized.[38]

Thereafter, Banzhaf and his front organization, Action on Smoking and Health (ASH), were directly involved in three other antismoking decisions made by various federal agencies: the FAA's decision to limit smoking on domestic airline flights (1973) and the ICC's rules to limit smoking on buses (1974) and on trains (1976). Banzhaf's machinations were also instrumental in the FDA decision to include antismoking health warnings on all birth control devices.[39] According to Banzhaf, ASH focused its energies on regulatory agencies like the FCC, the ICC, the FAA, and the FDA precisely because they are more democratic in the classical sense; that is, they are more responsive to the will of individuals. In Banzhaf's words: "We pick very carefully areas where they [the tobacco interests] cannot use their muscle, more precisely where the outcome doesn't depend solely on muscle."[40]

Even groups who have no resources at all can find a way to make their cases before regulatory agencies thanks to the advent of "intervener funding." During the 1970s, a number of federal agencies, including the FTC, began providing resources to "needy" (i.e., cash-poor) citizens' groups so that those groups could meet the expenses of participating in the regulatory process.[41] Intervener funding is designed to redress somewhat the advocacy and information imbalance in public hearings previously dominated by regulated industries. In addition, many other agencies that do not contribute funds directly to private organizations have, according to the U.S. comptroller general, "inherent authority to use appropriated funds to pay reasonable fees of attorneys and expert witnesses and other costs of needy interveners . . . provided their participation could 'reasonably be expected to contribute substantially to a fair and full determination.'"[42]

In the end, the history of cigarette sales and advertising regulation suggests that the existence of widespread public support for antismoking measures is not always sufficient to motivate legislators to act contrary to the interests of a powerful tobacco industry.[43] At the same time, this history suggests that administrative agencies can act as a democratic counterweight to the legislature. It has been said that the court serves as the "great equalizer"; the counterbalance to the power of economically powerful factions in the democracy. Maybe the same could be said for the bureaucracy, at least in the case of smoking and politics, where economically strong and politically well-connected supporters of the status quo, members of the tobacco subsystem, have seen their clout erode substantially over time, thanks in part to the participation of private, public-interest-minded interveners in the regulatory process.

MEDIA AS WATCHDOGS

The media also play a role as an intervener, of sorts. While the ability of bureaucrats to manipulate the media provides agencies, with a potentially important lever of political power, the media may also serve an important watchdog function, intervening in the policy process by calling agencies to task for acting undemocratically. The Iran-Contra scandal is a prime example of the critical role media can play, both in initially uncovering possible misdeeds of bureaucrats, and in keeping citizens abreast of developments as they unfold. The Freedom of Information Act often comes into play here, making it possible for investigative journalists to monitor and keep private citizens abreast of agency activity.

Generally speaking, members of the media make government accessible to the general public and make it possible for the citizenry to become better informed. Informed public opinion is an increasingly important element in our mass democracy.[44] Indeed, informed public support has become a critical dimension of an agency's power base in these days of tight budgets and cut-back management, and the media—with its access to the policy process guaranteed by the FOIA, the APA, written record requirements, and various sunshine provisions of statutory law—play a key role in what opinions will be formed and what agencies will be favored by the public and its representatives in Congress.

REFLECTIVE REPRESENTATION AND BUREAUCRATIC PLURALISM

Some might argue that Congress has, in theory, the best chance of being the most representative institution of government because it is dependent on the electoral process. Yet practical experience has cast doubts on the notion that democratic representation can best be achieved through elections. Studies of voters, elections, and the power structure of Congress have demonstrated that Congress frequently falls short of representative ideals. One-party jurisdictions, the seniority system, incumbency advantages, and the concentration of power in congressional committees make it difficult, if not impossible, for a majority to work its will inside or outside Congress.

In contrast, we have noted that the bureaucracy operates in an environment of highly developed procedural constraints (e.g., requirements of the APA and the *Federal Register*) in which a number of agents (e.g., administrative law judges, members of advisory committees, private sector interveners, and the media) play potentially important parts in the policy-making process. All of these aspects of the regulatory process help to keep the bureaucracy in check and provide avenues for individuals and groups with interests beyond those of an economic or electoral nature to have a say in how the public is governed.

In addition, it has been argued by Charles Goodsell and others, that the makeup of the bureaucracy is much more representative, in a demographic sense, than the makeup of either the legislature or the judiciary.[45] In theory, this characteristic of the bureaucracy—a characteristic we call "reflective representation"—leads the bureaucracy on a more populist course than it might tend to take otherwise.[46] Given trends in federal hiring in recent decades, Norton Long's observation of 1952 is more true today than ever before:

> . . . The bureaucracy now has a very real claim to be considered much more representative of the American people in its composition than the Congress. This is not merely the case with respect to the class structure of the country, but equally significantly, with respect to the learned groups, skills, economic interests, races, nationalities, and religions. The diversity that makes up the United States is better represented in the civil service than anywhere else.[47]

Bureaucrats also work within a framework of shared political-cultural traditions, and this too helps keep the regulatory process in line with the will of the mass public. Bureaucrats not only tend to "look" (demographically) like the general public, they tend to think and act in accordance with widely shared beliefs about their relatively restricted role in the constitutional system. In fact, Goodsell presents data that suggests that government employees share a mind set that can be characterized as significantly more democratic and less autocratic than the mind set shared by their counterparts in the general public.[48]

There is also the issue of "bureaucratic pluralism" to consider: The vast array of opinions and positions represented by groups in the general population that is typically reflected in the bureaucracy itself. Decision making in the executive branch of government is diffused among many individuals and agencies and often takes place in piecemeal, two-steps-forward-one-step-backward fashion.[49] There is considerable overlapping of functions within the bureaucracy, and this overlap inevitably leads to a considerable overlapping of interests and opinions, making it difficult for any single agency to capture and hold for itself an area of policy over long periods of time. Indeed, challenges to agency predominance by other agencies with affected constituencies are frequent. In particular, challenges to agency predominance are regularly mounted by the Office of Management and Budget, which operates under the President's direction with presidential priorities clearly in mind.

In the initial stages of the cigarette controversy, bureaucratic pluralism helped to maintain the status quo. For example, there was little agreement on policy between the Department of Agriculture, which sought to protect its tobacco farmer constituents, and the FTC. There was also disagreement *within* the Department of Health, Education and Welfare (HEW) when Surgeon General Luther Terry took a position quite different from that of Anthony Celebrezze, secretary of HHS and ostensibly, Terry's boss. All of this pluralism made change very difficult to initiate.

Even after change agents began to transform the cozy tobacco subsystem into a more amorphous and permeable tobacco network, disagreements between departments continued, and this served to slow the rate of change that could be effected. For example, friction and accommodation were evidenced by the clash between two of President Carter's Cabinet secretaries late in the 1970s. Joseph Califano, the outspoken secretary of HHS who was actively engaged in efforts to discourage smoking pulled his punches when it came to agricultural issues. In the words of Bob Bergland, Carter's secretary of agriculture at the time, "I'm not going to get into a question of whether tobacco is healthy or unsafe—I'm not qualified to judge in that regard, and Joe Califano assured me that he's not going to get into the price support issue."[50]

In the 1980s, another clash—this one between the Department of Health and Human Services and the office of the U.S. Trade Representative (USTR)—was very much in evidence. Officials at HHS were attempting to continue playing a lead role in government efforts in the area of smoking cessation and health promotion. At the same time, officials at the U.S. Trade Representative's office were involved in efforts to force foreign countries to ease trade barriers to U.S. exporters of tobacco products. In some cases, USTR bureaucrats actually threatened to bring trade sanctions to bear on countries that did not freely accept imports of tobacco products from U.S. manufacturers.[51] Curiously, one part of the federal bureaucracy was attempting to diminish the incidence of smoking while federal agents in other quarters were attempting to encourage the use of tobacco products.

In the end, Americans won both ways. The rate of smoking continues to decline in America, and the incidence in related disease is also on the wane. This is good news for those who are concerned with the state of the nation's health, and related issues of health care spending. Meanwhile, tobacco exports are on the rise. The U.S. is currently the leading exporter of tobacco products in the world, accounting for 26 percent of world cigarette exports,[52] and that is good news for those who fret about the state of the American economy, in general, and the health of the agricultural sector in particular. Somehow, the bureaucratic policy-making process found a way to appease competing constituencies in our pluralistic society. This was possible largely because the bureaucracy is nothing more, or less, than a reflection of the interests and positions found within the general public.

In the end, if one takes both reflective representation and bureaucratic pluralism into account, it may be that, as institutions go, the federal bureaucracy is *more* representative than Congress. Add to this the heightened emphasis placed on accountability of federal bureaucrats stemming from the Civil Service Reform Act of 1978 (there is nothing quite parallel to this act guiding the behavior of legislators), and it begins to become clear that there may be reasons to be more suspicious of legislators than of bureaucrats when it comes to making policy in the public interest.

THE POLICY-MAKING ROLE OF BUREAUCRACIES RECONSIDERED

There are numerous ways to check agency power at the national level of government. Individually, each of the checks on bureaucratic power is inadequate in one way or another. But bureaucrats typically face many of these checks simultaneously; the degree of freedom to make policy enjoyed by an agency is always limited to one degree or another. Autonomy may ebb and flow with time, but it is rarely if ever absolute or uncontrolled (see Figure 9-1).

As a result, capricious or arbitrary action is not as serious a problem in national government as it may be in state or local governments where political institutions are often too weak or disorganized to challenge the bureaucracy.[53] The problem in Washington is more often one of persuading the bureaucracy to act when its members know from experience that doing as little as possible is the safest and easiest course. Hardening of administrative arteries can be more serious in the long run than agency aggressiveness. Ironically, an abundance of safeguards does not guarantee responsive government, because their ready availability can make it easier for small, special interest groups to stop proposed changes in policy. Certainly a wide range of

Figure 9–1 External and Internal Controls on Agency Power

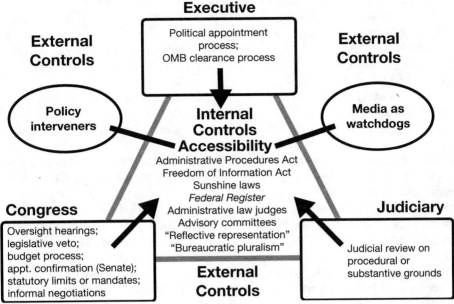

safeguards served to restrain the Federal Trade Commission from acting in the public interest during various phases of the cigarette labeling controversy.

In addition, it is important to put the role played by American bureaucracies into comparative context. The situation in France is illustrative. As Robert A. Kagan and David Vogel point out, "French political culture and tradition endorses strong control of government over business, with policy making by elite educated bureaucrats who are relatively insulated from political pressure groups."[54] Indeed, bureaucrats play a lead role in formulating policy in France and many other Western democracies where parliamentary systems operate, and where once the executive branch endorses the proposed course of action, legislative approval is essentially pro forma. Such countries have well-developed traditions of public authority and political structures that are less sensitive to the interests of the business community.

In the United States, the political culture is more liberal and individualistic, less statist and communalistic. As a result, government in America is, de facto, more sensitive to the selfish interests of economically powerful groups. All this is to suggest that whatever the bureaucracy has accomplished in the United States, its clout is relatively limited when compared to what bureaucracies in other Western countries have accomplished and are capable of accomplishing.[55] Certainly, bureaucratic accomplishments in America in the area of regulating tobacco seem puny when compared to the magnitude of the problem, with related health care costs totaling in the billions, annually, and with over a thousand Americans dying each day as a result of smoking-related diseases.

Ultimately, the existence in America of a bureaucracy with policy-making powers assures a more broadly representative decision-making process than one that relies solely on a legislature. Bureaucrats, if they wish, can afford to take a somewhat broader view of an issue because, unlike members of Congress, they are not always directly answerable to a narrow constituency. Members of Congress generally have to respond to specialized interests, particularly when those interests are well organized and well financed. How an institution of government operates alone is not as important as how it works in concert with other institutions. America's rather unique combination of bureaucratic and congressional policy-making powers can make important contributions to a system of government based on checks and balances in which expanded participation in democratic policy making is the goal.

At times, agencies may fall into the legislative trap and fail to make positive contributions to representation because they respond only to the small, powerful interest groups upon which they may depend for their political strength. At the same time, the existence of discretionary authority in the bureaucracy does make it possible, for agencies—working together with sympathetic members of Congress and with advocates in the private sector—to break the grip of economically and politically powerful interests on the policy-making process. The time, money, and energy required to gain government acceptance of the cigarette health warning illustrates well, however, a reality that will be reassuring for some and sobering for others: Those who would challenge the status quo in American government make advances slowly, even with the assistance of agencies that enjoy a fair measure of policy-making power.

NOTES

1. The tobacco industry's strength in Congress and the state legislatures, though diminished over the years, continues to pose significant hurdles to those who would advance the anti-tobacco cause. In 1986, for example, the Tobacco Institute was credited with helping to defeat approximately 90 percent of 560 bills considered by state legislatures in that year. At the federal level, not one of the 160 smoking-related bills

opposed by the Tobacco Institute were passed by Congress. Karen L. Fernicola, "Where There's Smoke . . . There's the Tobacco Institute," *Association Management,* July 1987, pp. 20–25.

2. The political science literature is replete with examples of this argument. For the classic, and still one of the best; expositions on this theme, see Theodore J. Lowi, *The End of Liberalism: The Second Republic of the United States,* 2nd ed. (New York: W. W. Norton, 1979).

3. The classic argument about the supposed dichotomy between politics and administration was made by former President and political scientist Woodrow Wilson late in the nineteenth century, and early in the twentieth century by Frank J. Goodnow, one of the founders and the first president of the American Political Science Association. The position advanced by Wilson and Goodnow—that politics (policy making) and administration (the neutral implementation of policy) could be and were separate—became the public administration orthodoxy in the twentieth century as a stream of scholars reiterated this normative claim and attempted to support it empirically. See Woodrow Wilson, "The Study of Administration" (1887) and Frank J. Goodnow, "Politics and Administration," both reprinted in *Classics of Public Administration,* 2nd ed., Jay M. Shafritz and Albert C. Hyde, eds. (Chicago, Ill.: Dorsey Press, 1987).

4. Elizabeth B. Drew, quoted in Kenneth Michael Friedman, *Public Policy and the Smoking-Health Controversy* (Lexington, Mass.: Lexington Books, 1975), p. 59.

5. For an elaboration of this point in a comparative perspective, see Friedman, *Public Policy,* pp. 154–155.

6. Peter Woll, *American Bureaucracy,* 2nd ed. (New York: W.W. Norton, 1977), pp. 248–249.

7. Helen Dewer, "Congress Doing Battle with a Monster of Its Own Creation. . . ," *The Washington Post,* October 21, 1979, p. A6.

8. There are several versions of the legislative veto, each of which give either a congressional committee, one house, or both houses of Congress acting together, the authority to veto a rule written by an administrative agency. In June 1983, the Supreme Court dealt a blow to the idea of the legislative veto in *Immigration and Naturalization Service* v. *Chadha* (634 F. 2d 408 433 [9th Cir. 1980]) where it was held that the Congress cannot unilaterally veto actions of an independent agency or an executive department without giving the opportunity to the President to override the legislative veto. Otherwise, the principle of separation of powers among the branches of government would be compromised. New authorizing legislation for the FTC thus included the provision for presidential authority to override a legislative veto of regulations.

9. Quoted in Friedman, *Public Policy,* pp. 38–39.

10. Ibid., p. 43.

11. Ibid.

12. Edward F. Cox, Robert C. Fellmeth, and John E. Schulz, *The Nader Report on the Federal Trade Commission* (New York: Grove Press, 1969), p. 77. The American Bar Association report was released on September 16, 1969. A lengthy summary of the report was published that day in *The New York Times.* Practically the only complimentary comment for the commission was the notation of the adoption of the new procedure: "To place our criticism, in perspective, we wish to emphasize that recent years have witnessed an improvement in several aspects of the FTC's operations. The FTC has sought to improve its rules of practice and procedure. It has experimented with new administrative techniques such as the trade regulation rule. . . ."

13. B. Dan Wood and Richard W. Waterman, "The Dynamics of Political Control of the Bureaucracy," *American Political Science Review* 85 (September 1991), pp. 801–828 at pp. 808–809.

14. Ibid., p. 822.

15. In some agency actions, statutes prohibit or limit court review. The Federal Trade Commission Act, for example, contains one of the common statutory limits on

judicial review of administrative actions: "The findings of the Commission as to the facts, if supported by the evidence, shall be conclusive." This section of the commission's act indicates one area of law where agencies and the courts have come to some agreement on the subject of review, at least at a high level of generalization.

16. For this reason, adjudicatory proceedings of agencies are subject to closer judicial scrutiny than rule making. Agency rule-making procedures can be as lax as those of congressional committees; as such, there are far fewer grounds upon which an agency rule might be appealed to the courts.

17. The Administrative Procedures Act of 1946 is an example of a general statute that guides the regulatory process, while the Public Health Cigarette Smoking Act of 1969 represents a statute that specifically prescribes certain agency procedures. The 1969 act requires that the FTC give six months' warning of any intentions to initiate rule-making procedures that would affect the tobacco industry.

18. In *Miranda*—a decision binding on local, state, and federal law enforcement officials—the Supreme Court held that confessions of an individual charged with a crime were not admissible if the charged individual was not first advised of his or her rights to remain silent. See 87 S. Ct. 11 (1968). In *Brown,* the Supreme Court ruled that separate schooling for children of different races was inherently unequal, and mandated that public schools at all levels of government be integrated with "all deliberate speed." See 347 U.S. 483 (1954).

19. *National Petroleum Refiners Association* v. *Federal Trade Commission,* 482 F. 2d 672 (D.C. Cir. 1973), reversing 340 F. Supp. 1343 (D DC 1972), cert. denied 415 US 951 (1974).

20. Bernard Rosen, *Holding Government Bureaucracies Accountable* (New York: Praeger, 1982), p. 110.

21. 60 Stat. 237 (1946). In 1966, the act was incorporated in Title 5 of the *United States Code.* The *Code* is supplemented annually and revised every six years.

22. The rule-making section of the Administrative Procedure Act states that requirements for notice and hearing need not be followed "in any situation in which the agency for good cause finds . . . that notice and public procedure . . . are impracticable, unnecessary, or contrary to the public interest." The courts may declare invalid any rule made if an agency acted arbitrarily or capriciously in failing to give notice of rule making and/or failing to hold hearings.

23. Quoted in Rosen, *Holding Government Bureaucracies Accountable,* p. 112.

24. *Panama Refining Company* v. *Ryan,* 293 US 388 (1935).

25. The Office of the Federal Register, a part of the National Archives, publishes the *Register* daily, Monday through Friday. Thousands of individual copies are distributed to various courts, executive agencies, and members of Congress. Copies also are mailed to lawyers, representatives of special interest groups, and other interested parties for about $450 per year. Currently, there are approximately 40,000 paid subscribers.

26. Wood and Waterman, "The Dynamics of Political Control of the Bureaucracy," p. 824.

27. In addition to the requirements of the FOIA and the Federal Register, regulatory commissions such as the FTC also are guided by a sunshine law, approved by Congress in 1976. This law prohibits private communications between commission members and parties affected by commission decisions. It also requires that top officials open their meetings to the public unless agency officials vote to close a particular meeting for a reason (e.g., individual right to privacy; national security) permitted by law. Even when meetings are closed, agencies are required to keep a verbatim transcript so that the decision to close the meeting can be challenged in court on its merits. The burden of proof in these cases falls on the agency, and any parts of the transcript found by a federal court not to meet the exemption standards set out by the sunshine law are then released to the public.

28. On August 19, 1972, an executive order eliminated the title "hearing examiner" and created the title "administrative law judge" (37 *Federal Register* 162, August 19, 1972). The change had been sought for many years by the hearing examiners' association, the Federal Trial Examiners Conference (now called the Administrative Law Judges Conference).

29. The number of administrative law judges grew rapidly between 1968 and 1981, increasing from 600 to over 1,000. This growth reflected the increase in rulemaking and adjudicatory powers exercised by agencies in those years. The number of "ALJs" dipped below 1,000 in the 1980s, the result of a deemphasis upon regulation during the Reagan administration, but rebounded again thereafter.

30. Only three agencies have more than 20 judges assigned to them: Health and Human Services (858), the Department of Labor (71), and the National Labor Relations Board (70). Most agencies have less than a dozen judges; the modal number of judges assigned to an agency is between four and five. U.S. Office of Personnel Management, Career Development Program, Office of Training and Operations; FAX in response to a query, June 6, 1994.

31. Judges are also subject to their own internal set of checks. The qualifications for appointment are quite rigorous. In addition to being a member of the bar, one must have had at least seven years of experience in preparation and presentation of cases in courts or before administrative agencies. A board of examiners within the Office of Personnel Management evaluates the written materials and recommendations of applicants and administers oral examinations. As such, administrative law judges are considered to be a select, prestigious group fully capable of playing the role assigned them in the regulatory process.

32. Avery Leiserson, in *Administrative Regulation: A Study in Representation of Interests* (Chicago: University of Chicago Press, 1942), discusses the history and early use of advisory councils in bureaucracies. For a more recent discussion of the role played by advisory committees in participative decision making, see James W. Felser and Donald F. Kettl, *The Politics of the Administrative Process* (Chatham, N.J.: Chatham House Publishers, 1991), pp. 192–193.

33. Robert J. Donovan, *Eisenhower: The Inside Story* (New York: Harper Brothers, 1956), p. 341.

34. *Interim Report of the Antitrust Subcommittee on the Judiciary on WOC's and Government Advisory Groups*, U.S. House of Representatives, 84th Congress, 2nd Session (1956), p. 99. An excellent analysis of business influence in government, including a discussion of the use and abuse of advisory councils, can be found in Grant McConnell, *Private Power and American Democracy* (New York: Alfred A. Knopf, 1966) pp. 276–279.

35. The law stipulates, generally, that all committees should be strictly advisory. More specifically, the following rules of committee operations are also charted: (1) Any committee whose duration is not fixed by law must terminate its activities no more than two years after it is established; (2) all meetings have to be called by a government employee; (3) the agency retains the right to draft the agenda; (4) all meetings are open to the public; and (5) meetings must be conducted by an agency employee who is empowered to adjourn the meeting whenever he or she determines that adjournment would be in the public interest.

36. See Charles T. Goodsell, *The Case for Bureaucracy: A Public Administration Polemic*, 3rd ed. (Chatham, N.J.: Chatham House, 1994), Chapter 2.

37. In the FCC's words, "The licensee . . . is presenting commercials using the consumption of a product whose normal use has been found by the Congress and the Government to represent a serious potential hazard to public health. . . . This obligation to inform the public of the other side of the matter stems not from any esoteric requirements of a particular doctrine but from the simple fact that the public interest means nothing if it does not include such a responsibility." U.S. Federal Communications Commission, Memorandum Opinion and Order in the Matter of Television Station

WCBS-TV, New York, N.Y.; Applicability of the Fairness Doctrine to Cigarette Advertising, Washington, D.C., 1967, pp. 42, 43. Quoted in Friedman, *Public Policy*, p. 50.

38. *John H. Banzhaf, III* v. *Federal Communications Commission*, 405 F. 2d 1082 (1968).

39. Ronald J. Troyer and Gerald E. Markle, *Cigarettes: The Battle over Smoking* (New Brunswick, N.J.: Rutgers University Press, 1983), p. 85.

40. Banzhaf estimates that the Tobacco Institute alone spent $4.5 million in 1978, compared to ASH revenues in that year, which totaled less than $300,000, one-fifteenth the Tobacco Institute total. Ibid., pp. 83, 100, 105. This helps explain why ASH activities were directed almost exclusively toward influencing regulatory agencies. From its inception in 1967 through 1979, ASH had filed over 150 complaints with regulatory agencies and provided input (testimony, briefs, petitions, etc.) in 45 other cases. Meanwhile, less than a dozen contacts between ASH and the legislative branch could be documented. Ibid., p. 85.

41. Other agencies involved in the provision of intervener funding include the Environmental Protection Agency, the National Highway Transportation Safety Administration, and the Department of Energy. Rosen, *Holding Government Bureaucracies Accountable*, p. 74.

42. Comptroller General of the United States, B-139703, December 1976, quoted in Rosen, *Holding Government Bureaucracies Accountable*, p. 74. This decision has an effect similar in type to the Equal Access to Justice Act, which requires federal agencies to pay the legal expenses of needy individuals (net worth under $1 million), businesses (net worth under $5 million), and nonprofit organizations (regardless of financial status) who bring suit against agencies in federal court. Rosen, p. 95.

43. This point is made at the state level of analysis by Peter D. Jacobson, Jeffrey Wasserman, and Kristina Raube, "The Politics of Anti-Smoking Legislation," *Journal of Health Politics, Policy, and Law*, 18, no. 4 (Winter 1993).

44. The Cable Satellite Public Affairs Network (popularly known as C-SPAN) has advanced the ball significantly in this respect. This network not only provides unedited gavel-to-gavel coverage of the House of Representatives (C-SPAN) and the U.S. Senate (C-SPAN II); it also covers the proceedings of a wide variety of administrative agencies, replaying highlights of these and other public affairs events at various times, 24 hours a day. The commercial networks have also become heavily involved in public affairs programming. Today a myriad of television news magazines and special investigative reports regularly compliment the ever-popular *60 Minutes* program. These shows often deal explicitly and critically with the machinations of administrative agencies.

45. For the general argument, Goodsell, *The Case for Bureaucracy*, Chapter 5. For a specific demographic comparison between the general public and public employees, see Goodsell, p. 107 (Table 5.1). We should note in qualification, however, that even though it appears that the bureaucracy is relatively reflective of the general public, the table does not discriminate between street-level bureaucrats and senior-level policy makers. The percentage of women and racial minorities at the senior levels of the bureaucracy, where policy is made, is substantially lower than the percentage of the general population accounted for by members of these groups.

46. In the words of democratic theorist Simon Stern, to be truly representative a decision-making body should, in its makeup, reflect the general population, "precisely as a map brings before us the mountains and dales, rivers and lakes, forests and plains, cities and towns." Quoted in W.J.M. MacKinzie, *Free Elections* (London: George Allen and Unwin LTD, 1950), p. 77.

47. Norton E. Long, "Bureaucracy and Constitutionalism," *The American Political Science Review*, 46 (September 1952), 808–819. For more recent extensions of this argument, see John Rohr, *To Run a Constitution: The Legitimacy of the Administrative State* (Lawrence, Kans.: University Press of Kansas, 1986).

48. Goodsell, *The Case for Bureaucracy*, p. 87.

49. Friedman, *Public Policy,* p. 154.

50. Carter, "Cabinet Astir over Tobacco, Health Issue," *The Washington Post,* June 28, 1977, p. D9.

51. See General Accounting Office, *Trade and Health Issues: Dichotomy Between Tobacco Export Policy and Anti-smoking Initiatives* (GAO/NSIAD-90-190, May 15, 1990).

52. Exports increased from 64 billion cigarettes in 1985 to 142 billion cigarettes in 1989, while domestic sales declined. This helps to account for the substantial increase in tobacco production by U.S. farmers (29 percent increase for flu-cured tobacco and 38 percent increase for burley tobacco) during a time when domestic consumption was declining. GAO, 1990, p. 39.

53. For example, some state legislatures are poorly organized, relatively weak institutions whose members serve for little compensation and with almost no staff support only a few months every other year. These kinds of institutions can hardly be expected to provide the sort of check on bureaucratic policy making at the state level that the U.S. Congress exerts on the federal agencies.

54. Robert A. Kagan and David Vogel, "The Politics of Smoking Regulation: Canada, France, and the United States," in *Smoking Policy: Law, Politics, and Culture,* eds. Robert L. Rabin and Stephen D. Sugarman (New York: Oxford University Press, 1993), p. 34.

55. This is certainly true at least with regard to levels of tobacco taxes and control of cigarette advertising, both of which are minimal compared to taxes and controls in Canada and France, for example. Ibid., pp. 44–45.

Appendix
I

Chronology of Important Events in the Cigarette Regulation Controversy

1865–1894: Cigarette smoking becomes popular and socially acceptable among adult American men. Meanwhile the sale of cigarettes to minors is banned in 26 states.

1881: Invention of the cigarette-making machine improves quality control of commercially produced cigarettes and dramatically lowers their unit price, making cigarette smoking an affordable habit for adult men, and some women, to acquire and continue.

1895–1917: The Anti-Cigarette League becomes organized and active. By 1909, cigarettes are legally banned in 14 states.

1906: Support for the Food and Drug Act of 1906, creating the Food and Drug Administration (FDA), is generated among members of Congress from tobacco-producing states after tobacco is stricken from the list of substances the new FDA would be allowed to regulate.

1918: Cigarettes become identified with the war effort as a symbol of courage and dignity. Citizens' groups organize to send cigarettes to soldiers.

1918–1930: Manufacturers and merchants organize to repeal existing bans on the sale of tobacco products. By 1930, all laws prohibiting the sale of cigarettes to adults are repealed.

1939: The first scientific study linking smoking and lung cancer is published.

1950–1954: Fourteen major studies are completed, all of which link cigarette smoking and serious diseases. Among the most influential is a study done at the Sloan-Kettering Cancer Institute in which tobacco extract painted on the backs of mice was found to cause the development of tumors. Meanwhile, the FDA reprimands tobacco manufacturers for attributing health value and medicinal properties to their products.

1954: Cigarette manufacturers set up the Council for Tobacco Research (CTR, originally called the Tobacco Industry Research Committee). The CTR—headquartered one floor below the New York offices of the public relations firm Hill and Knowlton (with a Hill and Knowlton staffer installed as the first executive director)—is a public relations organization that doles out more than $200 million over the next 40 years in funding research that it hopes will cast doubt on the link between smoking and health problems.

The industry faces its first tobacco liability lawsuit: *Pritchard* v. *Liggett and Myers.* The suit is dropped by the plaintiff in 1966.

1955: The FTC holds a Trade Practices Conference in which voluntary advertising guidelines prohibiting claims about the tar and nicotine content of various brands of cigarettes is reached with manufacturers.

1957: Four health organizations issue a report citing a causal relationship between cigarette smoking and lung cancer and call for government action. This leads to the first congressional hearings on smoking and health.

1958: The Tobacco Institute is established by major United States cigarette manufacturers as the primary lobbying and public relations organization for the industry.

1960: The FTC bans advertising regarding the health effects of filters.

1962: The Advisory Committee on Smoking and Health is formed by Surgeon General Luther Terry and its members meet for the first time.

1964: In January, after two years of study, the Surgeon General issues the report written by the Advisory Committee on Smoking and Health. The report summarizes existing research on the hazards of smoking and becomes the first of what will become an important stream of nearly annual reports on the subject.

One week after release of the *Smoking and Health* report, the Federal Trade Commission (FTC) issues its notice of rule making pertaining to the advertising and labeling of cigarettes (29 *Federal Register* 530-532, January 22, 1964).

The Public Health Service (PHS) discontinues distribution of free cigarettes to the 16 Public Health Service hospitals and 50 Indian hospitals under its control. The Veterans Administration and the Department of Defense soon follow suit in their medical installations.

Several members of Congress introduce legislation related to the cigarette controversy and call for hearings. Meanwhile, the National Association of Broadcasters amends its television advertising code to discourage portrayal of cigarette smoking as a habit worthy of imitation by youngsters.

In April, the cigarette manufacturers announce the establishment of their voluntary Cigarette Advertising Code.

The Federal Trade Commission promulgates its Trade Regulation Rule on Cigarette Labeling and Advertising (29 FR 8325, July 2, 1964).

The National Interagency Council on Smoking and Health, a coalition of health advocacy groups, is established.

The FTC agrees to delay the January 1, 1965, implementation date of its new Trade Regulation Rule in order to allow Congress the opportunity to hold hearings and act, if it chooses.

R. J. Reynolds Jr. (58)—son, namesake, and heir to the founder of R.J. Reynolds Tobacco Co.—dies of emphysema and congestive heart failure after years of smoking.

1965: Congressional hearings are held on the cigarette labeling issue in the spring, leading to passage of the Cigarette Labeling and Advertising Act of 1965 (CLAA, signed into law by President Johnson on July 27). The new law requires that a health warning appear on all packages of cigarettes and bans federal agency regulation of the tobacco industry for four years.

In October, Congress appropriates funds to establish the National Clearinghouse for Smoking and Health in the Public Health Service.

1966: The warning "Caution: Cigarette Smoking May Be Hazardous to Your Health" begins appearing on packages of cigarettes on January 1.

1967: The Federal Communications Commission (FCC) rules that the fairness doctrine applies to cigarette advertising and requires licensees who broadcast cigarette ads to provide free media time for antismoking public service announcements (PSAs) in a ratio that approximates one PSA for every three paid cigarette ads.

In its first report to Congress since passage of the CLAA of 1965, the FTC renews its call to require that health warnings be part of any cigarette advertisement. Later in the year, the FTC releases the tar and nicotine ratings of 59 brands as measured in its new testing laboratory.

1968: Secretary of Health, Education and Welfare Wilbur J. Cohen endorses the FTC position in calling on Congress to extend health warnings to advertising.

The U.S. Court of Appeals upholds the FCC's decision to apply the fairness doctrine to cigarette advertising.

1969: In February, the FCC proposes a rule to ban all cigarette advertising from radio and television.

With the ban on FTC rule making due to expire in July, 90 members of Congress introduce or co-sponsor bills on the subject of cigarette industry regulation, and congressional hearings commence. Many members push bills that are antagonistic to cigarette interests, but those backing measures sympathetic to the tobacco industry continue to have more clout.

The FTC begins holding hearings on a new health warning and extension of the warning to advertising on July 1, the first day after the congressional ban on such activities expires.

The Television Code Review Board of the National Association of Broadcasters endorses the phasing out of cigarette ads on radio and television within five years.

The New York Times states that all cigarette ads in its pages must carry the health warning required on packages, beginning in 1970. Shortly thereafter, R.J. Reynolds, Philip Morris, and the American Tobacco Company announce they will no longer advertise in that paper.

1970: After 12 months of contentious hearings and conferences, Congress passes the Public Health Cigarette Smoking Act of 1969 (signed into law by President Nixon on April 1). The new law (1) bans ads from radio and television; (2) extends the rule-making prohibition on the FTC for another year; and thereafter (3) requires that the FTC give Congress six months' notice of any pending rule making concerning cigarettes. The new law also strengthens the wording of the package warning from "*Caution:* Cigarette Smoking *May Be Hazardous* to Your Health" to "*Warning: The Surgeon General Has Determined That* Cigarette Smoking *Is Dangerous* to Your Health." (Italics indicate differences in the language of the two warnings.)

The World Health Organization takes a public position against cigarette smoking. This action marks widespread international support for antismoking movements, which were growing rapidly in most Western cultures at the time. This same year, and National Conference on Smoking and Health is staged to highlight the public health dimensions of the issue in the United States.

Six radio station owners file suit to enjoin the government from enforcing the new legislation banning cigarette advertising from the airwaves. In October 1991 the U.S. Court of Appeals upholds the congressional ban on radio and television advertising. The owners file an appeal to the Supreme Court, which upholds the congressional action in March 1972.

The FCC rules that television and radio stations may continue to carry antismoking commercials, but they will not be required to carry prosmoking ads under the provisions of fairness doctrine.

With prodding from the FTC, cigarette manufacturers volunteer to include disclosure of tar and nicotine content of cigarettes in all advertising.

1971: January 1 is the last day for cigarette advertising on radio and television in the United States.

The Surgeon General proposes a governmental initiative to ban smoking in public places. Nonsmokers in smoke-filled rooms experience a health hazard, he claims.

On April 15, at the urging of the FTC, seven of nine major cigarette companies agree voluntarily to include a health warning in all printed advertising, beginning immediately. Later in the year, the commission registers its dissatisfaction with this agreement, noting its intent to proceed against the major cigarette companies for false and deceptive advertising if they do not agree to make their health ad warnings more "clear and conspicuous" to the consumer.

The congressional prohibition against the FTC rule making in cigarette regulation expires on July 1, 1971. With this as added bargaining power, the FTC convinces six major cigarette companies to agree, as part of a consent order, to include a "clear and conspicuous" health warning in all cigarette advertisements.

1972: In February, the Secretary of HEW issues a policy directive to establish "no-smoking" rules in departmental conference rooms, auditoriums, sections of cafeterias, and in certain work areas, and the National Clearinghouse for Smoking and Health moves within HEW to become a part of the department's Center for Disease Control. The reorganization indicates emphasis of the point of view that smoking is a preventable health problem.

In an April decision that called into question the FTC's authority to regulate the cigarette industry, a U.S. district court declares that the FTC lacks statutory authority to issue trade regulation rules in cases involving posting of octane ratings on gasoline pumps. The U.S. Court of Appeals reverses this decision in June 1973, reaffirming the rule-making authority of FTC. The U.S. Supreme Court denies certiorari in the octane case, thereby allowing to stand the U.S. Court of Appeals' decision confirming the FTC's rule-making authority.

1973: The Federal Aviation Administration requires that smokers and nonsmokers be segregated by section on commercial airlines.

At the urging of the FTC, Congress passes a law banning ads for "little cigars" (cigars made the same size and shape as cigarettes by the tobacco companies to avoid regulation).

1974: The Interstate Commerce Commission (ICC) restricts smoking to the rear 20 percent of all commercial interstate buses.

1975: The FTC Improvements Act (Magnuson-Moss) is signed into law by President Ford on January 4. The new law gives the FTC a statutory basis for rule-making authority and provides easier consumer access to FTC proceedings.

The U.S. District Court rules that the Consumer Product Safety Commission (CPSC) has authority to regulate tar and nicotine.

1976: In a blow to the antismoking forces, Congress passes and President Ford signs legislation that exempts tobacco from CPSC regulation. Meanwhile, other parts of the federal bureaucracy become more bold in their antismoking decisions: The ICC implements rules segregating smoking on trains, the GSA issues smoking guidelines for buildings in which nearly one million government employees work, and the National Parks Service bans smoking in federally owned caves.

1978: Health, Education and Welfare Secretary Califano announces a "vigorous" antismoking campaign on fourteenth anniversary of the Surgeon

General's report and declares smoking to be "Public Enemy Number One."

1979:   Negative reaction to Califano's antismoking initiatives by members of Congress from tobacco-producing states helps precipitate the hasty dismissal of Califano as HEW Secretary.

1980:   A new FTC Improvements Act passes limiting commission jurisdiction and establishing a legislative veto system for FTC rules.

1981:   The Surgeon General's annual report calls for study of the addictive nature of smoking.

After five years of study, the FTC calls for a new, more effective health warning system including a sterner warning on packages that is set in larger type.

Reversing its position of 15 years, the American Medical Society calls for an end to tobacco price supports.

A concerted effort to kill the 48-year-old tobacco price support program dies in the House on a 231 to 184 vote.

1982:   Surgeon General C. Everett Koop issues the annual report on smoking and health and declares that "cigarette smoking is clearly identified as the chief preventable cause of death in our society."

Congress increases the excise tax on cigarettes for the first time since 1951, doubling the per-pack levy from 8 to 16 cents.

The National academy of Sciences releases a report stating that it is "doubtful" that there are any health benefits to switching to a cigarette lower in tar and nicotine.

1984:   The National Cancer Institute of the Department of Health and Human Services launches a long-range "Cancer Prevention Awareness Campaign," with a major effort aimed at smoking cessation, which the institute estimates could save 95,000 lives each year.

Congress passes and President Reagan signs into law the Comprehensive Smoking Education Act. The new law replaces the 1970 version of the package warning with four stronger, more specific warnings.

1985:   The American Medical Association calls for a ban on all advertising of tobacco.

1986:   On January 27 President Reagan signs into law the Comprehensive Smokeless Tobacco Education Act of 1986. The new law extends ad limits and warning label requirements to smokeless tobacco.

The Surgeon General's annual report identifies smokeless tobacco as an oral cancer risk factor and highlights the problem of side stream or second-hand smoke. The National Research Council publishes a report on environmental tobacco smoke (ETS) with the same conclusions. Shortly thereafter, the GSA, the DoD, and the VA establish smoke-free rules for common work areas and the DoD undertakes an antismoking campaign. The Environmental Protection Agency (EPA) issues its own draft report citing second-hand smoke as carcinogenic and appoints a panel of experts to review the EPA's findings.

An administrative law judge dismisses an FTC complaint filed against R.J. Reynolds for misrepresenting results of the Multiple Risk Factor Intervention Trial (known as the "MR FIT" study). The FTC appeals the decision and two years later, R.J. Reynolds agrees, via an FTC consent order, to settle charges the company made false and misleading advertising claims regarding MR FIT, and the FTC drops its adjudicatory appeal.

1987: Congress bans smoking on domestic airline flights of two hours or less.

1988: The case of Rose Cipollone (*Cipollone* v. *Liggett Group*) is decided in favor of the plaintiff by a jury trial. The jury decision finds one of the companies—Liggett Group Inc.—liable to Cipollone's heirs for $400,000. However, in January 1990, a federal appeals court throws out the damage award, ruling that the plaintiffs had not proved Cipollone either saw or believed the claims made by Liggett about the health benefits of smoking.

1989: Congress bans smoking on all commercial airline flights regardless of length (excepting flights to Alaska and Hawaii).

1990: ICC bans smoking on regularly scheduled interstate buses.

Tobacco companies scrap plans to market two new brands of cigarettes targeted to reach specific populations. (*Uptown* was to be geared toward African Americans and *Dakota* was designed to appeal to blue-collar women.) Public protests, prompted by HHS Secretary Dr. Louis Sullivan identified these marketing strategies as predatory and irresponsible.

Secretary Sullivan testifies before the Senate Labor and Human Resources Committee in February that cigarette smoking costs the nation $52 billion in health expenses and time lost from work, and points out that "cigarettes are the only legal product that when used as intended, cause death." Later in the year, Sullivan asks sports fans and promoters to boycott sports events sponsored by tobacco companies in a speech to the First International Conference on Smokeless Tobacco.

In December, a distinguished panel of scientific experts, several of whom had links to research organizations funded by the tobacco industry (including panel chairman Walter Lippmann), endorse the EPA's draft report citing the health dangers of second-hand smoke and support the EPA proposal to classify second-hand smoke as a cause of cancer in non-smokers.

1991: In November, seven flight attendants file a class-action suit against six major tobacco companies on behalf of 60,000 flight attendants. The suit, filed in a Florida state court, alleges that the plaintiffs suffered an increased risk of lung cancer and other diseases as a result of their long periods of exposure to second-hand cigarette smoke.

An article published in a December issue of the *Journal of the American Medical Association* reports that Old Joe Camel, the cartoon mascot appearing in Camel ads beginning in 1987, entices minors to smoke Camel cigarettes. The article cites results of a survey in which 98 percent of the teenage respondents correctly identified the Old Joe character (compared to 72 percent of adult respondents) and that 33 percent of teenage smokers in the survey identified Camel as their favorite brand (compared to 9 percent of the adult smokers in the survey).

1992: In February, federal prosecutors begin a criminal investigation into whether major tobacco companies misled the public about risks of smoking through company-sponsored research organizations like the CTR.

The U.S. Supreme Court rules in *Cipollone* v. *Liggett Group* that federally required warning labels provide a substantial, but not an invincible, shield from tort liability for cigarette manufacturers, suggesting that plaintiffs could successfully bring suit if they could prove that the industry perpetrated a fraud or a conspiracy by hiding or distorting the health risks inherent in cigarette smoking.

1993: The EPA issues its final report on second-hand smoke, labeling it as serious a cancer risk as asbestos and radon. Five months later, Philip Morris sues the EPA for citing secondary smoke as a carcinogen without enough scientific evidence to support the claim.

President Clinton bans smoking in the White House shortly after being inaugurated.

1994: **February**—Six former Surgeons General from four Republican and two Democratic administrations testify before the House Subcommittee on Health and Environment (chaired by Henry Waxman, D.-California) in support of the Smoke Free Environment Act.

McDonald's decides to ban smoking in all of its 9,000 chain-owned restaurants. Taco Bell and Jack in the Box follow suit.

Surgeon General Joycelyn Elders attacks cigarette marketing geared toward youths, calling on the FTC to prohibit use of the Joe Camel cartoon promotions of Camel cigarettes. She also reveals research that demonstrates the presence of chemicals from passive smoke in fetuses.

Dr. David Kessler, commissioner of the FDA, threatens to regulate cigarettes as drugs if it can be determined that cigarette manufacturers have manipulated nicotine levels in their products over the years in an effort to better "hook" consumers.

March—Congress passes and President Clinton signs legislation that prohibits smoking in schools and in Head Start and community health centers.

DoD bans smoking in all indoor spaces on military bases, worldwide (except in restaurants, recreational areas, and domiciles).

Thousands of tobacco workers are given the day off and are bused to Washington for a demonstration in opposition to the proposed raise in the cigarette tax to finance health care reform.

Philip Morris sues ABC, seeking $10 billion in a defamation case for a program in which ABC charged Philip Morris with lacing its cigarettes with extra nicotine to make them more addictive.

The Labor Department's Occupational Safety and Health Administration (OSHA) announces its intention to prohibit smoking in workplaces (*including* restaurants and bars where food is served) in the roughly 6 million enclosed business sites under its jurisdiction nationwide.

A class action suit is filed in federal court (U.S. Eastern District of New Orleans) against major tobacco companies for manipulating nicotine levels in cigarettes (*Castano* v. *American Tobacco*). Some of the most prestigious lawyers in the country are among the 100 attorneys from 60 firms representing a class of 40 million current, former, and deceased smokers.

April—Top executives of the leading tobacco companies appear before the Waxman subcommittee for a "grilling" about their promotional and manufacturing practices.

May—Internal papers from the Brown and Williamson Tobacco Company are leaked to key members of Congress supporting the claim that the industry knew as early as the 1940s that cigarettes were addictive.

Mississippi sues tobacco companies to recover smoking-related health care costs paid by the state (*Mississippi* v. *American Tobacco et al*).

Florida passes a bill that would make it much easier for the state to sue tobacco companies for the state's share of Medicaid costs associated with smoking-related illness.

June—FDA Commissioner David Kessler testifies before the Waxman subcommittee about manipulation of nicotine levels by the tobacco industry.

Thomas E. Sandefur, Jr., chairman and chief executive of Brown and Williamson, denies Kessler's charges regarding the manipulation of nicotine to hook smokers, arguing that nicotine levels were varied to enhance the taste of the products sold.

Attorney General Janet Reno announces that the Justice Department will undertake a preliminary review of complaints brought by members of Congress that tobacco company executives misled them in the congressional testimony taken earlier in the year.

R.J. Reynolds III (60), grandson, namesake, and heir to the founder of R.J. Reynolds Tobacco Co., dies—like his father—from emphysema and congestive heart failure after years of heavy smoking.

August—Blue Cross and Blue Shield of Minnesota joins the state's attorney general in a lawsuit that accuses cigarette manufacturers of conspiring for decades to hide information about the dangers of smoking, in violation of Minnesota's antitrust and consumer protection statutes. Plaintiffs will attempt to recover much of the estimated $350 million spent annually on health care costs in the state attributable to smoking-related disease. The case is the first in which a plaintiff state has been joined by an insurer.

September—"Mortality from Smoking in Developed Countries, 1950–2000," is published. This report, prepared by scientists and epidemiologists from the Imperial Cancer Research Fund (Oxford, U.K.), the World Health Organization (Geneva, Switzerland), and the American

Cancer Society (Atlanta, Ga.) pegs the long-term death rate of smokers from smoking-related diseases at 50 percent. According to the study, 8,000 people die every day worldwide from smoking-related illnesses.

October—A judge in Dade County, Florida, certifies the legitimacy of a class-action suit, *Engle* v. *R.J. Reynolds,* in which plaintiffs—a group of smokers who claim to be addicted to nicotine—are requesting $200 billion in damages.

Seventy-five health, consumer, and religious groups begin a nationwide petition drive to encourage the enactment of a law that would have the FDA regulate tobacco as an addictive substance. The effort, led by former Surgeon General C. Everett Koop, includes the American Lung Association, the American Cancer Society, the American Heart Association, the American Medical Association, the American Academy of Pediatrics, and the March of Dimes.

November—After spending over $500 million on research over ten years, R. J. Reynolds announces plans to introduce a new kind of cigarette, marketed under the brand name "Eclipse." The new brand delivers as much nicotine to smokers as conventional brands, but it produces little smoke or odor and purportedly cuts the delivery of cancer-causing tars by up to 90 percent.

1995:   February—In a major blow to the tobacco companies, a federal district judge certifies the class action motion in the Castano case involving nearly 1 million Americans. (See the Castano lawsuit entry at March 1994.) Cigarette manufacturers maintain that their products are not dangerous or addictive and have denied charges that they have manipulated nicotine levels in order to "hook" smokers. Lawyers for R.J. Reynolds say they will appeal the certification. Damages, if awarded, could exceed $4 billion.

Florida files a lawsuit against 21 tobacco companies and their consulting and public relations firms seeking $1.4 billion in damages under the new law passed in that state in May 1994. The suit is aimed at recovering Medicaid expenses that are attributable to health care spending for residents who suffer from smoking-related illnesses. The suit also aims to halt the marketing of cigarettes to teenagers through "Joe Camel" and other such campaigns that appeal specifically to children under 18.

President Boris Yeltsin of Russia issues a decree banning all advertisements for tobacco and alcohol products, effective immediately. Television, radio, newspapers, and magazines are being required to either drop ads for the effected products or turn over any revenue gained to the Ministry of Health for public education programs. Only the U.S., China, and the European Union represent larger markets for tobacco products, and most American tobacco companies have been actively vying for a share of this market since 1992 through advertising and by investing in the dozens of cigarette manufacturing facilities scattered across Russia.

Appendix

II

Federal Trade Commission's Trade Regulation Rule on Cigarette Labeling and Advertising (29 FR 8325) Subchapter D— Trade Regulation Rules

---

Part 408 UNFAIR OR DECEPTIVE ADVERTISING AND LABELING OF CIGARETTES IN RELATION TO THE HEALTH HAZARDS OF SMOKING

Part 408 is added to Chapter I, Title 16, Code of Federal Regulations, reading as set forth below.

The Federal Trade Commission, pursuant to the Federal Trade Commission Act, as amended, 15 U.S.C. sections 41, et seq., and the provisions of Subpart F of the Commission's Procedures and Rules of Practice, 28 F.R. 7083-84 (July 1963), has conducted a proceeding for the promulgation of a Trade Regulation Rule, or Rules, for the prevention of unfair or deceptive acts or practices in the sale of cigarettes. Notice of this proceeding, including a set of proposed rules, was published in the FEDERAL REGISTER on January 22, 1964 (29 F.R. 530-532). Interested parties were thereafter afforded an opportunity to participate in the proceeding through the submission of written data, views and argument and to appear and express orally their views as to the proposed rules and to suggest revisions thereof and amendments and additions thereto. In adopting this rule, the Commission has given due consideration to all such views, data and argument together with all other relevant matters of fact, law, policy and discretion.

Sec. 408.1 The rule
    408.2 Definitions.
    408.3 Petition to reopen rulemaking proceeding.
    408.4 Effective dates.

AUTHORITY: The provisions of this Part 408 issued under Federal Trade Commission Act, as amended, 38 Stat. 717, as amended; 15 U.S.C. 41–58; 16 CFR 1.61–1.67.

§408.1 The Rule.

The Commission, on the basis of the findings made by it in this proceeding as set forth in the accompanying Statement of Basis and Purpose of Trade Regulation Rule, hereby promulgates as a trade regulation rule its determination that in connection with the sale, offering for sale, or distribution in commerce (as "commerce" is defined in the Federal Trade Commission Act) of cigarettes it is an unfair or deceptive act or practice within the meaning of section 5 of the Federal Trade Commission Act (15 U.S.C.§ 45) to fail to disclose, clearly and prominently, in all advertising and on every pack, box, carton or other container in which cigarettes are sold to the consuming public that cigarette smoking is dangerous to health and may cause death from cancer and other diseases.

§408.2 Definitions.

For purposes of the rule in this part:

(a) "Cigarette" means any roll of tobacco wrapped in paper or otherwise commonly considered a cigarette.

(b) "Advertising" includes all radio and television commercials, newspaper and magazine advertisements, billboards, posters, signs, decals, matchbook advertising, point-of-sale display material, and all other written or other material used for promoting the sale or consumption of cigarettes, but does not include the labeling of packs, boxes, cartons and other containers in which cigarettes are sold to the consuming public.

§408.3 Petition to Reopen Rulemaking Proceeding.

In the event that any person subject to the rule in this part is of the opinion that new or changed conditions of fact or law, the public interest, or special circumstances require that the rule in this part be suspended, modified, waived, or repealed as to him, or otherwise altered or amended, such person may file with the Secretary of the Commission a petition to reopen this rulemaking proceeding, stating the changes desired and the grounds therefor. The Commission will act on the petition as provided in §1.66 of this chapter (the Commission's Procedures and Rules of Practice).

§408.4 Effective Dates.

(a) Except with respect to advertising, the rule in this part shall become effective on January 1, 1965.

(b) With respect to advertising, the rule in this part shall become effective on July 1, 1965: *Provided, however,* That the Commission will entertain an application filed prior to May 1, 1965, by an interested party to postpone the effective date or otherwise suspend, modify, or abrogate the provisions of the rule in this part as to advertising, upon a showing of such change in circumstances as to justify such requested action in the public interest.

Issued: June 22, 1964.
By the Commission.   Joseph W. Shea
[SEAL]   *Secretary*

Suggestions
for Further Reading

Anderson, Douglas D., *Regulatory Politics and Electric Utilities.* Boston: Auburn House Publishing Company, 1981.

Anderson, James E., *Politics and the Economy.* Boston: Little, Brown, 1966.

Appleby, Paul, *Big Democracy.* New York: Alfred A. Knopf, 1945.

Bauer, Raymond A., Ithiel De Sola Pool, and Lewis Anthony Dexter, *American Business and Public Policy: The Politics of Foreign Trade.* New York: Atherton Press, 1963.

Bendiner, Robert, *Obstacle Course on Capitol Hill.* New York: McGraw-Hill, 1964.

Bernstein, Marver H., *Regulating Business by Independent Commission.* Princeton, N.J.: Princeton University Press, 1955.

Blau, Peter M., *Bureaucracy in Modern Society.* New York: Random House, 1956.

Boyer, William W., *Bureaucracy On Trial: Policy Making by Government Agencies.* Indianapolis: Bobbs-Merrill, 1964.

Breyer, Stephen G., *Breaking the Vicious Circle: Toward Effective Risk Regulation.* Cambridge, Mass.: Harvard University Press, 1993.

Breyer, Stephen, *Regulation and Its Reform.* Cambridge, Mass.: Harvard University Press, 1982.

Cary, William L., *Politics and the Regulatory Agencies.* New York: McGraw-Hill, 1967.

Clarkson, Kenneth W., and Timothy J. Muris (eds.), *The Federal Trade Com-*

mission Since 1970: Economic Regulation and Bureaucratic Behavior. New York: Cambridge University Press, 1981.

Cox, Edward F., Robert C. Fellmeth, and John E. Schulz, *The Nader Report on the Federal Trade Commission.* New York: Grove Press, 1969.

Cushman, Robert E., *The Independent Regulatory Commission.* New York: Oxford University Press, 1941.

Davidson, Roger H., and Walter J. Oleszek. *Congress and Its Members,* 2nd ed. Washington, D.C.: Congressional Quarterly Press, 1985.

Davis, Kenneth Culp, *Administrative Law and Government.* St. Paul, Minn.: West, 1960.

Davis, Kenneth Culp, *Discretionary Justice: A Preliminary Inquiry.* Urbana, Ill.: University of Illinois Press, 1969.

Derthick, Martha, and Paul Quirk, *The Politics of Deregulation.* Washington, D.C.: The Brookings Institution, 1985.

Dror, Yehezkel, *Public Policymaking Reexamined.* San Francisco: Chandler Publishing, 1968.

Dunlop, John T. (ed.), *Business and Public Policy.* Cambridge, Mass.: Harvard University Press, 1980.

Eads, George S., and Michael Fix, *The Reagan Regulatory Strategy: An Assessment.* Washington, D.C.: Urban Institute Press, 1984.

Fisher, Louis, *Constitutional Conflicts Between Congress and the President.* Princeton, N.J.: Princeton University Press, 1985.

Freedman, James O., *Crisis and Legitimacy: The Administrative Process and American Government.* Cambridge: Cambridge University Press, 1978.

Freeman, J. Leiper, *The Political Process: Executive Bureau-Legislative Committee Relations.* New York: Random House, 1965.

Friedman, Kenneth Michael, *Public Policy and the Smoking-Health Controversy: A Comparative Study.* Lexington, Mass.: Lexington Books, 1975.

Fritschler, A. Lee, and Bernard H. Ross, *How Washington Works: The Executive's Guide to Government.* Cambridge, Mass.: Ballinger Publishing, 1987.

Froman, Lewis A., Jr., *People and Politics: An Analysis of the American Political System.* Englewood Cliffs, N.J.: Prentice Hall, 1962.

Gawthrop, Louis C., *Administrative Politics and Social Change.* New York: St. Martin's Press, 1971.

Gilmour, Robert S., and Alexis A. Halley, *Who Makes Public Policy? The Struggle for Control between Congress and the Executive.* Chatham, N.J.: Chatham House, 1994.

Goodin, Robert E., *No Smoking: The Ethical Issues.* Chicago: University of Chicago Press, 1989.

Goodsell, Charles T., *The Case For Bureaucracy: A Public Administration Polemic,* 3rd ed. Chatham, N.J.: Chatham House, 1994.

Harris, Joseph P., *Congressional Control of Administration.* New York: Doubleday Anchor Books, 1965.

Henderson, Gerard C., *The Federal Trade Commission: A Study in Administrative Law and Procedure.* New Haven, Conn.: Yale University Press, 1924.

Herring, Pendleton, *Public Administration and the Public Interest.* New York: McGraw-Hill, 1936.

Hymneman, Charles S., *Bureaucracy in a Democracy.* New York: Harper and Brothers, 1950.

Ingram, Helen, and Steven Smith (eds.), *Public Policy for Democracy.* Washington, D.C., The Brookings Institution, 1993.

Institute for the Study of Smoking Behavior and Policy, *The Policy Implications of the 1986 Surgeon General's Report on Involuntary Smoking.* Cambridge, Mass.: John F. Kennedy School of Government, 1987.

Jacob, Charles E., *Policy and Bureaucracy.* New York: D. Van Nostrand Co., 1966.

Jones, Charles O., *An Introduction to the Study of Public Policy.* Belmont, Calif.: Wadsworth, 1970.

Jones, Charles O., *The Presidency in a Separated System.* Washington, D.C.: The Brookings Institution, 1994.

Katzmann, Robert A., *Regulatory Bureaucracy: The Federal Trade Commission and Antitrust Policy.* Cambridge, Mass.: MIT Press, 1980.

Kerwin, Cornelius M., *Rulemaking: How Government Agencies Write Law and Make Policy.* Washington, D.C.: CQ Press, 1994.

Kohlmeier, Louis M., Jr., *The Regulators: Watchdog Agencies and the Public Interest.* New York: Harper and Row, 1969.

Krislov, Samuel, and Lloyd D. Musolf, *The Politics of Regulation: A Reader.* Boston: Houghton Mifflin, 1964.

Leiserson, Avery, *Administrative Regulation: A Study in Representation of Interests.* Chicago: University of Chicago Press, 1942.

Long, Norton E., *The Polity.* Chicago: Rand McNally, 1966.

Lowi, Theodore J., *The End of Liberalism: The Second Republic of the United States,* 2nd ed. New York: W.W. Norton, 1979.

McConnell, Grant, *Private Power and American Democracy.* New York: Alfred A. Knopf, 1966.

Magnuson, Warren G., and Jean Carper, *The Dark Side of the Market Place.* Englewood Cliffs, N.J.: Prentice Hall, 1968.

Mitchell, William C., *The American Polity: A Social and Cultural Interpretation.* New York: Free Press, 1962.

Mund, Vernon A., *Government and Business,* 4th ed. New York: Harper & Row, 1965.

Nadel, Mark V., *Corporations and Political Accountability.* Lexington, Mass.: D.C. Health, 1976.

Neuberger, Maurine B., *Smoke Screen: Tobacco and the Public Welfare.* Englewood Cliffs, N.J.: Prentice Hall, 1963.

Pennock, J. Roland, *Administration and the Rule of Law.* New York: Rinehart and Company, 1941.

Pertschuk, Michael, *Revolt Against Regulation: The Rise and Pause of the Consumer Movement.* Berkeley: University of California Press, 1982.

Powell, Norman John, *Responsible Public Bureaucracy in the United States.* Boston: Allyn and Bacon, 1967.

Quirk, Paul J., *Industry Influence in Federal Regulatory Agencies.* Princeton, N.J.: Princeton University Press, 1981.

Rabin, Robert L., and Stephen D. Sugarman (eds.), *Smoking Policy: Law, Politics, and Culture.* New York: Oxford University Press, 1993.

Redford, Emmette S., *Democracy in the Administrative State.* New York: Oxford University Press, 1969.

Ripley, Randall, and Grace Franklin, *Congress, the Bureaucracy and Public Policy,* 3rd ed. Homewood, Ill.: Dorsey Press, 1984.

Rohr, John, *To Run a Constitution: The Legitimacy of the Administrative State.* Lawrence, Kans.: University Press of Kansas, 1986.

Rourke, Frances E., *Bureaucracy, Politics, and Public Policy,* 3rd ed. Boston: Little, Brown, 1984.

Rourke, Francis E., ed., *Bureaucratic Power in National Politics.* Boston: Little, Brown, 1965.

Schattschneider, E. E., *The Semi-Sovereign People.* New York: Holt, Rinehart & Winston, 1960.

Schnitzer, Martin C., *Contemporary Government and Business Relations.* Chicago: Rand McNally College Publishing, 1978.

Schooler, Dean, Jr., *Science, Scientists, and Public Policy.* New York: Free Press, 1971.

Schwartz, Bernard, *The Professor and the Commissions.* New York: Alfred A. Knopf, 1959.

Troyer, Ronald J., and Gerald E. Markle, *Cigarettes: The Battle over Smoking.* New Brunswick, N.J.: Rutgers University Press, 1983.

Welborn, David M., *Governance of Federal Regulatory Agencies.* Knoxville: University of Tennessee Press, 1977.

Woll, Peter, *American Bureaucracy,* 2nd ed. New York: W.W. Norton, 1977.

Index

Abell, Bess, 26
Action on Smoking and Health (ASH),
  39, 123n9, 144
Adjudication (administrative):
  compared with rule making, 62–63
Administrative Conference of the
    United States, 60n3
Administrative law judges (ALJ), 133,
    153n29, n30
  in adjudication, 138–39
  duties, 139
  history, 138–39
  in rule making, 116, 139
Administrative agencies:
  policy-making process, 4, 12–14
Administrative Procedure Act (APA), 95,
    133–37, 139, 145, 152n17, n22
Advertising Federation of America, 12
Advisory Committee on Smoking and
    Health, 41–43, 45, 89, 96, 116,
    121, 128, 141–42
  membership, 42, 46n7, 140
  operating procedures, 42
  report, 43–44
Agriculture, Department of (USDA), 5,
    9, 16, 18n13, 147
  against health warnings, 31
  interest in tobacco, 30, 31

Allen, George V., 16, 25
American Cancer Society, 6, 22, 35n4,
    46n5, 95, 97, 109–10
American Heart Association, 35n4, 95
American Medical Association (AMA), 6,
    35n9, 102n10
American Medical Association Educa-
    tion and Research Foundation,
    35n9
American Newspaper Publishers Asso-
    ciation, 12
American Tobacco Company, 28, 29, 54
American Tobacco Company v. U.S.,
    60n8
Americans for Democratic Action, 100
Arnold and Porter, 109
Association of National Advertisers, 12,
    78
Austern, H. Thomas, 16, 76, 78, 82

Banzhaf, John F., 39, 109–10, 143–44
Bass, Ross, 94
Belli, Melvin, 30
Bennett, Wallace, 35n1, 98, 102n4
Bergland, Bob, 16, 147
Blatnik, John A., 27
Bolling, Richard, 91, 102n6
Boyer, William, 19n26

Brewster, Daniel, 99–100
British Ministry of Health, 22
Brown and Williamson Tobacco Corporation, 36n23, 120
Bureaucracy:
  advisory committees, 41
  conflict within, 17, 30
  policy-making, 14, 15, 34, 41, 45, 114, 127–29, 140, 148–50
  powers of, 126, 140
  procedural constraints, 145
  role of, 4, 146
  tobacco regulation, 150
Bureaucratic pluralism, 146–48
Bureau of the Budget (now Office of Management and Budget), 34
Business Advisory Council (BAC), 140–41

Califano, Joseph, 118–20, 147
Carper, Jean, 35n6, 45n1
Carter, Jimmy, 117, 131, 142, 147, 155n50
Cary, William L., 57, 61n18
Celebrezze, Anthony, 16, 32–34, 147
Chandler, Alfred D., 18n11
Cigarette Advertising Code, Inc., 25
Cigarette Labeling and Advertising Act, 89, 92, 100, 104, 106, 110, 114, 126, 128
Cigarettes:
  advertising, 1, 9–10, 12–13, 18n17, 26, 27, 73, 88, 135, 137
  ban on advertising, 6, 108, 114
  consumption, 2, 10, 29, 32, 41, 106, 123n12
  deaths attributed to, 7, 21–23
  government promotion of, 27
  health risks, 2, 18n22, 21, 23, 29, 30, 40, 81, 119, 124n20, 141
  health studies, 21, 89
  health warning required, 38, 84n9, 89
  lobbyists, 98
  regulation of advertising, 31, 32, 67, 126
  sales, 2, 10, 17n3, 89, 144
  smoking in public places, 6, 106
  smoking policies, 124n27
Cipallone v. *Liggett Group*, 30, 36n19
Civil Service Reform Act of 1978, 148
Clare, Donald, 19n24
Clark, Joseph, 102n4
Clayton Act, 54–55
Clements, Earle C., 16, 25–26, 92–94, 97–98
Code of Federal Regulations, 81, 84n8

Cohen, David, 94
Cohen, Wilbur J., 106
Cohn, Victor, 123n2
Commerce, Department of, 16, 141
Commerce, Senate Committee on, 91, 93–94, 97, 100, 112
Comprehensive Smoking Education Act of 1984, 116
Congress:
  bans radio and TV ads, 73, 113–14, 117
  committees, 5, 6 (*see also* Committee on Commerce [Senate]; Interstate and Foreign Commerce Committee [House])
  delegation of authority, 12–13, 48–49, 51–52, 55–56, 79, 86, 130
  hearings on cigarette labeling, 97–98, 100
  influence over regulatory commissions, 131
  legislative veto, 130, 151n8
  oversight functions, 49, 86–88, 104, 130
  part of subsystem, 5, 6
  policy-making, 45, 54, 150
  powers granted by, 62, 115
  powers in, 15, 85–86
  requires health warnings, 87, 90
  rule-making authority, 78–79, 88
  tobacco power in, 27, 39, 82, 119, 126, 130
Congressional Office of Technology, 23
Consent order, 66
Consumer:
  legislation, 38
  protection, 131
Cordtz, Dan, 36n26
Coser, Lewis, 18n7
Council for Tobacco Research (CTR) (originally Tobacco Industry Research Committee), 16, 24, 35n1
Covington and Burling, 76, 109
Cox, Edward F., 151n12
Cullman, Joseph, 112

Dallos, Robert E., 123n8
Davis, Kenneth Culp, 60n6
Dawson, William L., 36n2
Delegation of authority:
  congressional, 12–13, 48–49, 51–52, 55–56, 79, 86, 130
  Supreme Court, 50–51, 55–56
Democratic Study Group, 91, 102n6
Department of Defense, 7, 117
Dewer, Helen, 18n14, 151n7
Dirksen, Everett M., 85

Dixon, Paul Rand, 69, 74–75, 82, 95,
  98, 108
Donovan, Robert J., 153n33
Douglas, Paul, 102n4
Drew, Elizabeth Brenner, 102n7,
  151n4
Dryden, Franklin B., 18n16, 103n14
Dunlop, John T., 18n11

Elders, Joycelyn, 129
Elman, Philip, 68, 74, 131
Entrepreneurial politics, 124n22
Environmental Protection Agency
  (EPA), 117
Environmental Tobacco Smoke (ETS),
  124n25, n26, 141
Evans, Rowland, 35n10

Fahey v. Mallonee, 61n15
Fair Labor Standards Act, 139
Fairness doctrine, 110
Federal Advisory Committee Act of
  1972, 46n8
Federal Aviation Administration (FAA),
  6, 117, 144
Federal Communications Commission
  (FCC), 50, 104, 108–9, 111, 114,
  143
Federal Register, 46n12, 81–82, 84n8,
  111, 133, 137, 145
Federal Register Act (1935), 136–37
Federal Trade Commission (FTC):
  adjudication and rule-making, 51,
    67–68
  advertising guidelines, 31, 45, 58–59
  ban on cigarette advertising, 59,
    108
  hearings on cigarettes, 72–73, 75–76,
    88
  hearings on health consequences, 27,
    98
  history of, 52, 54
  impact of TV advertising, 36n25
  on health warnings, 13, 17, 17n2,
    32, 35n9, 47, 65, 88, 115
  policy-making, 47, 49, 56, 67, 101
  powers limited, 52, 87, 126
  report to Congress, 108, 123n4
  rule on cigarette labeling, 45, 50, 64,
    68, 73, 97, 99
  rule making, 60, 61n23, 63, 65–66,
    70, 74, 79, 84n3, n4, 88, 92, 115,
    124n15, 128, 135, 137
  task force on cigarettes, 70
  voluntary code, 82
Federal Trade Commission Act, 51, 68,
  77, 79–80, 101, 151n15

Federal Trade Commission Improve-
  ments Act, 115–16, 130–31
*Federal Trade Commission v. Curtis
  Publishing Company*, 61n20
Federal Trade Commission v. Klesner,
  61n20
Federal Trade Commission v. Raladam,
  61n20
Federal Trade Commission v. Ruberoid,
  60n1, n2
*Federal Trade Commission v. Warren,
  Jones and Gratz*, 61n20
Fellmeth, Robert C., 151n12
Ferber, Mark F., 102n6
Fernicola, Karen L., 151n1
Field v. Clark, 61n13
First Amendment Rights, 140
Food and Drug Act of 1906, 33
Food and Drug Administration (FDA),
  7, 32–34, 46n5, 118
Foote, Emerson, 96, 103n16, 106
Ford, Gerald, 115
Fortas, Abe, 26
Frank, Stanley, 107
Freedom of Information Act (FOIA),
  136, 145
Freeman, J. Leiper, 18n6
Freeman, Orville, 16, 31
Friedman, Kenneth Michael, 45n3,
  155n49
Fritschler, A. Lee, 18n12, 19n26
Fur Products Labeling Act of 1945,
  77–78

Galbraith v. R. J. Reynolds Industries,
  30, 139
Gaskill, Nelson B., 61n19
General Services Administration (GSA),
  7, 117
Golden, Charles, 107
Goodnow, Frank J., 151n3
Goodsell, Charles, 146, 153n36,
  154n45, n48
Government in the Sunshine Act,
  46n8
Gray, Bowman, 99
Green v. American Tobacco Co., 28–29,
  36n14, n15, n17
Greenberg, D. S., 18n22
Guthrie, Eugene H., 42

Hammond, E. Cuyler, 21, 35n2
Harris, Oren, 16, 82, 91, 93
Harris, Richard, 36n28
Hartke, Vance, 94
Hazardous Substances Labeling Act,
  33

Health, Education and Welfare, Department of (HEW), (now Department of Health and Human Services), 16, 32, 35n3, 44, 45n2, 96–98, 106–7, 147

Health Warning Label, 1–4, 7, 11–13, 17n1, 23, 29, 30, 35n1, 73, 90–92, 98, 107, 113, 144

Hearings, FTC:
commissioner's role, 72–74, 77–79
health testimony, 73
tobacco testimony, 76–77
witnesses, 75–76
(*see also* Federal Trade Commission; Cigarettes)

Heclo, Hugh, 121, 125n29

Helms, Jesse, 9

Henderson, Gerard C., 60n9

Hill and Knowlton, 93

Hockett, Robert C., 35n5

Home Owners Act of 1933, 56

Horn, Daniel, 21, 35n2

Huff, Darrell, 99

Humphrey, Hubert, 26

Immigration and Naturalization Service v. Chadha, 151n8

Interstate and Foreign Commerce Committee (House), 32, 91, 93, 111–12

Interstate Commerce Commission (ICC), 6, 54, 83n3, 84n4, 117, 138, 141, 144

Issue Networks, 121, 125n29

John F. Banzhaf III v. Federal Communications Commission, 123n7, 154n38

Johnson, Lyndon B., 26, 34, 89, 92, 100–101, 128, 136

Jones, Mary Gardiner, 74

Jones, Walter, 16, 109

Judicial policy-making, 63

Judicial proceedings, 133
suits against cigarette manufacturers, 28, 29
under the Sherman Act, 53–55

Justice, Department of, 121, 142

Kagan, Robert A., 123n13, 124n24, 149, 155n54

Katzmann, Robert A., 61n17, 102n12

Kefauver, Estes, 33, 39, 74

Kennedy, John F., 40, 142

Kennedy, Robert F., 13, 45n3, 102n4

Kessler, David, 119–20, 129

Kilbourne v. *Thompson*, 60n12

Koop, Everett C., 107, 128

Kornegay, Horace, 16, 93

Legislative policy-making, 63

Leiserson, Avery, 153n32

Liggett and Myers Tobacco Co., 36n22

Loevinger, Lee, 50, 60n2

Long, Norton E., 102n11, 146, 154n47

Lowi, Theodore J., 18n6, 19n27, 151n2

MacIntyre, Everette A., 16, 74

McLellan, David S., 19n24

Magnuson, Warren G., 35n6, 36n21, 45n1, 91, 94, 105, 109, 112

Markle, Gerald E., 124n23, 154n39

Marsee v. *U.S. Tobacco*, 30, 35n19

Media watchdog function, 145

Meserve, William G., 123n1

Miller, James III, 132

Mississippi v. *American Tobacco et al.*, 120

Morton, Thurston, 16, 94

Moss, John, 91, 98, 111–12

Multiple Risk Factor Intervention Trial (MR FIT), 116, 139–40

Nadel, Mark V., 123n10

Nader, Ralph, 39, 110, 131

National Association of Broadcasters (NAB), 12, 16, 84n11, 100, 109

National Cancer Institute, 35n4

National Clearinghouse for Smoking and Health (also Office of Smoking and Health), 17n3, n5, 90, 105

National Heart Institute, 35n4

National Institute on Drug Abuse, 7

National Interagency Council on Smoking and Health, 96, 103n16

National Petroleum Refiners Association, 51

National Petroleum Refiners Association v. Federal Trade Commission, 152n19

National Rifle Association, 12

National Tuberculosis Association, 46n5, 95

Nelson, Gaylord, 102n4

Neuberger, Maurine B., 32–33, 35n11, 39, 46n6, 71, 94, 98, 100, 112, 123n9

Neuberger, Richard, 35n1

New England Journal of Medicine, 8

Nicholson, James M., 108

Nicot, Jean, 9, 10

Nixon, Richard M., 142

Novak, Robert, 35n10

Occupational Safety and Health Administration (OSHA), 117, 142
Office of Management and Budget, 15, 147
Office of Personnel Management (OPM), 139
Office of Science and Technology, 46n5
Office of the Federal Register, 152n25
Office on Smoking and Health, 3, 45n2, 90, 125n28
Office to the U.S. Trade Representative, 16

Panama Refining Co. v. *Ryan,* 60n5, 152n24
Parker, Roy, Jr., 103n15, n19
Penn Tobacco Company (FTC proceedings), 70n2
Pershing, General John J., 11
Pertschuk, Michael, 112, 123n12, 132
P. Lorillard Company v. *Federal Trade Commission,* 61n22
Policy-making process, 121, 123, 126
    agencies and Congress, 143
    stages of, 49
Post Office, Department of, 13
Presidential powers, 56–57
Prohibition of cigarette sales, 10, 11
Public Health Cancer Association, 22
Public Health Cigarette Smoking Act, 17n1, 113, 127, 152n17
Public Health Service (PHS), 17n3, 21, 32–33, 40–43, 45, 45n2, 69, 90, 96–97, 105–6, 114, 125n28
Public interest, 49

Rabin, Robert L., 35n7, 36n20, 123n13
Radio Advertising Bureau, 12
Reagan, Ronald, 116, 123n28, 132
Reilly, John, 74, 128
Reilly, William, 142
Reynolds, R. J., Company, 99, 116, 140
Robinson, Jackie, 106
Rockefeller, Nelson A., 89
Rosen, Bernard, 123n14
Rosenblatt, Roger, 35n5
Ross, Bernard H., 18n12, 19n26
Rourke, Francis Edward, 19n26

Schattschneider, E. E., 18n7
Schlechter Poultry Corp. v. *U.S.,* 60n5
Schulz, John E., 151n12
Schwartz, Gary T., 36n20
Sears, Roebuck and Co. v. *Federal Trade Commission,* 61n16
Securities and Exchange Commission (SEC), 57, 80

Securities and Exchange Commission v. *Chenery Corporation,* 84n6
Separation of powers, 4, 5, 55–56, 131, 133
Shapiro, David L., 70n1
Sherman Act, 53–55, 59
Silver v. *Federal Trade Commission,* 61n21
Simmel, George, 18n7
Sinclair, Upton, 38
Smoke-Free Environment Act, 118
Smoking and Health (*see* Advisory Committee on Smoking and Health)
Staggers, Harley, 16, 93
Standard Oil Company, 54
Standard Oil Company v. *U.S.,* 60n8
Stewart, William H., 23
Stillman, Richard J. II, 125n29
Subsystem, 5–7, 11, 17n6, 45
    tobacco, 5–7, 11, 83, 116, 119, 121, 123, 141, 147
Sugarman, Stephen D., 35n7, 123n13
Sullivan, Louis, 119, 128
Supreme Court:
    congressional delegations, 50–51
    FTC, 58
    rule-making, 78–79
    "rule of reason," 54
Surgeon General, 2, 17n5, 40, 42–44, 59–60, 69–70, 74, 83, 89, 97–99, 105–6, 116–18, 121, 128 (*see also* Advisory Committee on Smoking and Health)

Task Force on Smoking and Health, 106
Terry, Luther D., 33, 40, 44, 103n16, 116, 127, 141–42, 147
Tobacco:
    causes of death, 23
    dissidents, 122
    expenditures for advertising, 8
    exporter, 148
    FDA regulation, 7
    health effects, 24, 42, 107
    lobbyists, 50, 124n21
    major producing states, 7, 74
    product safety, 147
    subsystem, 5–7, 11–12, 17, 34, 44, 83, 88, 116, 119, 122–23, 141, 147
Tobacco industry:
    liability, 120
    promotes cigarettes, 129
    research committee, 16, 24, 35n5
    self-regulation, 82, 126
    strength in Congress, 150

Tobacco Institute, Inc., 16, 25, 46n5,
    51, 60n7, 75–79, 84n3, 88, 93, 96,
    100, 103n14, 108, 112, 150n1
Tobacco Network, 121–22
Tobacco producers code membership,
    84n10
Tobacco Tort Liability, 36n20
Trade Practices Conference, 66, 68
Trade regulation rules, 51, 72, 80–82,
    84n5, n7
Troyer, Ronald J., 124n23, 154n39

Unfair trade practices, 79, 81
United States Code, 81, 152n21
U.S. Fire Administration, 7
*U.S. v. Chicago, Minneapolis and St.
    Paul Railroad Co.,* 61n14

U.S. Trade Representative (USTR),
    147

Veterans Administration, 7, 117
Vogel, David, 123n13, 124n24, 149,
    155n54

Warner, Kenneth E., 18n10
Warning (*see* Health warning label)
Waxman, Henry, 118–19
Wegman, Richard A., 36n13
Weil, Gilbert H., 78
Welborn, David M., 102n12
Wheeler-Lea Act, 59
Wilson, James Q., 124n22
Wilson, Woodrow, 151n3
Woll, Peter, 19n26, 129, 151n6